AF335445

Managing Public Trust

Barbara Kożuch • Sławomir J. Magala
Joanna Paliszkiewicz
Editors

Managing Public Trust

Editors
Barbara Kożuch
Jagiellonian University
Krakow, Poland

Sławomir J. Magala
Rotterdam School of Management
Erasmus University
Rotterdam, The Netherlands

Joanna Paliszkiewicz
Warsaw University of Life Sciences
Warsaw, Poland

ISBN 978-3-319-70484-5   ISBN 978-3-319-70485-2   (eBook)
https://doi.org/10.1007/978-3-319-70485-2

Library of Congress Control Number: 2018935568

This Palgrave Macmillan imprint is published by Springer Nature
The registered company is Springer International Publishing AG
The registered company address is: Gewerbestrasse 11, 6330 Cham, Switzerland

To our fellow brain trust members, with a mild warning: How much trust would a brain trust trust if a brain trust could trust trust?

CONTENTS

LIST OF CONTRIBUTORS

Marek Bugdol Jagiellonian University, Kraków, Poland

Fatih Çetin Niğde Ömer Halisdemir University, Niğde, Turkey

Chun-Yu Chien Asia University, Taichung, Taiwan

Michał Chmielecki University of Social Sciences, Warszawa, Poland

Agnieszka Chrisidu-Budnik University of Wroclaw, Wroclaw, Poland

Özge Demiral Niğde Ömer Halisdemir University, Niğde, Turkey

Barbara Filipczyk University of Economics in Katowice, Katowice, Poland

Jerzy Gołuchowski University of Economics in Katowice, Katowice, Poland

Adam Jabłoński WSB University in Poznań, Poznań, Poland

Dorota Konieczna University of Economics in Katowice, Katowice, Poland

Jerzy Korczak University of Wroclaw, Wrocław, Poland

Barbara Kożuch Jagiellonian University, Krakow, Poland

Lee, Tzong-Ru (Jiun-Shen) National Chung Hsing University, Taichung, Taiwan

Regina Lenart-Gansiniec Jagiellonian University, Kraków, Poland

Yang Liu Jinan University, Guangzhou, China

Sławomir J. Magala Rotterdam School of Management, Erasmus University Rotterdam School of Management, Rotterdam, The Netherlands

Jagiellonian University, Krakow, Poland

Florinda Matos ICLab – ICAA – Intellectual Capital Accreditation Association, Santarém, Portugal

Ana Josefa Matos ICLab – ICAA – Intellectual Capital Accreditation Association, Santarém, Portugal

Joanna Paliszkiewicz Warsaw University of Life Sciences, Warsaw, Poland

Katarzyna Sienkiewicz-Małyjurek Silesian University of Technology, Gliwice, Poland

Ari Sivula University of Vaasa, Vaasa, Finland

Jaakko Sivusuo University of Vaasa, Vaasa, Finland

Łukasz Sułkowski Jagiellonian University, Kraków, Poland

István Takács Óbuda University Budapest, Budapest, Hungary

Katalin Takács-György Óbuda University Budapest, Budapest, Hungary

Josu Takala University of Vaasa, Vaasa, Finland

Valter Vairinhos ICLab – ICAA – Intellectual Capital Accreditation Association, Santarém, Portugal

Vesa-Jukka Vornanen University of Vaasa, Vaasa, Finland

LIST OF FIGURES

LIST OF TABLES

CHAPTER 1

Introduction

Barbara Kożuch, Sławomir J. Magala,
and Joanna Paliszkiewicz

Contemporary management goes beyond individual organizations. The increasing frequency of international encounters has led to crises of greater complexity and variety. Sorting out and solving these crises requires fundamental trust, which is a very fragile component of organizational interactions. Trust is difficult to establish and sustain, but it can be destroyed very easily. People create expectations about others, believing that they will behave in a way that is beneficial and not harmful for the parties in an interaction. Trust is a very important part of social and organizational life, especially in situations where the trustor depends on the trustee's future actions to achieve her or his own goals and objectives. This is of great importance in managing public organizations. The necessity of establishing conditions of creating public trust is becoming omnipresent (Denhardt 2011; Lane 2009). Thus, trust must be taken into account in the operations of any public organization.

B. Kożuch (✉)
Jagiellonian University, Krakow, Poland

S. J. Magala
Rotterdam School of Management, Erasmus University,
Rotterdam, The Netherlands

J. Paliszkiewicz
Warsaw University of Life Sciences, Warsaw, Poland

1

B. Kożuch et al. (eds.), *Managing Public Trust,*
https://doi.org/10.1007/978-3-319-70485-2_1

Some researchers have described public trust as "an important goal of governmental organisations" (Feldheim and Wang 2004, p. 63). However, this seems to be a too narrow definition of trust. A deep examination into the literature of the field indicates that trust is a means to achieve the goals of public organizations, not the end goal itself. There is also a view that the public trust experienced in all situations can be defined as social capital, which enhances problem solving, reduces conflicts, and enables more satisfying relationships (Fukuyama 1995; Carnevale 1995). That approach seems to be too wide when research revolves around the organizational perspective of public trust. Some aspects of this perspective can be traced in the works of researchers such as Bourdieu (2008) and Putnam et al. (1993). Bourdieu (2008, p. 248) referred correctly to social capital as the "aggregate of actual or potential resources which are linked to the possession of a durable network or more or less institutionalised relationships of mutual acquaintance of recognition," whereas Putnam et al. (1993, p. 167) emphasized the "features of social organization, such as trust, norms and networks". Therefore, according to these authors, trust is a feature of an organization: in the case of a public organization, this feature remains to be public trust. Today, more and more frequently, people share an opinion that public trust is the glue that holds a given democracy together. However, from the perspective of our research, this seems to be too general.

Other authors have proposed a highly meticulous approach to trust (Llewellyn et al. 2013; Hardin 2006), with a distinction between trust and confidence. For instance, Hardin wrote about a meaningful distinction between these phenomena, claiming that public confidence may be more linked to indications of good performance, whereas trust is more driven by perceptions of public integrity and shared values. At the same time, he stressed that trust and confidence are interwoven. Thus, both of these concepts can be analyzed jointly in the discussions on confidence as a subcomponent of trust.

The literature in the field offers some attempts to explain the essence of public trust. A compilation of the main indicators of public trust listed good governance as one of them (Bouckaert and Van de Wall 2003a). The same authors connected the notion of public trust with "citizens' perceptions of their government, and of their administration more specifically" (Bouckaert and Van de Walle 2003b, p. 303). An interesting way of understanding public trust was provided by Bouckaert (2012) who distinguished three types of trust: (1) the trust of citizens and organizations in government and the public sector; (2) the trust of government and the public sector in citizens and organizations; (3) trust within government and the public sector.

In this book, public trust is understood as a type of organizational trust (Kożuch and Dobrowolski 2014) that takes into consideration the specificity of managing public organizations. It is related to the belief that the organizational objectives of public bodies, their competences, shared norms and values, organizational principles, processes and procedures, codes of conduct, and attention to the interests of workers and citizens lead to the adoption of policies and public programs that serve the public interest and represent citizens.

We think that creating a trust-enhancing organizational context has become one of the most important analyses of public trust (Six 2004). Furthermore, we fully share a view that trust has to be built and managed (Klijn and Eshuis 2013). We claim that trust has a crucial role to play when public organizations aim at innovations and successful operations or to pave the way to the next public service generation (Harisalo and Stenvall 2004; Heichlinger and Vanebo 2013). The purpose of this book is to bring together the theory and practice of managing public trust. The book is divided into five parts, as follows.

Part 1: Trust and Public Trust: Background and Definitions
Part 1 contains two chapters that cover the concept of trust and public trust. The first chapter presents the concept of trust as a multifaceted notion based on critical literature review. In this chapter, the definitions of trust are presented. Next, the types, dimensions, and roles of trust in management are described. The second chapter provides a framework for interpreting the specificity of trust in public organizations in the context of concepts of publicness, particularly the linkage of public trust and effectiveness of public organizations, as well as the processes of creating, regaining, and sustaining public trust in public organizations. This chapter reports on the current state of knowledge about public trust and helps to further a deeper understanding of creating public trust within and between organizations.

Part 2: Organizational Challenges and Public Trust
Part 2 contains five chapters explaining the relationship of public trust with different organizational activities. It includes a description of the relationship between public trust and aspects of organizing and managing

activities such as organizational change, organizational learning, human resource management, and strategic partnership. Chapter 5 is devoted to the issue of building and maintaining trust in academic institutions, as illustrated by the example of Poland. Chapter 6 discusses how to manage human resource processes to develop and maintain a high level of trust as an element of social capital. In Chap. 7, the concept of trust in organizations is dissected and analyzed within the framework of national culture. The aim of Chap. 8 is to clarify and explore trust, partnership, and dynamic capabilities.

Part 3: The Development of Public Trust
Part 3 contains two chapters. In Chap. 9, the authors present the impact of social media on the development of public trust. Public trust is analyzed in three dimensions—competence, benevolence, and integrity—in an example of communication via Twitter during a participative budgeting process in Poland's voivodships. Chapter 10 presents the relationship between public service design and public trust management in the context of ensuring the continuity of public trust-based organizations. It is particularly important to pay attention to the criteria of this continuity with regard to the various interpretations of the sustainability concept. The scope of the chapter includes the principles of building a concept of sustainable management with respect to ethics, economics, and ecology toward meeting the expectations of stakeholders in public organizations.

Part 4: The Dynamics of Public Trust in Organizational Cooperation
Part 4 contains three chapters. The authors of Chap. 11 describe the results of research conducted in Finland that is related to mutual trust. Chapter 12 uses the game theory to introduce and explain how information asymmetry among members of the society and differences between the interests of the partners influence public trust. The last chapter in this part covers the aspects of trust in integrated territorial investment projects.

Part 5: Public Trust in Different Countries
Part 5 contains four chapter in which the meaning of public trust is presented from different cultural perspectives. Chapter 14 provides an overview of the meaning of trust, the studies on trust, and trustworthy behaviors in Turkish culture. In next chapter, the authors describe four cases to demonstrate the characteristics of relevance, psychology, risk,

goodwill, and decision-making of public trust in Taiwan. In Chap. 16, an example from Poland is presented. The authors present trust as a vital instrument that enables collaboration between different parties engaged in complex planning processes. Chapter 17 presents an overview of the relationship between intellectual capital indicators and trust in the public administration of European countries. In other words, it highlights the empirical evidence that countries with better indicators of trust are also those with better intellectual capital management.

Overall, this book provides a look at the current state of public trust, including a comprehensive global overview of both the research and practical applications of managing public trust by presenting research from different countries, including Finland, Poland, Hungary, Taiwan, and Turkey. We argue that managing public trust effectively is necessary for successful interactions with internal and external stakeholders, as well as for fruitful organizational collaboration. Furthermore, the book demonstrates how public trust is built, maintained, and rebuilt in various organizational contexts in different countries. The book aims to unify the extant research on public trust in and between organizations and to stimulate new research directions. Finally, this book brings together conceptual thinking and empirical research on the nature, meaning, and development of managing public trust. The main purpose of this publication is to demonstrate relevance of the processes of building and developing public trust as a foundation for creating and sustaining effective intra- and interorganizational relationships, as illustrated through examples of public organizations from different countries around the world.

REFERENCES

Bouckaert, G. (2012). Trust and public administration. *Administration, 60*(1), *93–94.*

Bouckaert, G., & Van de Wall, S. (2003a, January). Comparing measures of citizen trust and user satisfaction as indicators of 'good governance': Difficulties in linking trust and satisfaction indicators. *International Review of Administrative Sciences, 69*(3), 329–343.

Bouckaert, G., & Van de Wall, S. (2003b). Quality of public service delivery and trust in government. In A. Salminen (Ed.), *Governing networks: EGPA yearbook.* Amsterdam: IOS Press.

Bourdieu, P. (2008). *Research for the sociology of education.* New York: Greenwood.

Carnevale, D. G. (1995). *Trustworthy government: Leaderships and management strategies for building trust and high performance.* San Francisco: Jossey Bass.

Denhardt, R. B. (2009/2011). *Theories of public organization* (International Edition). Boston: Wodsworth Cengage Learning.

Feldheim, M. A., & Wang, X. (2004). Ethics and public trust. *Public Integrity, 6*(1).

Fukuyama, F. (1995). *Trust: The social virtue and the creation of prosperity.* New York: Free Press.

Hardin, R. (2006). *Trust.* Cambridge: Polity Press.

Harisalo, R., & Stenvall, J. (2004). Citizens' trust in ministers. In M. Huotari & M. Iivonen (Eds.), *Trust in knowledge management and systems in organizations* (pp. 147–117). Hershey: Idea Group Publishing.

Heichlinger, A., & Vanebo, J. O. (2013). *Public sector and the new ("old") technology* (pp. 81–97). Oslo: Universitetsforlaget.

Klijn, E. H., & Eshuis, J. (2013). Trust and networks. In S. Llewellyn, S. Brookes, & A. Mahon (Eds.), *Trust and confidence in government and public services* (pp. 52–54). New York: Routledge.

Kożuch, B., & Dobrowolski, Z. (2014). *Creating public trust. An organisational perspective.* Frankfurt am Main: Peter Lang GmbH.

Lane, J.-E. (2009). *State management.* New York: Routledge.

Llewellyn, S., Brooks, S., & Mahon, A. (2013). *Trust and confidence in government and public services.* New York: Routledge.

Putnam, R. D., Leonardi, R., & Nanetti, R. (1993). *Making democracy work: Civic traditions in modern Italy.* Princeton: Princeton University Press.

Six, F. (2004). *Trust and trouble. Building interpersonal trust within organizations.* Rotterdam: Erasmus Research Institute of Management.

Trust and Public Trust: Background and Definitions

CHAPTER 2

Trust: A Multifaceted Notion

Joanna Paliszkiewicz

2.1   Introduction

Trust is an important factor in business, society, and individual life. Researchers and practitioners have highlighted the significance of this concept (Mayer et al. 1995; Grudzewski et al. 2007; Sztompka 1999; Bugdol 2010; Paliszkiewicz 2013; Paliszkiewicz et al. 2015; Kożuch and Lenart-Gansiniec 2017). Trust is essential to establish cooperation between people (Isik et al. 2015), improve communication, increase engagement at work, and improve organizational performance (Cho and Poister 2014; Koohang et al. 2017). Trust helps people to live in risky and uncertain situations (Deutsch 1962; Mayer et al. 1995) and to reduce organizational complexity and uncertainty (Hummels and Roosendaal 2001). It influences the quality of social relationships (Rempel et al. 1985; Savolainen et al. 2014) and the quality of public relations (Bekmeier-Feuerhahn and Eichenlaub 2010). It has also been identified as a critical factor in leadership effectiveness (Tyler 2003). Trust decreases transaction costs by reducing the necessity of monitoring (Mayer et al. 1995). Trust influences the level of knowledge sharing between people (Casimir et al. 2012) and innovativeness (Ellonen et al. 2008). Trust has also been shown to influence technology adoption, online transactions, cloud adoption, social

J. Paliszkiewicz (✉)
Warsaw University of Life Sciences, Warsaw, Poland

B. Kożuch et al. (eds.), *Managing Public Trust*,
https://doi.org/10.1007/978-3-319-70485-2_2

media, and website usage decisions (e.g., Bahmanziari 2003; Gefen et al. 2003; Habib et al. 2012; Paliszkiewicz and Koohang 2016). Trust is a multifaceted and multidisciplinary issue that has been widely studied in different fields of science, including psychology, social psychology, sociology, economics, management, and information technology. Trust is a very fragile and intangible asset.

The purpose of this chapter is to present the concept of trust as a multifaceted notion based on a critical literature review and to propose future research in this area. The definitions of trust, its different types and dimensions, and the role of trust in management are presented. Finally, conclusions and future directions are proposed.

2.2   The Meaning of Trust

Trust has been defined in many ways in prior research. The literature reveals at least four different perspectives of trust understanding: an individual feature from the viewpoint of personality theories, individual expectations, a part of a relationship, and a part of social and economic exchange. Viewed from the individual level, trust is best understood by looking at the psychology of the person. According to Wrightsman (1966) and Rotter (1967), trust is a personality trait that reflects the general expectations of the trustworthiness of others. These expectations depend on the process of socialization and previous personal experiences. Gibb (1978) insisted that trust is instinctive and as a feeling is close to love.

In the second group of definitions, researchers treat trust as an individual expectation or belief. The definitions given by Deutsch (1958), Sako (1992), Lewicki and Bunker (1995), Mayer et al. (1995), Bhattacharya et al. (1998), and Paliszkiewicz (2013) can be regarded as an example of the second category. Deutsch (1958) defined trust as an individual's optimistic expectation about the outcome of an event. According to Sako (1992), trust can be treated as a state of mind, an expectation held by one partner about another, that the other behaves or responds in a predictable and mutually acceptable manner. Lewicki and Bunker (1995) claimed that trust is a state involving confident positive expectations about another's motives regarding oneself in situations of risk. Mayer et al. (1995) defined trust as the willingness of a party to be vulnerable to the actions of another party based on the expectation that the other party will perform a particular action important to the trustor, irrespective of the ability to monitor or control that other party. Bhattacharya et al. (1998)

insisted that trust is an expectancy of positive (non-negative) outcomes that one can receive based on the expected action of another party in an interaction characterized by uncertainty. Paliszkiewicz (2013) described trust as the belief that another party (a) will not act in a way that is harmful to the trusting party, (b) will act in such a way that it is beneficial to the trusting party, (c) will act reliably, and (d) will behave or respond in a predictable and mutually acceptable manner.

Lewis and Weigert (1985) stressed that individuals would have no occasion or need to trust apart from their relationships with others. Trust is described as an essential ingredient in the initiation and maintenance of stable social relationships, so it has a sociological function. Definitions presented by Zand (1972), Morgan and Hunt (1994), and Doney and Cannon (1997) can be considered as belonging to the third category. According to Zand's definition (1972), trust is the willingness of one person to increase his or her vulnerability to the actions of another person, whose behavior he or she could not control. Morgan and Hunt (1994) claimed that trust is one party's confidence in an exchange partner's reliability and integrity. Doney and Cannon (1997) described trust as a willingness to rely on another.

According to Blau (1964), social exchange is the voluntary action of individuals who are motivated by the returns they are expected to bring from others (not priced in terms of a single quantitative medium of exchange), while economic exchanges are moored on a formal contract that specifies the exact amount to be exchanged. Economic and social exchange are different but both depend on trust (Buskens 1998; Doney et al. 1998; James 2002). Some definitions related to trust as a part of social and economic exchanges have been described by Hosmer (1995), Sztompka (1999), and James (2002). Hosmer (1995) presented trust as the reliance by one person, group, or firm upon a voluntarily accepted duty on the part of another person, group, or firm to recognize and protect the rights and interests of all parties engaged in a cooperative endeavor or economic exchange. Sztompka (1999) defined trust as the expectation that other people, groups, or institutions with whom we interact will act in ways conducive to our well-being. James (2002) described trust from an economic standpoint as an expectation that people will not be exploited by others, which exists when there are no strong incentives for people to behave opportunistically.

Das and Teng (2004) confirmed that people vary in terms of when and how much they are willing to trust. People's readiness to trust depends on the nature of their personalities (Luhmann 1979), their developmental experiences and cultural backgrounds (Mayer et al. 1995), propensity to trust (Sankowska and Paliszkiewicz 2016), people's estimation of the probability that those trusted will reciprocate the trust (Tyler and Kramer 1996), and people's willingness to depend on their interactional partners (McKnight et al. 2002).

2.3   THE TYPES OF TRUST

Trust is a complex concept, and researchers have proposed many different types of trust. The most common types of trust are conditional, unconditional, general, specific, simple, blind, basic, organizational, and individual. Some researchers classify trust by taking into consideration its foundations, such as institutional-based, characteristic-based, process-based, calculus-based, knowledge-based, identification-based, affect-based, and cognition-based trust. Other propositions that appear in the literature are self, rational, structural, transactional, horizontal, and vertical trust.

Jones and George (1998) described conditional and unconditional trust. Unconditional trust can appear when the relationship is very significant, whereas conditional trust is based on positive expectations to other parties. Siegrist et al. (2005), Ding et al. (2011), and Chen (2013) described two types of trust: general and specific. General trust is presented as trust toward people in general, and specific trust refers to trust specifically related to the given referent. General trust is treated as an individual trait that is founded on moral values (Uslaner 2002) and refers to the disposition to trust. In Solomon and Flores (2001), general trust is called basic trust. Apart from this type, they also distinguished another three types: simple, blind, and authentic. Simple trust appears when people do not question each other's trustworthiness and do not have suspicions. Blind trust means that people think that other parties cannot act against them (also known as unconditional trust). Authentic trust is the most mature type of trust and is based on previous individual experiences. Trust also can be divided by organizational and individual types, where the former is connected to the reputation of the organization and the latter is related to interpersonal relations. Puusa and Tolvanen (2006) added a group type to this classification, in which the trust is linked with project teams.

Zucker (1986) proposed three types of trust: institutional-based trust, characteristic-based trust, and process-based trust. The first type is related to formal societal structures, second to a person, and third to expected or past experience (i.e., reputation). Lewicki and Bunker (1995) distinguished the following types: calculus-based, knowledge-based, and identification-based trust. The first type will develop if the relationship will pay off, the second type is based on previous experience, and third can appear when people know each other and may predict other's behavior. McAllister (1995) described a distinction between affect-based and cognition-based trust. Trust is affective-based when we develop emotional bonds toward other individuals over time. Trust is cognition-based when we choose whom we will trust in which respects and under what circumstances.

Bibb and Kourdi (2004) proposed four different types of trust: self, rational, structural, and transactional trust. Self-trust is very important in the lives of all people because it is central to building trust with others. If people do not trust themselves, it is unlikely that others will trust them. Rational trust is based on previous experience, like a general type of trust, and is established over time. Structural trust is similar to organizational trust, as it is directed to different institutions. Transactional trust is a specific type of trust that pertains to a particular context at a particular time. Loon (2007) and Krot and Lewicka (2012) distinguished horizontal trust (between co-workers) and vertical trust (between managers and employees).

As shown, scholars have distinguished different types of trust based on certain characteristics of the trustee and perceptions of the trustor. Trust is dynamic, difficult to build, and very easy to destroy. Trust cannot be compulsory. Trust overcomes risk and uncertainty in interpersonal relationships. Trust may be confirmed or revoked depending whether the other person respects or misuses it.

2.4   THE DIMENSIONS OF TRUST

Trust is a complex and multidimensional concept. To measure and understand trust, it is important to identify the dimensions of trust. In the literature, we can find different ideas on how to classify the dimensions of trust: reliability and integrity (Morgan and Hunt 1994); ability, benevolence, and integrity (Mayer et al. 1995); benevolence, honesty, competency, and predictability (McKnight and Chervany 1996); competence, openness, reliability, and caring (Mishra 1996); credibility and benevolence (Ganesan and Hess 1997); competence, goodwill, and contractual promise keeping (Sako 1998), reliability, honesty, and predictability (Zaheer et al. 1998); and competence and goodwill (Das and Teng 2001). These examples illustrate that trust can have different foundations. In this chapter, the three dimensions proposed by Paliszkiewicz and Koohang (2016) are discussed: competence, benevolence, and integrity. These dimensions were also described by Morgan and Hunt (1994), Dietz and Den Hartog (2006), Schooman et al. (2007), and Ellonen et al. (2008).

2.4.1   Competence

Most trust-related research concurs that the trustee's competence within a certain domain plays a key role (Lewis and Weigert 1985; Gulati 1995; McAllister 1995; Mishra 1996; Hart and Saunders 1997; Luhmann 2000; Brownlie and Howson 2005). Trust increases when people are perceived as competent (Sonnenberg 1994): "Competence is the ability of a person to do what needs to be done" (Paliszkiewicz and Koohang 2016, p. 92). This includes a trustee's ability to perform job responsibilities (McKnight et al. 2002) or interpret information correctly (Mishra 1996).

2.4.2   Benevolence

Benevolence can be defined as care about others, extraordinary behavior that enhances the trustor's well-being, or a willingness to act with consideration and sensitivity to the trustor's needs and interests. Benevolence is also a willingness and desire to do favors for others. Hovland et al. (1953) believed that benevolence is the basis for trust between the trustee and the trustor and displays a trustor's belief that the trustee has his or her best interests in mind. Similarly, other authors have defined benevolence as a trustee's attempt to do good for the trustor without any condition (Ingenhoff and Sommer 2010). According to Jarvenpaa and Leidner (1999), benevolent behaviors are expressions of altruism, care, and concern for others that go beyond profit motives or future gains.

2.4.3   Integrity

Integrity is established by following a set of rules and ethical standards of conduct. According to Schoorman et al. (2007), integrity is the extent to which the trustee's actions reflect values that are acceptable to the trustor. According to Butler and Cantrell (1984), integrity is the reputation for honesty and truthfulness. It is related to the broad emphasis on social justice and sincerity (Marcus et al. 2007). According to Ingenhoff and Sommer (2010), integrity "is measured by the perception of the trustor" (p. 341) and the "extent a congruency exists between the activities and the promises a party gives and whether the trustee develops a procedural fairness and transparency toward the trustor" (p. 341). Integrity is the ability of the trustee to be truthful, honest, authentic, keep promises, and show sincerity.

The described dimensions of competence, benevolence, and integrity are very important foundations to build trust in private and business lives. A study promoting such understanding would shed light on how innovativeness could be enhanced by building up trust (Ellonen et al. 2008). Managers of public and private organizations could consider more carefully how the different dimensions of interpersonal trust based on competence, benevolence, and integrity affect organizational innovativeness.

2.5   THE ROLE OF TRUST IN MANAGEMENT

The role of trust in management in public and private organization is very important. In the literature, different aspects of the role of trust in management are discussed, such as the following:

- Trust increases team performance (Klimoski and Karol 1976; Costa et al. 2001; Costa 2003).
- Trust enhances voluntary collaboration (Ganesan 1994; Morgan and Hunt 1994; Jap 1999, Bijlsma and Koopman 2003; Paliszkiewicz 2013).
- Trust facilitates long-term relationships (Ring and Van den Ven 1992; Ganesan 1994; Morgan and Hunt 1994).
- Trust facilitates management coordination among different organizational units (McAllister 1995; Doney et al. 1998).
- Trust improves the organizational climate by reducing the level of interfunctional conflicts (Das and Teng 1998).
- Trust contributes to the effective implementations of strategies (Doney et al. 1998).
- Trust reduces control-based monitoring (McAllister 1995; Das and Teng 1998, 2001; Castaldo 2007).

- Trust facilitates more open communication and sharing of knowledge, especially the enhanced exchange of tacit knowledge (McAllister 1995; Lewis and Weigert 1985; Chowdhury 2005; Seppanen et al. 2007; Hardwick et al. 2013).
- Trust helps to overcome the tension between knowledge sharing and protection (Bogers 2011).
- Trust increases job satisfaction, reduces stress, and increases organizational commitment and productivity (Kramer 1999).
- Trust enhances organizational performance and is a source of sustainable competitive advantage (Cho and Poister 2014; Paliszkiewicz et al. 2014).

Trust is very fragile and is a very dynamic process. It is built up gradually based on previous positive experiences and the number and quality of interactions. Trust is very easy to destroy and difficult to rebuild. It needs time to develop. In the literature, different types of behaviors that support trust building in organizations are presented, such as the following:

- Show that you understand the needs of the person and/or group; establish the guiding principles of how you will operate; explain the resources you will use in this work; keep to the principles you have elaborated; engage in constant, honest, two-way communication; and reinforce trust through consistent behaviors (Galford and Drapeau 2002).
- Be transparent, responsive, caring, sincere, and trustworthy (Bracey 2002).
- Be open, share influence, delegate, and manage mutual expectations (Six 2005).
- Talk straight, show respect, create transparency, right wrongs, show loyalty, deliver results, get better, confront reality, clarify expectations, practice accountability, listen first, keep commitments, and extend trust (Covey 2009).

It is important to remember that all presented behaviors need to be balanced (i.e., talk straight needs to be balanced by show respect). Any behavior pushed to the extreme becomes a weakness. Most scholars agree that trust involves positive expectations regarding the actions of others and the willingness to be vulnerable to the actions of others.

2.6   Chapter Summary

The theory of trust is still developing. Many definitions, types, and dimensions of trust are presented in the literature. This chapter presented trust as a multifaceted notion. Trust influences many aspects of organizational life in public and private organizations. Trust is needed when there is interdependence between actors—that is, when the interests of one party cannot be achieved without reliance upon another.

The review of empirical studies has brought about a number of possible research directions, such as how to measure public trust and how to rebuild public trust. Researchers should also examine how to create trust in social media, the Internet, and new technology, as well as among the people who use this technology. It will be challenging in the future research to study how trust is assessed and signaled in an online environment. Studies are needed to develop theories on how to build, manage, and measure online trust. In addition, instruments are needed for online risk and security assessment. Another important issue is how to balance between trust and distrust related to the successful use of the Internet, especially when we estimate the reliability of information. Furthermore, the following general areas need more attention and development.

- *Country comparisons:* More studies are needed to understand trust building in different societies, as well as what influences the development of public trust on a national level.
- *Cultural comparisons:* Research should consider cultural differences between people.
- *Long-term studies:* It would be interesting to see how the level of public trust has changed over time in countries or different cultures.

The review of literature presented in this chapter reveals that the body of knowledge regarding trust is still limited and further research is needed.

References

Bahmanziari, T., Pearson, J. M., & Crosby, L. (2003). Is trust important in technology adoption? A policy capturing approach. *The Journal of Computer Information Systems, 43*(4), 46–54.

Bekmeier-Feuerhahn, S., & Eichenlaub, A. (2010). What makes for trusting relationships in online communication? *Journal of Communication Management, 14*(4), 337–355.

Bhattacharya, R., Devinney, T., & Pillutla, M. (1998). A formal model of trust based on outcomes, (special topic forum on trust in and between organizations). *Academy of Management Review, 23*(3), 459–473.

Bibb, S., & Kourdi, J. (2004). *Trust matters for organizational and personal success* (p. 10). Basingstoke: Palgrave Macmillan.

Bijlsma, K., & Koopman, P. (2003). Introduction: Trust within organizations. *Personnel Review, 32*, 543–555.

Blau, P. (1964). *Exchange and power in social life.* New York: Wiley.

Bogers, M. (2011). The open innovation paradox: Knowledge sharing and protection in R&D collaborations. *European Journal of Innovation Management, 1*(14), 93–117.

Bracey, H. (2002). Building trust. In *How to get it! How to keep it!* Taylorsville: Hyler Bracey.

Brownlie, J., & Howson, A. (2005). Leaps of faith and MMR: An empirical study. *Sociology, 39*(2), 221–239.

Bugdol, M. (2010). *Wymiary i problemy zarządzania organizacją opartą na zaufaniu* [Dimensions and problems of trust-based organization management]. Kraków: Wydawnictwo Uniwersytetu Jagielońskiego.

Buskens, V. (1998). The social structure of trust. *Social Networks, 20*, 265–289.

Butler, J. K., & Cantrell, R. S. (1984). A behavioral decision theory approach to modeling dyadic trust in superiors and subordinates. *Psychological Reports, 55*, 19–28.

Casimir, G., Lee, K., & Loon, M. (2012). Knowledge sharing: Influences of trust, commitment and cost. *Journal of Knowledge Management, 16*(5), 740–753.

Castaldo, S. (2007). *Trust in market relationship.* Cheltenham/Northampton: Edwar Elgar.

Chen, W. (2013). The effects of different types of trust on consumer perceptions of food safety. *China Agricultural Economic Review, 5*(1), 43–65.

Cho, Y. J., & Poister, T. H. (2014). Managerial practices, trust in leadership, and performance: Case of the Georgia department of transportation. *Public Personnel Management, 43*(2), 179–196.

Chowdhury, S. (2005). The role of affect- and cognitions-based trust in complex knowledge sharing. *Journal of Managerial Issues, 17*(3), 310–326.

Costa, A. C. (2003). Work team trust and effectiveness. *Personnel Review, 32*, 605–622.

Costa, A. C., Roe, R. A., & Taillieu, T. (2001). Trust within teams, the relation with performance effectiveness. *European Journal of Work and Organisational Psychology, 10*, 225–244.

Covey, St. M.R. (2009). How the best leaders build trust. *Leadership Now*, Retrived from https://www.leadershipnow.com/pvcovey.html. Accessed 13 Sept 2017.

Das, T. K., & Teng, B. S. (1998). Between trust and control: Developing confidence in partner cooperation in alliances. *Academy of Management Review, 23*(3), 491–512.

Das, T. K., & Teng, B. S. (2001). Trust, control and risk in strategic alliances: An integrated framework. *Organization Studies, 22*(2), 251–283.

Das, T. K., & Teng, B. S. (2004). The risk-based view of trust: A conceptual framework. *Journal of Business and Psychology, 19*(1), 85–116.

Deutsch, M. (1958). Trust and suspicion. *Journal of Conflict Resolution, 2*, 265–279.

Deutsch, M. (1962). Cooperation and trust: Some theoretical notes. *Nebraska Symposium on Motivation, 10*, 275–318.

Dietz, G., & Den Hartog, D. N. (2006). Measuring trust inside organizations. *Personnel Review, 35*(5), 557–588.

Ding, Y. L., Veeman, M. M., & Adamowicz, W. L. (2011). The impact of generalized trust and trust in food system on choice of a functional GM food. *Agribusiness, 27*, 1–13.

Doney, P. M., & Cannon, J. P. (1997). An examination of the nature of trust in buyer–seller relationships. *Journal of Marketing, 61*, 35–51.

Doney, P. M., Cannon, J. P., & Mullen, M. R. (1998). Understanding the influence of national culture on the development of trust. *Academy of Management Review, 23*(3), 601–620.

Ellonen, R., Blomqvist, K., & Puumalainen, K. (2008). The role of trust in organisational innovativeness. *European Journal of Innovation Management, 11*(2), 160–181.

Galford, R., & Drapeau, A. S. (2002). *The trusted leader. Bringing out the best in your people and your company*. New York: Free Press.

Ganesan, S. (1994). Determinants of long-term orientation in buyer – Seller relationships. *Journal of Marketing, 58*(2), 1–19.

Ganesan, S., & Hess, R. (1997). Dimensions and levels of trust: Implications for commitment to a relationship. *Marketing Letters, 8*(4), 439–448.

Gefen, D., Karahanna, E., & Straub, D. W. (2003). Trust and TAM in online shopping: An integrated model. *MIS Quarterly, 27*(1), 51–90.

Gibb, J. R. (1978). *Trust, a new view of personal and organizational development*. International College, Los Angeles: Guild of Tutors Press.

Grudzewski, W. M., Hejduk, I. K., Sankowska, A., & Wańtuchowicz, M. (2007). *Zarządzanie zaufaniem w organizacjach wirtualnych* [Trust management in virtual organization], Difin Warsaw.

Gulati, R. (1995). Does familiarity breed trust? The implications of repeated ties for contractual choice in alliances. *Academy of Management Journal, 38*(1), 647–664.

Habib, S. M., Hauke, S., Ries, S., & Mühlhäuser, M. (2012). Trust as a facilitator in cloud computing: A survey. *Journal of Cloud Computing, 1*(1), 1–18.

Hardwick, J., Anderson, A. R., & Cruickshank, D. (2013). Trust formation processes in innovative collaborations. *European Journal of Innovation Management, 16*(1), 4–21.

Hart, P., & Saunders, C. (1997). Power and trust: Critical factors in the adoption and use of electronic data interchange. *Organization Science, 8*(1), 23–42.

Hosmer, L. T. (1995). Trust: The connecting link between organizational theory and philosophical ethics. *Academy of Management Review, 20*(2), 379–403.

Hovland, C. I., Janis, I. L., & Kelley, H. H. (1953). *Communication and persuasion.* New Haven: Yale University Press.

Hummels, H., & Roosendaal, H. E. (2001). Trust in scientific publishing. *Journal of Business Ethics, 34*(2), 87–100.

Ingenhoff, D., & Sommer, K. (2010). Trust in Companies and in CEOs: A comparative study of the main influences. *Journal of Business Ethics, 95*(3), 339–355.

Isik, M., Timuroglu, M. K., & Aliyev, Y. (2015). The relationship between teamwork and organizational trust. *International Journal of Research in Business and Social Science, 4*(1), 133–149.

James, H. S. (2002). The trust paradox: A survey of economic inquiries into the nature of trust and trustworthiness. *Journal of Economic Behavior & Organization, 47,* 291–307.

Jap, S. D. (1999). Pie-expansion efforts: Collaboration processes in buyer – Supplier relationships. *Journal of Marketing Research, 36*(4), 461–475.

Jarvenpaa, S. L., & Leidner, D. E. (1999). Communication and trust in global virtual teams. *Organization Science, 10*(6), 791–815.

Jones, G., & George, J. (1998). The experience and evolution of trust: Implications for cooperation and teamwork. *Academy of Management Review, 23*(3), 531–548.

Klimoski, R. J., & Karol, B. L. (1976). The impact of trust on creative problem solving groups. *Journal of Applied Psychology, 61,* 630–633.

Koohang, A., Paliszkiewicz, J., & Gołuchowski, J. (2017). The impact of leadership on trust, knowledge management, and organizational performance: A research model. *Industrial Management & Data Systems, 117*(3), 52–537.

Kożuch, B., & Lenart-Gansiniec, R. (2017). Trust and knowledge sharing. In L. Liebowitz, J. Paliszkiewicz, & J. Gołuchowski (Eds.), *Intuition, trust, and analytics.* Boca Raton: CRC Press, Taylor & Francis Group, Auerbach Publications.

Kramer, R. M. (1999). Trust and distrust: Emerging questions, enduring questions. *Annual Review of Psychology, 50,* 569–598.

Krot, K., & Lewicka, D. (2012). The importance of trust in manager-employee relationships. *International Journal of Electronic Business Management, 10*(3), 224–233.

Lewicki, R. J., & Bunker, B. B. (1995). Developing and maintaining trust in work relationships. In R. M. Kramer & T. R. Tyler (Eds.), *Trust in organizations: Frontiers of theory and research* (pp. 114–139). Thousand Oaks: Sage Publications.

Lewis, J. D., & Weigert, A. (1985). Trust as a social reality. *Social Forces, 63*(4), 967–985.

Loon, H. S. (2007). Is interpersonal trust a necessary condition for organisational learning? *Journal of Organisational Transformation and Social Change, 4*(2), 149–156.

Luhmann, N. (1979). *Trust and power.* Chichester: John Wiley.

Luhmann, N. (2000). Familiarity, confidence and trust problems and alternatives. In D. Gambetta (Ed.), *Trust: Making and breaking cooperative relations.* Oxford: University of Oxford.

Marcus, B., Lee, K., & Ashton, M. C. (2007). Personality dimensions explaining relationships between integrity tests and counterproductive behavior: Big five, or one in addition? *Personnel Psychology, 60*(1), 1–34.

Mayer, R. C., Davis, J. H., & Schoorman, F. D. (1995). An integrative model of organizational trust. *Academy of Management Review, 20*(3), 709–734.

McAllister, D. J. (1995). Affect and cognition based trust as foundations for interpersonal cooperation in organizations. *Academy of Management Journal, 38*(1), 24–59.

McKnight, D. H., & Chervany, N. L. (1996). *The meanings of trust.* Retrieved from http://www.misrc.umn.edu/workingpapers/fullpapers/1996/9604_040100.pdf. Accessed 27 Apr 2015.

McKnight, D. H., Choudhury, V., & Kacmar, C. (2002). Developing and validating trust measures for e-commerce: An integrative typology. *Information Systems Research, 13*(3), 334–359.

Mishra, A. K. (1996). Organizational responses to crises: The centrality of trust. In R. M. Kramer & T. Tyler (Eds.), *Trust in organizations.* Beverly Hills: Sage.

Morgan, R. M., & Hunt, S. D. (1994). The commitment-theory of relationship marketing. *Journal of Marketing, 58*(3), 20–38.

Paliszkiewicz, J. (2013). *Zaufanie w zarządzaniu* [Trust in management]. Warszawa: Wydawnictwo Naukowe PWN.

Paliszkiewicz, J., & Koohang, A. (2016). *Social media and trust: A multinational study of university students.* Santa Rosa: Informing Science Press.

Paliszkiewicz, J., Koohang, A., & Horn Nord, J. (2014). Management trust, organizational trust, and organizational performance: Empirical validation of an instrument. *The Online Journal of Applied Knowledge Management, 2*(1), 28–39.

Paliszkiewicz, J., Gołuchowski, J., & Koohang, A. (2015). Leadership, trust, and knowledge management in relation to organizational performance: Developing an instrument. *Online Journal of Applied Knowledge Management, 3*(2), 19–35.

Puusa, A., & Tolvanen, U. (2006). Organizational identity and trust. *Electronic Journal of Business Ethics and Organization Studies, 11*(2), 29–31.

Rempel, J. K., Holmes, J. G., & Zanna, M. P. (1985). Trust in close relationships. *Journal of Personality and Social Psychology, 49*(1), 95–112.

Ring, P. S., & Van den Ven, A. H. (1992). Structuring cooperative relationships between organizations. *Strategic Management Journal, 13*(7), 483–498.

Rotter, J. B. (1967). A new scale for the measurement of interpersonal trust. *Journal of Personality, 35*, 651–665.

Sako, M. (1992). *Prices, quality and trust, inter-firm relations in Britain & Japan.* Cambridge: Cambridge University Press.

Sako, M. (1998). Does trust improve business performance. In C. Lane & R. Buchmann (Eds.), *Trust within and between organizations: Conceptual issues and empirical applications.* Oxford: Oxford University Press.

Sankowska, A., & Paliszkiewicz, J. (2016). Dimensions of institutionalized organizational trust and Firm's innovativeness. *Journal of Computer Information Systems, 56*(2), 168–174.

Savolainen, T., Lopez-Fresno, P., & Ikonen, M. (2014). Trust-communication dyad in inter-personal workplace relationships – Dynamics of trust deterioration and breach. *Electronic Journal of Knowledge Management, 12*(4), 232–240.

Schoorman, F. D., Mayer, R. C., & Davis, J. H. (2007). An integrative model of organizational trust: Past, present, and future. *Academy of Management Review, 32*(2), 344–354.

Seppanen, R., Blomqvist, K., & Sundqvist, S. (2007). Measuring inter-organizational trust – A critical review of the empirical research in 1990–2003. *Industrial Marketing Management, 36*, 249–265.

Siegrist, M., Gutscher, H., & Earle, T. C. (2005). Perception of risk: The influence of general trust and general confidence. *Journal of Risk Research, 8*(2), 145–156.

Six, F. (2005). *The trouble with trust. The dynamics of interpersonal trust building.* Bodmin: MPG Books.

Solomon, R. C., & Flores, F. (2001). *Building trust in business, politics, relationships, and life.* Oxford: Oxford University Press.

Sonnenberg, F. K. (1994). Trust me.... Trust me not. *Journal of Business Strategy, 15*, 14–16.

Sztompka, P. (1999). *Trust: A sociological theory.* Cambridge: Cambridge University Press.

Tyler, T. R. (2003). Trust within organisations. *Personnel Review, 32*(5), 556–568.

Tyler, T. R., & Kramer, R. M. (1996). Wither trust? In R. M. Kramer & T. R. Tyler (Eds.), *Trust in organizations: Frontiers of theory and research* (pp. 1–15). Thousand Oaks: Sage Publications.

Uslaner, E. M. (2002). *The moral foundation of trust.* New York: Cambridge University Press.

Wrightsman, L. S. (1966). Personality and attitudinal correlates of trusting and trustworthy behaviors in a two-person game. *Journal of Personality and Social Psychology, 4,* 328–332.

Zaheer, A., McEvily, B., & Perrone, V. (1998). Does trust matter? Exploring the effects of inter-organizational and interpersonal trust on performance. *Organization Science, 9*(2), 141–159.

Zand, D. (1972). Trust and managerial problem solving. *Administrative Science Quarterly, 17,* 229–239.

Zucker, L. G. (1986). Production of trust: Institutional sources of economic structure, 1840–1920. *Research in Organizational Behavior, 8,* 53–111.

CHAPTER 3

Understanding Public Trust

Barbara Kożuch

3.1 Introduction

Public management is one of the fastest-growing disciplines. However, the specificity of public organizations and their management, including public trust, are still not fully understood. This chapter first discusses the nature of public organizations. The literature analysis examines the state of knowledge in the scope of the publicness concepts. Based on this analysis, public trust in the context of organizational publicness is defined. Finally, the issues related to creating, regaining, and sustaining public trust within and between organizations are discussed. The main assumption made in this work is that relationships based on trust within and between public organizations and their efficient functioning are mutually conditioned.

3.2 Theoretical Background

3.2.1 *The Nature of Public Organizations*

In this chapter, the investigation into the differences between private and public organizations was focused on their specifics. According to Tholen (2016), this stage of researching the nature of public organizations is

B. Kożuch (✉)
Jagiellonian University, Kraków, Poland

© The Author(s) 2018
B. Kożuch et al. (eds.), *Managing Public Trust*,
https://doi.org/10.1007/978-3-319-70485-2_3

mirrored in following definitions of the public. The nature of the public organization is as follows:

1. Concerns the whole citizenry (Rosenbloom and Goldman 1989, p. 8);
2. Considers societal and democratic values (conversely, a private organization considers managerial values; Raadschelders 2003, p. 202)
3. Inevitably shares public goods or public opinion (John 1998, pp. 4, 206)
4. Public concerns are chosen by the government (Dye 1992, p. 2)

Thus, understanding the nature of public organizations or a notion of publicness is related to different traditional considerations.

Bozeman (1987, p. xi) developed a highly cited definition of publicness, stating the degree to which organizations are affected by political authority. He also developed the dimensional publicness theory (1984, 1987, 2007, 2013), which identifies the distinct dimensions of public organizations as the instruments for the implementation of public purposes. The model expounds that public and private characteristics are dimensions rather than dichotomies, and organizations can be more or less public in each of these dimensions. Based on his scientific findings and the achievements of other scholars (Boyne 2002; Rainey 1983, Rainey et al. 1976; Rainey and Bozeman 2000; Rainey 2014; Noordegraf 2015), the theory of publicness has widened its scope.

According to Bozeman and Bretschneider (1994), the most relevant criteria of publicness in organizational studies include the following:

– Distinction from the private sector
– The scope and composition of its service recipients,
– The magnitude and intensity of its socioeconomic role
– The degree of its public accountability
– The level of its public trust (Haque 2001, p. 67)

In this way, publicness is related to democratic political systems, as well as to action and policies.

As Bozeman and Moulton noted (2011), from the outset, there were two different approaches to the publicness theory. In that discourse, one approach was used by political science and public administration researchers, to whom the uniqueness of public organizations was obvious. In the other approach, organization theorists claimed that any empirical difference between public and private organizations was a result of misunderstanding and researcher errors. The former is a generic approach, whereas the latter is a core approach. These differences have been overcome in the comparison studies within the well-known book, "Understanding and Managing Public Organizations" by Hal G. Rainey (2014). The distinctiveness of public organizations has been proven.

Investigations into the nature of public organizations have attempted to develop an integrative approach to describing publicness. Bozeman and Molton (2011) asserted that two types of publicness should be considered for a better understanding of the contemporary public organization: (1) empirical publicness, which focuses on resource publicness, personnel publicness, and on organizational behaviors and outcomes, and (2) normative publicness, which seeks to infuse values. This approach embraces publicness as the production of public goods, as well as a way for public organizations to meet public interest (Apelt 2014; Riccucci 2012). Examples of such activities include the following: (1) pursuing the interests of a given public organization, as well as the people served by this organization, by cultivating relationships with different classes of stakeholders, such as citizens, elected officials, and employees; (2) exerting varied forms of stakeholders' empowerment; (3) exercising political skills transparently and without bias; (4) practicing honesty and integrity by trusted public managers while expecting the same from those around them (Cooper and Bryer 2012). All approaches provide a field-level depiction of publicness that is useful for achieving public value outcomes.

3.2.2   Distinctive Features of Public Organizations

When interpreting the nature of the public organization, the dimensional publicness theory, which was developed by Bozeman (1984) and elaborated by his followers, can be used. Particularly useful are Boyne's (2002) method of dealing with organizational publicness and interpretations of this approach (Kożuch 2011; Kożuch and Dobrowolski 2014). Such an approach highlights the distinctive features of organizational relationships and the relationships that characterize public organizations.

The theory of publicness is about the nature of internal connections as well as the types of interorganizational relationships. The publicness of the organization is formed in four dimensions: in concrete relationships with its environment, distinguishing goals, specific structure, and values (Boyne 2002). When interpreting this idea, the starting assumption should be underlined. The emerging needs of individuals forming a society can be met by private goods or public goods. All goods are private and public to varying degrees. Everyone must compete for a private good. In contrast, no one needs to compete for a public good, nor can anyone be excluded from the consumption. Bearing this in mind, public organizations can be understood as those whose primary function, or mission, is to meet the public needs of the citizenry by providing public goods and services. What is most important is the extent to which the public organization retains the ability to satisfy users of these goods and services.

Public organizations are obliged to provide publicly available public services. Civic organizations, or even business entities, can be the implementers of these services, especially when there is a convergence of the objectives of the cooperating organizations. However, in no case do these organizations guarantee public services—they only deliver them directly to citizens. The public nature of these services exists when public organizations fund specific services and take responsibility for the citizens.

Understanding the essence of organizational publicness makes it easier to list the characteristics of business organizations versus public organizations. A very important difference is that public organizations are subjected to more political control than market control. Furthermore, there is a greater likelihood of conflicts, as there is often more than one source of power in public organizations. The publicness is characterized by a combination of characteristics of its particular dimensions, as indicated by the majority of British and American researchers. The relationships of public organizations with their external environment are distinguished from other organizations by four circumstances (Pollitt 1990; Boyne 1998): greater complexity of environmental influences, greater openness to environmental influences, less stable operations, and less pressure (or a lack of pressure) on the part of competitors.

The interactions of public organizations with their external environment are characterized by great complexity. The recipients of public goods and services are diverse social groups. In addition, other organizations and individuals are interested in the results of public actions. Numerous and diverse stakeholders direct their expectations and preferences to the managers of public organizations, which are often contradictory. It should be noted that public organizations often operate through a network of independent organizations, which aim to achieve their own goals (Agranoff 2006; Klijn 2008; Kożuch and Małyjurek 2013).

One of the most important attributes of an organization is its openness to the influence of the environment. In the case of public organizations, a greater degree of openness is taken into consideration. The impact of the environment is desirable, because the interactions of the organization and its external environment are conducive to matching their activities to the real needs of the public. Such a high level of openness serves both the interests of the organizations and the environments in which they operate.

The less stable environment of public organizations is due to their links with politics. This is reflected in frequent operational changes. Public managers often prefer short-term measures because they are under constant pressure to achieve rapid results. Public organizations also typically operate under less pressure from competitors. They generally occupy a dominant position in the market, sometimes operating under the conditions of a natural monopoly. Furthermore, in accordance with the expectations of the society, public organizations establish cooperation with other organizations, including private companies that offer similar goods and services.

The distinctive characteristics of the objectives of public organizations are not controversial. It is obvious that goals such as justice and accountability to citizens are absent in the business world. The goals of public organizations are rooted in the shared ownership of these organizations and the resulting drive to control the behavior of the organization, ensuring that collective goals are achieved. These goals require a different organizational process management in public organizations. These organizations need to address the multiple objectives formulated by different classes of stakeholders. The situation is different in business organizations, where the most important thing is to make a profit—a clear measure of success or failure. On the contrary, the main task of public organizations is to balance the influence of different stakeholder groups and reconcile or resolve emerging conflicts. A comparison of the objectives formulated in the business sector with the objectives of public organizations points to some imprecision and ambiguity of the latter objectives.

Publicness is reflected in an organizational structure, typically as the more formal nature of the organization, solving management problems in a bureaucratic manner, and less autonomy for managers. The organization's more formal nature is reflected in the decision-making process in public organizations. This process involves more formal procedures than in business; however, it evokes less flexibility and less willingness to take risks. This situation has its origin in several causes. The justification is, for example, the pursuit of monitoring of public decision-making processes in order to clarify accountability to stakeholders. The formalization of procedures is also important in the context of the specific control mechanisms. Red tape in public organizations is seen as a side effect of hierarchical governance. Its most common symptoms are the tendency to create countless documents that irritate people served by public organizations due to numerous delays and lack of progress in adapting the organization to the needs of the public.

In the literature, there is no consensus concerning the essence and range of publicness in certain features of an organization. Bozeman (1984, 1987, 2007, 2013) and his followers have claimed that all organizations are public to a varying extent. The basis for this reasoning is that the individual dimensions of public and private organizations can be compared separately. However, this concept omits that only public organizations act in the interest of the whole society. Furthermore, it is not surprising that the different types of organizations are similar.

When striving to understand the nature of an organization, one is supposed to concentrate on its specificity. Similarities are associated with belonging to a category of organizations, and this assertion does not bring anything new. As a result, the distinctiveness of public organizations needs to be defined. Generally, the distinctiveness of public organizations results from the fact that those organizations accomplish their aims mostly due to the influence on other organizations or directly on citizens. Consequently, public organizations take public actions, which will enable the realization of both their own aims and also the goals of the organization that is influenced by them. In doing so, they act in the public interest.

The nature of public organizations is clearly explained in the definition of organizational publicness, which refers only to public organizations by their interrelated five attributes, as follows (Kożuch et al. 2016):

1. A public organization pursues the public interest, which refers to the common values relevant to a given society. In practice, this interest is shared by the majority of citizens.
2. A public organization functions in complex and politically, economically, and socially unstable environments. The recipients of public goods and services are different classes of stakeholders. Traditionally, public organizations have focused solely on their own organizational goals. Current practice shows that public organizations increasingly operate through organizational networks.

3. A distinctive nature of the aims of public organizations ensures the simultaneous satisfaction of various stakeholder groups, without the support of which contemporary public organizations cannot exist.
4. Public organization use formalized decision-making processes to ensure their legitimacy, transparency, and accountability to citizens, what affects the shape of the organizational structure.
5. Public managers have steward roles that focus on empowerment, collaboration, and participation.

All of these identified attributes refer directly or indirectly to the general distinguishing feature of public organizations. Their organizational goals can be effectively achieved by employing collaborative approaches in strategic and operational public management. Thus, there is a need for public organizations as sociotechnical systems to build relationships based on trust.

3.3   Defining Public Trust

3.3.1   *Traditional Approaches to Public Trust*

Generally, public trust is connected with society and is defined on the bases of sociology and political sciences (Lynn 1981; Nutt and Backoff 1993; Candlin and Crichton 2013; Llewellyn et al. 2013; Bouckaert 2012; Hardin 2009; Blind 2006; Warren 2006; Sztompka 1999; Fukuyama 1996: Van de Walle et al. 2008). Trust in government or trust in citizens is the main focus of research. According to researchers, trust is a type of human and institutional interaction. Political trust is commonly identified with public trust. In that case, the term *public* comes from "the public" or citizenry. Public trust can be system-based and institution-based trust or social trust with social capital and civic engagement.

According to this approach, public trust means that citizens judge the government and its institutions, policymaking, and the behaviors of the individual political leaders. In this context, it is understood as a central indicator of the public's feelings about public policies and their implementations. When motivation-based public trust is analyzed, rational political trust and psychological public trust are distinguished. Political trust is an interest-based calculation linked with public actions taken by governments and political leaders. This type of trust can be referred to as trust based on the maximization of self-interest. Psychological trust, on the other hand, includes an assessment of the publicly shared values and attributes associated with the public action performed by governments. It is significant that citizens expect integrity in the functioning of public institutions. Social trust—the "lubricant of interactions among people" (Arrow 1974, p. 23)—is the citizens' trust in each other as members of a social community. Both interpersonal trust and civic engagement in a community contribute to increased social trust in a society (Putnam 2000; Putnam et al. 1993).

Another approach to public trust was developed by Geert Bouckaert (2012), who distinguished three types of interactions and directions of relationship based on trust:

1. The trust of citizens and organizations in government and the public sector
2. The trust of the government and the public sector in citizens and organizations
3. The trust within the government and the public sector

This list considers the public sector as a whole, but the public organizations included in this sector are not taken into account. This is likely because publicness is defined as a collection of certain elements, but not as a set of specific dimensions of the nature of public organizations.

In traditional approaches to public trust, political, public, and social trust are at the core of the concept (Bozeman and Moulton 2011; Bouckaert 2012). The organizational aspects of functioning political and economic systems and organizations, as well as individual political leaders and public managers, are missed.

3.3.2 *Organizational Perspective of Public Trust*

In management and organization, specific attitudes and behavior models are linked with the concepts of trust (Sitkin and Roth 1993, p. 373; Blomquist and Stahle 2000, p. 4; Zucker 1986, p. 54; Zaheer et al. 1998, p. 143). The notion of trust in reference to organizational processes can be understood as follows:

- A belief in a person's competence to perform an organizational task under specific circumstances and positive expectations of the other party's competencies, goodwill, and appropriate organizational behaviors

– A set of expectations shared by all who are involved in an exchange
– Expectations that an individual can be relied on to fulfill obligations, behave in a predictable manner, and act and negotiate fairly when the possibility for opportunism is present

Investigating public trust from an organizational perspective requires a focus on the elements of the organization's functioning, particularly on management processes, where the impact of trust is considered in the context of formulating and achieving organizational goals. In the proposed approach, the overall organizational, intra-organizational, and inter-organizational perspectives of public trust can be distinguished. The overall perspective consists of elements that are the basis for organizational trustworthiness, such as the following:

1. The ability of an organization to effectively produce public goods or provide public services
2. A positive attitude toward the recipients of goods and services produced (i.e., toward steward citizens and other stakeholders)
3. Consistency of the proclaimed values and organizational practices relevant to public organizations

In the process of building trust in organizations, it is necessary to ensure appropriate conditions for the execution of organizational processes—for example, having appropriate competencies, organizational structures, coordination mechanisms, resource availability, and others. An adequate set of organizational competencies—including the propensity to trust, confidence, and the ability to take risks—are indispensable conditions for both building and restoring organizational trust. The same applies to the cohesion of proclaimed values and organizational practices, which enters the realm of the ethical behavior of people and organizations and the responsibility of the organization toward its stakeholders. Any violation of this cohesion negatively affects the level of trust in the organization.

The proposed understanding of the overall organizational perspective of trust was discussed by Mayer et al. (1995), who stated that competence, benevolence, and integrity are the three factors of perceived trustworthiness that determine trust in an organization. Competences are understood as reliable opportunities of a trusted party in a given field. Benevolence is an attitude to act in the best interests of a trusting person. Integrity in this approach implies the ability and will of a trusted party to achieve and maintain its moral and ethical values. According to the authors, perceived risk has an impact on trust relationships in the sense that positive or negative results will increase or decrease the impact of the anticipated risk. This perspective may provide a starting point for particular research perspectives, such as the organizational perspective of public trust.

Public trust refers to the situation where public organizations are competent, open, and honest, characterized by concern for stakeholders and responsibility to them, and identified with public goals, norms, and values (Shockley-Zalabak et al. 2003). In other words, from the organizational perspective, public trust can be defined as a relationship reflecting the degree to which all stakeholders trust the organization's competences, organizational goals, shared standards and values, organizational principles, processes, procedures, codes of conduct, and care for internal and external stakeholders. Intra-organizational trust relates to individuals employed in an organization or to a system which is that organization. Trust in the organization includes positive expectations for other members of the organization, groups, and the organization as a whole. It is more than cumulative trust in a given number of relationships. It also includes relationships between people and structures, as well as mechanisms for shaping organizational behaviors (Adams et al. 2008).

Understanding the specificity of public organizations makes it possible to know the mechanism for creating and maintaining public trust. Starting from the organizational perspective of public trust, this mechanism can be described in a simplified way using a model that consists of four components, through which positive characteristics and interdependence create or enhance the public trust within organizations and between them:

1. The ability of public organizations, including public managers and officials, to effectively provide public services
2. Positive attitudes toward citizens as stakeholders and responding to the collective needs of citizens
3. Consistency of proclaimed public values and organizational practices
4. Stakeholders' knowledge of public service delivery and the public organization's responsibility, particularly when it is acquired through prior experience in dealing with a given public organization.

The intra-organizational perspective of public trust is thus formed by the following processes (Shaw 1997; Shockley-Zabalak et al. 2010):

1. Signaling trust within public organizations due to knowledge of employees about the whole organization, propensity to trust, participation, and empowerment
2. Achieving planned outcomes by pursuing compliance of goals and means, effective implementation of the organizational strategy, and collaboration within the organization
3. Integrating activities by coherence of objectives, impartiality, and concern for public affairs
4. Creating conditions for organizational commitment by focusing on the delegation of power and fair treatment of employees

In turn, interorganizational trust is created by following components (Kożuch 2014):

1. Understanding intra-organizational public trust as the basis for shaping interorganizational trust relationships by employing the will and the ability of public organizations to serve the public interest
2. Pursuing the effective realization of organizational goals in collaboration with external stakeholders, such as establishing partnerships and initiating networking
3. Shaping general and specific competencies of public managers and appropriate attitudes to stakeholders, such as a high level of public management skills or implementation of modern management methods and techniques
4. Endowing stakeholders with knowledge about the ability to meet organizational goals and being responsible to citizens and other stakeholders, such as sending reliable communication and gaining knowledge of public organizations through joint actions or through other individuals or organizations

It must be stressed that when the organizational components of the public trust perspective are characterized by high ethical and efficiency standards, these organizations are able to achieve established organizational goals more effectively. However, when the factual characteristics are below standards, then a low level of intra-organizational trust results (below the expectations of the stakeholders), which limits the possibilities of establishing interorganizational public trust.

3.4   Chapter Summary

The research explored in this chapter indicates that a rethinking of contemporary public organizations is needed. In contrary to most public management scholars, organizational publicness should only refer to a subcategory of public organizations, not to each type of organization. Furthermore, the dimensions of public organizations need to be analyzed as interrelationships and considered as a set of characteristics. Such an approach increases one's understanding of the nature of contemporary public organizations as units of the public sector. Creating, regaining, and sustaining public trust have led to an understanding of this notion as the central category of public organizations. It is influenced by the organizational behavior of people and systems on both sides of the public service delivery processes, together with their material and nonmaterial instrumentation.

The analysis of intra-organizational public trust in this chapter indicates that this concept can be defined as a relationship based on knowledge about public organizations and the belief that public organizations are able to conduct public policies and programs that allow the public interest to be served by the public organizations. In turn, interorganizational public trust can be understood as a relationship based on the sound intra-organizational trust of each organization as a pre-condition of building future trust between interacting organizations. Other bases for creating, regaining, and sustaining trust include collaborative relationships with external stakeholders, shaping appropriate public management competencies, and establishing effective communication with other organizations.

References

Adams, B. D., Thomson, M. H., Brown, A., Sartori, J. A., Taylor, T., & Waldherr, S. (2008). *Organisational trust in the Canadian forces.* Toronto: HumanSystem.

Agranoff, R. (2006). Inside collaborative networks: Ten lessons for public managers. *Public Administration Review, 66*(1), 56–65.

Apelt, C. (2014). *Change in public organisations School of Management/Faculty of Business Queensland University of Technology.* Retrieved from https://eprints. qut.edu.au/73086/2/ Christina_Apelt_Thesis.pdf. 16 June 2017.

Arrow, K. (1974). *The limits of organization*. New York: Norton.

Blind, P. K. (2006, November). Building trust in government in the twenty-first century: Review of literature and emerging. *Issues*, 3–8.

Blomqvist, K., & Stahle, P. (2000). *Building organizational trust*. Paper presented at the 16th Annual IMP Conference, Bath.

Bouckaert, G. (2012). Trust and public administration. *Administration, 60*(1), 91–115, Retrieved from: http://unpan1.un.org/intradoc/groups/public/documents/un/unpan025062.pdf. 18 July 2017.

Boyne, G. A. (1998). Public services under new labour: Back to bureaucracy? *Public Money and Management, 18*(3), 43–50.

Boyne, G. A. (2002). Public and private management: What's the difference? *Journal of Management Studies, 39*(1), 97–122.

Bozeman, B. (1984). Dimensions of publicness: An approach to public organizational theory. In B. Bozeman & J. Straussman (Eds.), *New directions in public administration* (pp. 46–62). Belmont: Crooks/Cole.

Bozeman, B. (1987). *All organizations are public: Bridging public and private organizational theories*. San-Francisco: Jossey-Bass.

Bozeman, B. (2007). *Public values and public interest: Counterbalancing economic individualism*. Washington: Georgetown University Press.

Bozeman, B. (2013). What organization theorists and public policy researchers can learn from one another: Publicness theory as a case-in-point. *Organization Studies, 34*(2), 169–188.

Bozeman, B., & Bretschneider, S. (1994). The "publicness puzzle" in organization theory: A test of alternative explanations of differences between public and private organizations. *Journal of Public Administration Research and Theory, 4*(2), 197–223.

Bozeman, B., & Moulton, S. (2011). Integrative publicness: A framework for public management strategy and performance. *Journal of Public Administration Research and Theory, 21*(suppl 3), i363–i380.

Candlin, C. N., & Crichton, J. (2013). *Discourses of trust*. Basingstoke: Palgrave Macmillan.

Cooper, T. L., & Bryer, T. A. (2012). William Robertson: Exemplar of politics and public management rightly understood. In N. M. Riccucci (Ed.), *Serving public interest. Profiles of successful and innovate public servants* (pp. 48–58). Armonk: M.E. Sharpe.

Dye, T. R. (1992). *Understanding public policy*. Inglewood Cliffs: Prentice Hall.

Fukuyama, F. (1996). *Trust: Human nature and the reconstitution of social order*. New York: Free Press.

Haque, S. (2001). The diminishing publicness of public service under the current mode of governance. *Public Administration Review, 61*(1), 65–79.

Hardin, R. (2009). *Zaufanie* [Trust], Sic!, Warszawa.

John, P. (1998). *Analysing public policy*. London: Continuum.

Klijn, E. H. (2008). Governance and governance networks in Europe: An assessment of 10 years of research on the theme. *Public Management Review, 10*(4), 505–525.

Kożuch, B. (2011). *Skuteczne współdziałanie organizacji publicznych i pozarządowych* [Effective cooperation between public and non-governmental organszations]. Kraków: Instytut Spraw Publicznych, Uniwersytet Jagielloński.

Kożuch, B. (2014). Organizacyjna perspektywa zaufania publicznego: zarys koncepcji [An outline of an organisationorganizational perspective of public trust]. *Przedsiębiorczość i Zarządzanie: Zarządzane Humanistyczne, 1*, 41–51.

Kożuch, B., & Dobrowolski, Z. (2014). *Creating public trust. An organisational perspective.* Peter Lang: Frankfurt am Main.

Kożuch, B., & Sienkiewicz-Małyjurek, K. (2013). Collaborative networks as a basis for internal economic security in sustainable local governance. The case of Poland. In K. Raczkowski & F. Schneider (Eds.), *The economic security of business transactions.* Oxford: Chartridge Books Oxford.

Kożuch A., Kożuch B., Sułkowski Ł., Bogacz-Wojtanowska E., Lewandowski M., Sienkiewicz-Małyjurek K., Szczudlińska-Kanoś A., & Jung-Konstanty S. (2016). *Obszary zarządzania publicznego* [Areas of public management]. Kraków: Instytut Spraw Publicznych, Uniwersytet Jagielloński.

Llewellyn, S., Brooks, S., & Mahon, A. (2013). *Trust and confidence in government and public services.* New York: Routledge.

Lynn, L. E. (1981). *Managing the public's business.* New York: Basic Books.

Mayer, R. C., Davis, J. H., & Schoorman, F. D. (1995). An integrative model of organizational trust. *The Academy of Management Review, 20*(3), 709–734.

Noordegraaf, M. (2015). *Public management. Performance, professionalism and politics.* London: Palgrave.

Nutt, P. C., & Backoff, R. W. (1993). Organizational publicness and its implications for strategic management. *Journal of Public Administration Research and Theory, 3*(2), 209–231.

Pollit, C. (1990). *Managerialism and the public services.* Oxford: Blackwell.

Putnam, R. D. (2000). *Bowling alone: The collapse and revival of American community.* New York: Simon and Schuster.

Putnam, R. D., Leonardi, R., & Nanetti, R. (1993). *Making democracy work: Civic traditions in modern Italy.* Princeton: Princeton University Press.

Raadschelders, J. (2003). *Government. A public administration perspective.* Armonk: M.E. Sharpe.

Rainey, H. G. (1983). Public agencies and private firms: Incentive structures, goals, and individual roles. *Administration and Society, 15*, 207–242.

Rainey, H. G. (2014). *Understanding and managing public organizations* (5th ed.). San Francisco: Jossey-Bass.

Rainey, H. G., & Bozeman, B. (2000). Comparing public and private organizations. *Journal of Public Administration Research and Theory, 10*(2), 447–469.

Rainey, H. G., Backoff, R. W., & Levine, C. H. (1976). Comparing public and private organizations. *Public Administration Review, 36*(2), 233–244.

Riccucci, N. M. (Ed.). (2012). *Serving public interest. Profiles of successful and innovate public servants.* Armonk: M.E. Sharpe.

Rosenbloom, D. H., & Goldman, D. (1989). *Public administration: Understanding management, politics, and law in the public sector.* New York: Random House.

Shaw, R. B. (1997). *Trust in ballance.* San Francisco: Jossey-Bass Publishers.

Shockley-Zalabak, P., Ellis, K., & Cesaria, R. (2000/2003). *Measuring organizational trust: Crosscultural survey and index.* IABC Research Foundation, San Francisco. (after M.L. Watson, can there be just one trust? A cross-disciplinary identification of trust definitions and measurement. Retrieved from http://www.clayton.k12.mo.us/cms/lib/MO01000419/Centricity/Domain/2/NSPRA2009/2004_Watson.pdf. 31 July 2017.

Shockley-Zalabak, P., Morreale, S. P., & Hackman, M. Z. (2010). *Building the high-trust organization.* San Francisco: Jossey-Bass.

Sitkin, S. B., & Roth, N. L. (1993). Explaining the limited effectiveness of legalistic "remedies" for trust/distrust. *Organizational Science, 4,* 367–392.

Sztompka, P. (1999). *Trust: A sociological theory.* Cambridge: Cambridge University Press.

Tholen, B. (2016). Drawing the line: On the public/private distinction in debates on new modes of governance. *Public Integrity, 18*(3), 237–253.

Van de Walle, S., Van Roosbroek, S., & Bouckaert, G. (2008). Trust in the public sector: Is there any evidence for a long-term decline? *International Review of Administrative Sciences, 74*(1), 47–64.

Warren, M. E. (2006). Democracy and deceit. Regulating appearances of corruption. *American Journal of Political Science, 50*(1), 160–174.

Zaheer, A., McEvily, B., & Perrone, V. (1998). Does trust matter? Exploring the effects of interorganizational and interpersonal trust on performance. *Organization Science: A Journal of the Institute of Management Sciences, 9*(2), 141–159.

Zucker, L. G. (1986). Production of trust: Institutional sources of economic structure,1840–1920. In B. M. Staw & L. L. Cummings (Eds.), *Research in organizational behavior* (Vol. 8). Greenwich: JAI Press.

Public Trust and Organizational Challenges

CHAPTER 4

Public Trust and Organizational Change

Sławomir J. Magala

"The ceaseless pursuit of data to quantify the value of any endeavor is catastrophic to true understanding."
(Eggers 2014, 485)
"Neither the direction of cultural shift nor the intensity of change can be fully predicted solely on the basis of economic growth."
(Minkov 2011, 237)

4.1 Introduction

Organizations evolve, but the institutional landscape of large clusters of organizations changes more slowly. Technological inventions can undermine libraries and massive online open courses can push universities toward a more virtual mode of operation. However, political attempts to either reaffirm elite control in professional bureaucracies or to share some power and privileges with concerned corporate citizens and constituencies remain crucial in making and breaking trust. More frequent sampling of public trust (with new data farming techniques) would allow the rate and direction of organizational change to be traced in response to the growing criticism of online masses and transforming job markets for graduates.

S. J. Magala (⊠)
Erasmus University Rotterdam (em.), Rotterdam, The Netherlands

Jagiellonian University, Cracow, Poland

© The Author(s) 2018
B. Kożuch et al. (eds.), *Managing Public Trust*,
https://doi.org/10.1007/978-3-319-70485-2_4

One should not take the current dictatorship of expert elites for granted. Does knowledge management require a celebrity hierarchy, with Stanford, Oxford, and Harvard being the ruling dynasties of academically guaranteed wisdom? Will the new networks of educated and concerned citizens respect the privileges of academic elites? Or, will they pay lip service to Cambridge and Cornell, for example, and continue to work with Wikipedia and online clouds?

4.2   Organizing Trust

When a passenger on a KLM flight opens a chicken sandwich carton, she reads an assurance that the chicken, whose flesh she is about to eat, has led a happy life and died fulfilled and at peace with the world. Doe she trust this caption? Does she shop for food with a "biological," "ecological," or "green" label on a package because she feels like a steward and a trustee of the planet?

We try to answer such questions by a administering a standard consumer research questionnaire, conducted by programmed robots that send out e-mails and register responses. What cannot be answered by the robots is the question of public trust and its conscious or unconscious manifestations. Does a consumer's preference for "environmentally friendly" products mean that the citizen's heart, which is hiding behind his or her brain, trusts the "green" labels? Or, does it mean that the consumer pays lip service and a premium price, viewing it as a public sacrifice on the altar of the new, ecologically correct gods (i.e., snobbery and hypocrisy instead of a genuine conviction)?

The link between "green" consumer preferences and trust in market economies can be even weaker than the link between the levels of carbon dioxide in the earth's atmosphere and a real danger of a global warming disaster. Do we trust the expert reconstructions of the causal links between our activities and large-scale, long-distance consequences? Do we trust the advocates of ecologically correct choices translated into political ideologies? If we do trust them, is this trust justified, especially in view of the many suspect manipulations of Greenpeace and other ecological activists taking liberties with truths?

The questions of trust usually evolve around a number of simple assumptions. Sicilian grandfathers are said to be fond of the following exercise with their grandchildren: They ask the child to jump from a rock onto a sandy beach, promising to catch the child in their arms, which they proceed to do. At some point, however, they suddenly step back in the last moment so that the child crashes onto the sand. "Why," asks the grandson, swallowing tears. The supposed answer is, "In order to teach you not to trust anyone." This is an early lesson in conditional and limited trust in future relationships. Does it make Sicilians more skeptical, more critical, less naïve, and less credulous?

Sociologists distinguish three conceptual approaches to the manifestations of trust in social life (Sztompka 1999):

1. Trust as a relationship: A child trusts his grandfather, although he also learns to distrust his own unlimited trust from time to time. Relationships are not fixed but rather are dynamic and susceptible to change.
2. Trust as a personality trait: A child with a happy childhood is more likely to trust others in future encounters than is a child with an unhappy childhood filled with violence and abuse. Empirically detectable traits may nevertheless surprise us into modifying this commonsense view.
3. Trust as a cultural rule: Early in our socialization, we learn to trust medical doctors more than random passersby on matters of health and therapy.

Our trust is not stable. A second or third opinion does not have to be a manifestation of distrust, but a patient looking for them proves that her trust is not blind. These three concepts of trust overlap. Trust in a medical doctor is based on a cultural valorization of accepted medical practices; in our culture, we educate and validate our medical doctors so that they are better at avoiding mistakes which random individuals might make. However, trust in a medical doctor is also based on a relationship: a professionally trained and certified doctor is supposed to make an effort to focus on every single patient, recognize and diagnose this specific patient, and apply impartial expertise without any second thoughts (for instance, on profits linked to a recommendation of specific drugs). Having experienced a build-up of a relationship with a medical doctor and experiencing positive social valuation of his or her medical practices, a patient may develop trust as a personality trait, displayed in respective social encounters with approved professionals and triggered by display of professional props (white frock, brain scanner) and behaviors (structured interview, physical examination of our bodies). This trust can be transferred far beyond a single context, as the trust displayed by students executing the cruel orders from white-frocked experiment-managers studied by Stanley Milgram clearly demonstrated (Milgram 1974).

Therefore, in a pragmatic investigation of the role played by public trust in an organizational change (e.g., of a public institution), a narrower definition of trust will be accepted—one that might be attributed to Robert Putnam (the author of "Bowling Alone" and a co-author of "Better Together") and Richard Sennett (the author of "Together"; Putnam and Feldstein 2003, Sennett 2012). Trust is measured by willingness to cooperate, by assumed or experienced past cases of successful cooperation, and by positive outcomes of social learning. The emergence of this trust in individuals and institutions can be enhanced through creative touches to the evolution of social organizations and institutions. These sociological approaches are compatible with the uses made of the concept of trust by pragmatic institutionalists such as Christopher K. Ansell, who claimed that "evolutionary learning arises from a dynamic tension between context-independent concepts and context-dependent experiences" (2011, 39).

4.3   TRUSTING ORGANIZATIONS

A representative democracy—with a historical mix of a market economy that produces material welfare and parliamentary majorities that produce responsive governments—does not fare very well in the second decade of the twenty-first century. After the rise of the Polish "Solidarity" movement in 1980 against the Soviet-imposed communist rule in central Europe and after the fall of the Berlin wall in 1989, the neoliberal doctrine seemed to rule the waves of popular imagination. Francis Fukuyama, an American public intellectual and advisor to the President of the United States, announced the end of history as a blind evolutionary sequence of experiments and changes (Fukuyama 1992). According to the popular sentiment of Fukuyama's readers, the evolution has arrived at the final destination, and Hegel's cunning reason could stop inventing new political institutions. A proper mix of market economy and parliamentary democracy was supposed to offer the best available recipe for the sustained and unlimited growth of welfare shared by all members of society and by all societies in the world. In other words, Fukuyama claimed that the liberal democracy as an organizational matrix for a civil society is the desirable last station in the evolution of the forms of government. The spectacular collapse of the communist alternatives in Russia and China demonstrated, according to Fukuyama, the advantages of the political systems of the United States and European Union. This optimistic belief did not last. In commenting upon his 1989–1992 views in 2014, Fukuyama admitted that a balance of checks and a check of balances continue to evolve:

> Twenty-five years later, the most serious threat to the end of history hypothesis isn't that there is a higher, better model out there that will some day supersede liberal democracy: neither Islamic theocracy nor Chinese capitalism cuts it. Once societies get on the up escalator of industrialization, their social structure begins to change in ways that increase demands for political participation. If political elites accommodate these demands, we arrive at some version of democracy. (Fukuyama 2014, 2)

In fact, Fukuyama repeated the widespread views of most economists who believed in the historical necessity of triggering the increase of welfare and an evolution of political forms toward a representative democracy after some stages of material growth had been achieved. However, in 2017, the main threats to the liberal democracy as the dominant form of political organization of human societies do not come from Islamic theocracy (the Islamic State is being effectively eliminated in the Middle East) nor from Chinese capitalism (political and ecological limits to economic growth are gradually accumulating, building up pressures for political opening of the communist top to upwardly mobile new generations). Rather, they come from the populist challengers to the parliamentary system inside the democratic states and from the elitist attempts to defuse them. One may call it a generalized class struggle, except that class identities resemble not only hereditary affinities but also elective ones.

The main challenges also come from the global migrations that are shifting millions of individuals from outside of the United States, European Union, Canada, and Australia and bringing them into the abovementioned zones of higher living standards. Inside the European Union, the main ideological conflict manifested in Brexit and in the political initiatives of the Central European states challenging the power monopoly of the Paris-Berlin axis is being fought between a diluted leftist version of a single European state as a neutral economic space administered by a federalist bureaucracy in Brussels and a more modest and conservative (and more Christian) vision of the European Union as a democratic community of nations. This does not forgive the uncondemned communist genocide throwing shadows over Russia's contemporary wars of aggression, nor does it accommodate Islamic minorities without demanding reciprocity in accommodating Christianity. Voting citizens of the member states of the European Union are generally speaking more conservatively than leftist; however, the power elites, media professionals, and the most knowledge-intensive professions both in nation-states and in the EU offices in Brussels and Strasbourg and their mainstream mass media are populated by more cosmopolitan individuals, standardized by the *multi-culti* ideologies. (The ideology of a multicultural society was partly based on research on national and organizational cultures, originated by d'Iribarne and Hofstede; cf. d'Iribarne 2015, first edition—1979, Hofstede 1984.) To put it in a nutshell: the EU elites and media professionals distrust voting citizens in nation-states, viewing with suspicion the growth of the popular vote for the populist parties and the decline of social democrats (e.g., Le Pen in France, Wilders in the Netherlands). The EU citizens in all member states and the EU's southern and eastern societies in particular distrust the liberal leftist elites of the EU institutions and their media representatives. These not-so-silent majorities are viewing with suspicion the weakening of the nation-states and the dismantling of Christianity by EU censorship disguised as "political correctness" (e.g., the removal of the reference to the Christian roots of the European Union was largely resented). Are they conservative?

The labels "leftist" or "conservative" should be used with a pinch of ideological salt. Evolutionary learning of contemporary societies does not follow the neat distinctions between "the left" and "the right"—between the fans of a change and the fans of immutability. Changes do happen, and the political landscape of democracy varies with time and ideological climate; however, a differential rate of participation requires special attention. Social changes are built up both by the elites and the populations at large, and their participation varies. "Society," as a flow of the intertwined and overlapping processes of interactions and communications, "socializes" (i.e., facilitates individual learning). However, not all citizens are socialized to the same degree and not every person socializes herself or himself in the same way.

The making and breaking of the "elites," for instance, is an ongoing process, as is the process of challenging and opposing them by "populations." Trust plays a very important role in increasing social coherence. The populations should trust their hopes that upward mobility toward elite status is possible in order to generate enough commitment to the reproduction of social order. The elites should be trusted that they deserve their elite status in order to sustain belief in meritocracy and a fair playing field for the ambitious, upwardly mobile individuals. The recovery of the public image of the monarchs in the United Kingdom and in the Netherlands in the twenty-first century is a case in point. A successful media campaign led to the restoration of trust in an aristocratic subelite supported by taxpayers. However, the Italian and Polish judiciary have failed to defend their caste corruption and privileges. The recovery of public trust required a long and complex process of reforming the court system and breaking caste privileges.

The main point of the public trust in democratic institutions and the main manifestation of social ability to successfully learn and change is the willingness of concerned citizens to perform an action, make a choice, and contribute to the democratic process (Achen and Bartels 2016). As researchers studying democratic innovations in political institutions remind us: "income, wealth and education remain crucial variables in predicting participation" (Smith 2016, 164). They are crucial, but not exclusive: Changes of any social activity are never automatic consequences of a technological or economic innovation, and the less educated do not have to be less concerned as citizens. Technology's influence upon social practices is filtered through cultural standards and values. For example, the emergence of Uber was not an automatic consequence of the growth of the Internet and mobile cellular phones. It was a creative match between individual expectations (trusted, quickly available, and cheap car transportation in a city) and institutional standardization (universal training of the car owners certified with a trusted driving license). Similarly, the electoral victory of Donald Trump was not an automatic consequence of the right choice of advisers. It was the result of a creative match between the individual expectations of voters (attracted by an outsider who contrasted with political elites) and institutional standardization (Cambridge Analytics offered a market segmentation technology allowing them to comb very large databases).

Neither the market success of Uber nor Trump's victory can be ideologically labelled as right, left, or middle of the road. Because of the established conventions, Hilary Clinton was classified as closer to socialist, communist, or social-democratic "left" political parties, while Donald Trump was perceived to be closer the conservative, Christian-democratic, and pragmatic liberals. Pragmatics of electoral struggle made it easier to exploit the distrust of the Clinton family (by referencing their failures while in office) than the distrust of Trump (who held no public office before becoming the President of the United States; he could only be attacked for business practices or for alleged misbehavior in erotic relationships, both of which are less central to a presidential campaign than political record). Trust matters and distrust never sleeps, but the distrust in Clinton's abilities as a politician in office prevailed over the distrust of Trump as a flamboyant user of contemporary political marketing. In the long electoral run, heaping insults upon Trump—who could retaliate with much more focused criticisms of Clinton's political skills—misfired.

4.4   Trust in Academic Bureaucracy

One of the manifestations of trust in academic bureaucracy is the acceptance of certificates issued by universities and other institutions of higher learning (the so-called tertiary educational sector), such as bachelor, master, and PhD diplomas. Trust in diplomas is based on a tacit assumption that academic bureaucracies recognize and reward merit by issuing diplomas and act as gatekeepers against those who would like to cheat. Two of these three types of diplomas have been standardized in the European Union after the Bolonia agreement between ministers of education in 2000; thus, the criteria for granting a right to issue diplomas are fairly transparent and well-known. The third type, the PhD diploma, has also been partly standardized. However, there are far fewer PhD students than students in master or bachelor programs; thus, it remains by nature more elitist than the other two, leaving more space for individual idiosyncrasies in the creative process and its coaching.

The writing of a PhD thesis by an individual is allowed only after he or she has acquired a master diploma and after her or his research project has been accepted by a senior academic researcher, who coaches a PhD student as a "promoter." The relationship between a promoter and a PhD student is based on trust. The promoter trusts that a student is capable of writing a defensible PhD thesis. The PhD student trusts that his or her promoter can coach them towards the PhD defense.

There are basically two channels for a prospective PhD student. One is the fast track (sometimes explicitly leading to employment and potentially tenure), which is open to gifted graduates directly after their defense of a master thesis. They are perceived as the best and the brightest of the master student body, and it is assumed that they will pursue professional careers in academic bureaucracies or applied research institutions. The other path is the individual external project pursued outside of university programs. These PhD students are usually older than the fresh graduates; often called "externs," they are usually employed full time and write a PhD thesis at the expense of their leisure. Sometimes, they are already retired and write an "experience-based" PhD thesis. However, they have to be accepted by academic coaches and usually follow some formal courses and workshops on research methodology. When their coaches decide that the PhD thesis is ready for examination by a commission of senior academic professionals (usually tenured professors from different universities), these external PhD students can acquire a diploma. External PhD students usually need more time to complete their thesis (5–7 years as opposed to 3–4 years). The difference between a research-driven PhD project of a young graduate and an experience-driven PhD project of a part-time PhD student is sometimes quite considerable. Universities are trying to develop ways of dealing with this difference, which leads to a number of methodological compromises, such as a new focus on qualitative methodologies or organizational ethnography (or even para-ethnography; cf. Islam 2015).

Both regular and external PhD students have to submit their writing for plagiarism control. Specialized software is being used to track possible sources of unreported borrowings. In the case of a positive outcome, the relevant passages have to be either removed or placed in quotation marks with a proper reference to the original source. Such a case occurred at a Dutch university in 2014. An older external PhD student had successfully defended her PhD thesis. However, when the university granted her PhD diploma, newspapers reported on plagiarized fragments from her thesis. The highlight of the story was the fact that the promoter and other members of the commission had detected the plagiarism (because of the controls imposed on all theses) and urged the author to change the respective passages. For reasons that are still unclear, the author failed to implement the required corrections and the promoter, who took for granted that changes had been introduced, did not recheck the final submitted text. The incriminated passage was very short and not particularly significant, so the quality of the entire thesis was not compromised. However, to trust the diploma industry, one has to be certain that all PhDs are above the suspicion of plagiarism. The case also became widely known because of a conflict of interests: PhD students can make use of programs at the universities employing their coaches, such as part-time PhD assistance programs that offer workshops and guidance in the course of writing a thesis. They can also make use of specialized coaches, who advertise their services in academic writing instruction, research methods, and techniques for research reporting and presentation.

Both the university assistance programs and the specialized coach services require a financial contribution from the external PhD student. The non-university coaches usually follow a "no cure, no pay" principle, only requiring a fee if and when a student successfully defends the PhD thesis. The university assistance programs often require a down payment before offering courses, trainings, and workshops. The financial threshold varies: some programs ask for 5000–7000€ per year, whereas others demand 15,000–20,000€ for more comprehensive schemes. The person in question here—the negative heroine of the plagiarism story—had originally accepted the services of a professional coach from outside of the university, then switched to a university-based "part-time promotion" program, and finally defended her thesis with an uncorrected flaw. The flaw had been reported by the non-university coach, who considered the switch away from her to university-based services as a betrayal of trust and hoped to be recruited into university employment.

What happened next illustrates the trust restoration strategy of the university. First, the promoter of the thesis, whose duty it was to check the implementation of the anti-plagiarist advice, was suspended as a promoter and excluded from the pool of future promoters. All of the PhD theses he had coached as a promoter in the past were re-checked for possible plagiarism. Normally, retiring university professors continue to serve as promoters up to 5 years after their official retirement. The promoter in question had just retired and was thus deprived of the right to continue acting as a promoter of PhD theses. Second, the author was reprimanded and asked to remove or edit the respective passages to indicate a clearly reported source. The possibility of reversing the decision to grant a PhD title was briefly considered but not followed. (External experts agreed that the plagiarism was too marginal to influence the quality of the study and did not invalidate the thesis.) Third, a structural change was introduced to the PhD programs at the university and announced in the media. The "part-time promotion" program, within which the author had been coached toward the defense, was terminated. This closure reflected as much an attempt to symbolically purge the university in the eyes of printed media (newspapers reported the case but television channels did not, considering it too insignificant to bother) because it mirrored the internal power struggle between departments for control of the part-time PhD programs. A new program, with an obligatory course in research ethics, was introduced (at a much higher price and under control of another department of the faculty).

Has trust in the fairness of PhD coaching been restored? If the intake of new candidates for PhD projects is a manifestation of public trust in the fairness of research coaching and in the transparency in the process of granting a PhD diploma, then the answer is positive. However, the case of detected but not rectified plagiarism in a PhD thesis revealed a rather disturbing feature of the control that academic professionals exercise over the certificates of intellectual merit. Like medical doctors and judges in the courts of law, academic professionals are granted a collective monopoly on self-regulation. The case would never had reached a broader audience if one of the participants in the process was not an external, non-academic service provider.

Quality control of intellectual merit and of the institutional mechanisms for granting diplomas ("diploma mills" according to David P. Noble, cf. Noble 1998) remains firmly lodged in the self-governing structures of the academic community. Two attempts to curb this discretionary and monopolistic power have not been entirely successful. The new public management introduced professional deans and university presidents who imposed external, usually economic, sometimes political controls on academic professionals. Professional managers replaced senior researchers as a pool of eligible top university functionaries. Thus, the monopoly of academic professionals was frequently replaced by a monopoly of commercial interests or political correctness, as in the case of the required percentage of female academic professionals per university or faculty.

The attempt to broaden the reach of academic teaching by offering online courses (massive online open courses, or MOOCs) with lectures by academic stars resulted in asymmetric growth in the numbers of the academic proletariat (e.g., the lowest paid teaching assistants who service the followers of online lectures as virtual call centers for educational feedback). Do Porter, Kotler, or Fukuyama—just to mention some star performers in marketing, strategic management, and the geopolitical philosophy of power—increase public trust in the massive expansion of online educational services? Or, are they a distraction while a vast democratization of access to higher education is rapidly taking place, with peer-to-peer university platforms emerging in both the commercial and non-commercial, civic spheres of social communications? Was Innerarity

(2013) right when he claimed that the industrial division of work, which led to the iron and subsequently velvet cages of the social division of labor, has finally been replaced by a new social distribution of knowledge by virtual cages and filters of a social distribution of knowledge?

PhD students are quickly becoming the one of the crucial groups of knowledge producers, managers, and disseminators. They are the ones who do not have to take things only at the "interface value" (a term that was introduced by Turkle [1995] and recycled by Innerarity [2013]). They will emerge as the creative class in inventive urban clusters, dictating the new social contracts—or rather, designing and re-designing, organizing and re-organizing sociotemporal platforms for new social contracts with competitive, part-time, partitioned, and rotating elites.

4.5   Chapter Summary

Access to second and third opinions makes it more difficult to maintain public trust. Trust cannot be taken for granted, even by the most respected professional bureaucracies that are usually granted an elite status (e.g., medical doctors, judges in courts of law, university professors). Events that undermine this trust usually trigger actions, which are executed to punish those who cannot be trusted and to repair organizational routines and procedures. The detection of a plagiarized passage in a PhD thesis defended publicly at a Dutch university in 2014 is a case in point. The dean and top managers removed the promoter, reprimanded the author, and terminated the extramural PhD program (replacing it with a new, presumably more strictly controlled one). However, controls are slipping away from professional elites. The mass dissemination of knowledge and access skills have changed the overall institutional landscape. After bachelor and master programs, the PhD breeding projects are probably on the eve of a significant expansion and a gradual transfer of controls from senior professionals to a virtual automated online system. In robot we trust?

References

Achen, C., & Bartels, L. M. (2016). *Democracy for realists. Why elections do not produce responsive governments.* Princeton/Oxford: Princeton University Press.

Ansell, C. K. (2011). *Pragmatic democracy. Evolutionary learning as public philosophy.* Oxford/New York: Oxford University Press.

D'Iribarne, Ph. (2015). *La logique de l'honneur. Gestion des enterprises et traditions nationales*. Paris: le Seuil.

Eggers, D. (2014). *The circle*. New York/London: Penguin.

Fukuyama, F. (1992). *The end of history and the last man*. New York: Free Press.

Fukuyama, F. (2014, June 6). At the end of history still stands democracy. *The Wall Street Journal*, p. 2.

Hofstede, G. (1984). *Culture's consequences. International differences in work related-values*. Newbury Park/London/New Delhi: Sage.

Innerarity, D. (2013). *The democracy of knowledge*. Bloomsbury Academic: London/New York.

Islam, G. (2015). Practitioners as theorists: Para-ethnography and the collaborative study of contemporary organizations. *Organizational Research Methods, 18*(2), 231–251.

Milgram, S. (1974). *Obedience to authority: An experimental view*. New York: Harper & Row.

Minkov, M. (2011). *Cultural differences in a globalizing world*. Bingley: Emerald.

Noble, D. P. (1998). *Digital diploma mills: The automation of higher education*. New York: Monthly Review Press.

Putnam, R. D., & Feldstein, L. M. (2003). *Better together. Restoring the American community*. New York/London: Simon & Schuster.

Sennett, R. (2012). *Together. The rituals, pleasures and politics of cooperation*. London/New York: Allen Lane/Penguin.

Smith, G. (2016). *Democratic innovations. Designing institutions for citizen participation*. Cambridge: Cambridge University Press.

Sztompka, P. (1999). *Trust; a sociological theory*. Cambridge/New York: Cambridge University Press.

Turkle, S. (1995). *Life on the screen. Identity in the age of the internet*. New York: Touchstone.

CHAPTER 5

Public Trust and Organizational Learning in Academic Institutions in Poland

Barbara Kożuch, Katarzyna Sienkiewicz-Małyjurek, and Regina Lenart-Gansiniec

5.1 Introduction

The functioning of a contemporary organization is based on both internal and external relationships. External relationships are of particular significance because they directly affect the achieved results, the development possibilities, and the organization's position. These relationships make use of a wide spectrum of knowledge and partners' experience; thus, their integration may lead to innovation. Moreover, the possibility of common learning increases the probability of high collaborative performance (Wong and Tjosvold 2006). In the modern world of knowledge generation, an intangible organizational factor that has a significant impact on collaborative processes is trust (Huotari and Livonen 2004). Trust enables organizations to focus on the realization of a common goal, without fear of opportunistic behaviors. Organizational trust influences the organizational knowledge-sharing environment (McEvily et al. 2003) and is "an essential ingredient for building a knowledge base organization with

B. Kożuch (✉) • R. Lenart-Gansiniec
Jagiellonian University, Kraków, Poland

K. Sienkiewicz-Małyjurek
Silesian University of Technology, Gliwice, Poland

  57
B. Kożuch et al. (eds.), *Managing Public Trust*,
https://doi.org/10.1007/978-3-319-70485-2_5

the work groups" (Rahman et al. 2015). Therefore, the nature of external relationships is to a large extent conditioned by internal relationships, including organizational trust.

The relationship between organizational trust and learning seems to be logical. More significantly, many authors have reported the positive impact of trust on the learning processes (Swift and Hwang 2013; Casimir et al. 2012; Holste and Fields 2010). However, there is still a lack of thorough research in this field based on empirical analyses. The significance of the context of action realization has also been investigated, as the multidimensional nature of trust influences the learning processes and knowledge exchange depends on the area of an organization's activity (Swift and Hwang 2013). Taking this into account, the aim of this chapter was to investigate the relationships between organizational trust and higher education. The findings were based on desk research and a diagnostic survey.

This chapter first presents the theoretical outline of trust, organizational learning, and knowledge management, including public trust and organizational learning as tools of managing academic institutions. The literature search allowed for analysis of the current state of knowledge on the scope of the influence of public trust on organizational learning, including knowledge creation in academic institutions. Next, after the research method and sample are characterized, the results of the conducted questionnaire research are presented. These results cover the identification of communication forms, evaluation of the level of studying and knowledge sharing, impact of trust on interorganizational learning and knowledge creation, and opinions on the general level of trust in higher education institutions. As a result, the conducted research enabled identification of the levels of organizational trust, learning, and the relationships between them.

5.2   Theoretical Background

5.2.1   Trust as a Condition for Effective Organizational Relationships

Relationships constitute the basis for the functioning of every organization, whether public, private, or nongovernmental. They influence an organization's development and position in a given sector. They create a social context, which shapes relations both inside the organization and in its surroundings. They function according to feedback because a given behavior of one entity generates appropriate results in the behavior of other entities. Taking this into account, organizational relations influence the form of realized actions. They can proceed inside and between organizations (Gammelgaard et al. 2011; Li 2005). As Thomas Ritter wrote, these relations do not exist independently; rather, they are connected with each other and stimulate one another (Ritter 2000). What is more, relations inside the organization are the basis of relations between organizations (Kożuch et al. 2015). Their course is based upon the existing formal rules and informal conditions, among which trust is of priority significance (Li 2005; Kastberg 2016). Trust determines the strength of relationships, both inside and between organizations.

The shaping of trust is not an easy process. Its level depends on the factors related to the perception of collaborating parties. It includes above all the trustworthiness of a trustee, irrespective of the context of actions (Manu et al. 2015). Moreover, trust does not come into being on its own; rather, it is built in the long term based upon the quality of organizational relations and experience in interactions. It results from the sincerity, openness, and kindness of the collaborating parties. Trust is an abstract notion—an elusive phenomenon that may be easily squandered. However, taking into consideration the benefits it brings to collaboration and functioning of an organization, trust can be considered as one of the key factors of organizational relations. The principal benefits resulting from collaboration based upon trust include organizational efficiency, effectiveness, flexibility, performance, and successful change management (Pate et al. 2007); improving teamwork and creativity (Elangovan et al. 2007); reducing transaction and agency costs and increasing adaptation capabilities (Molina-Morales et al. 2011); and innovation, organizational learning, and knowledge sharing (Holste and Fields 2010; Dovey 2009). These benefits prove the important role that is played by trust in an organization's functioning. Taking into consideration the subject scope, in this chapter we focus on organizational learning and creating knowledge as the factors affecting the existing level of trust.

The approaches to organizational learning are diversified. Sometimes they are used interchangeably with the notion of an organization's learning. It should be emphasized that it is difficult to use them in an interchangeable way. An organization's learning is a process that results in gained knowledge, thus increasing the organization's capability to solve problems and take effective action (Rokita 2005). The participation of the organization's members in training that develops interpersonal and professional skills is emphasized here. Organizational learning is a condition necessary for an organization's adaptation, problem solving, effectiveness, and promotion of individual and collective learning (Jashapara 2006). It contributes to the understanding and organization of its dissemination and coordinated use (Mikuła 2005). Organizational learning may be a tool for organizational culture modification (Czerska 2003), internal integration of an organization (Watkins and Marsick 1999), and improvement of an organization's effectiveness, thus raising the quality of organizational products, possible actions, and behaviors (Lenart 2014). Most often, organizational learning is a process of a collective nature in which relationships based on trust play a significant role.

5.2.2   Public Trust and Organizational Learning as Tools for Managing Academic Institutions

The activity of public organizations consists of influencing other organizations and citizens in order to realize the public interest. They are of principal significance to national competitiveness, creating conditions of functioning in the private sector (Rashman et al. 2009). In academic institutions, this influence includes the shaping of knowledge and skills for future generations, which indirectly impacts the level of economic development in a given state or region. A society should believe that the contents provided to young people are up-to-date and useful. This level of trust in the competence and professionalism of academic institutions is defined as public trust, which as a general approach signifies the conviction of the citizens on the correctness of state officials' actions in the scope of realizing policies and programs (Kożuch and Dobrowolski 2014). Public trust is based upon rational conduct (i.e. common goals, routines, procedures), as well as existing relations (e.g., norms and values, codes of conduct; Blind 2006; Keele 2007; Thomas 1998). Taking this into account, two types of public trust are distinguished in the subject literature—rational and relational (Kożuch and Dobrowolski 2014; Kożuch et al. 2015). Rational trust points out the benefits coming from collaboration based on a continuous calculation of profitability. It results from an individual evaluation of the existing relations, experience in this scope, competencies of the collaborators and superiors, and the existing employee attitudes. It is of a normative nature (Pedersen et al. 2014) that results from a cognitive attitude (Frost-Arnold 2014). On the other hand, relational trust is built as a result of direct interactions. It is based upon common norms of conduct and communication practices. It results from convictions and good will (Faulkner 2007) and its characteristic feature is changeability in time (Tabak and Smith 2005). Public trust in academic institutions is based upon internal and external relations. In organizational learning, it concerns both information sharing, creating new knowledge resources, and acquiring knowledge from the outside.

Organizational learning includes all aspects of the organization's functioning and its interaction with the surroundings. The nature of these interactions is to a large extent determined by organizational learning within the organization. Its nature is multi-level and it is a result of tensions between absorbing of new knowledge and its practical usage. It includes cognitive processes that influence the organization to take action and vice versa—actions that generate cognitive processes (Crossan et al. 1999). Organizational learning is a broad area of knowledge. Fiol and Lyles defined it as "the process of improving actions through better knowledge and understanding" (Fiol and Lyles 1985). In turn, Daft and Weick conducted analyses assuming that organizational learning constitutes "knowledge about action outcome interrelationships between the organization's action and the environment (Daft and Weick 1984). Richard Boateng believed that "learning occurs when information is questioned and tested with existing knowledge to construct and reconstruct new knowledge" (Boateng 2011). In addition, organizational learning is a dynamic process that concerns tensions between exploration and exploitation and runs through many levels, with each level connected by social processes; it also combines cognition with action (Crossan et al. 1999). It runs in time with different intensity, depending on the number of interactions. One may achieve a high level of organizational learning during the realization of non-routine activities in an ambiguous context, developing diversified structures and rules, which occur in situations with a lack of control and also make use of heuristics and insights (Fiol and Lyles 1985). Furthermore, the problems of organizational learning concern an individual learning process or system, culture or metaphor, knowledge management, continuous improvement, innovation, and creativity (Wang and Ahmed 2003).

The main factors that influence organizational learning and knowledge sharing are the following: "features of the source organization (or unit); features of the recipient organization (or unit); the characteristics of the relationship between organizations (or units); and the environmental context" (Rashman et al. 2009). The features of the source organization define its ability to learn. In turn, recipient and source characteristics include organizational culture, structures, and systems. The organizational culture impacts the level of trust and supports organizational learning, while the structure and systems create conditions for an effective course of this process. It is emphasized that a decentralized, horizontal design fosters learning processes, as opposed to hierarchical structures of authority. The next set of factors—organizational relations—includes networks of connections as well as power and leadership in these networks, which determine the level of these relations. With the growth of the strength of relations, the possibilities of organizational learning grow. On the other hand, the environment and context cover the existing market, political, institutional, and social conditions. Therefore, it is dependent on the existing circumstances, which foster learning, and the intra- and inter-organizational relationships, which are the carriers of new knowledge.

In public organizations, taking into account the expectations of the interested parties, there is pressure to learn and transfer good practices between the employees and organizations (Rashman et al. 2009). This increases the professional competence of the employees, the scope of communication, and the organization of collaborative work. However, for the process to run smoothly, a high level of trust is required. Taking into account the specifics of academic institutions and their role in the development of existing knowledge and discovery of new areas, one may ascertain that their effective functioning is based upon public trust and continuous learning processes. These tools have a mutual effect on each other.

5.3   Research Results

5.3.1   Research Method

Public trust is one of the key elements evoked in the context of interorganizational learning and knowledge creation. In internal and interorganizational relations, it is one of the key conditions that initiate creation and also influence the maintenance of interorganizational relations. Although many authors (Makhija and Ganesh 1997; Kostova 1999) are convinced about the significant impact of trust on processes connected with intra- and interorganizational learning, there is a lack of deeper research in this area, particularly with reference to public trust. Based on literature research and earlier empirical research (Chenhall and Smith 2003; Ferres et al. 2005), it was assumed that one must become familiar with the opinions of the examined about the level and dominant forms of knowledge sharing and conditions of creating trust in an organizational environment (university, chair, institute, department) in order to examine the interdependence between public trust and organizational learning. Furthermore, importance was attached to communication with superiors and collaborators, the national and relational aspects of building organizational trust, and their opinions about relationships dominating their organizational environment.

The research in this chapter is of a learning nature and is focused on searching for connections between organizational trust and organizational learning, with an emphasis on academic institutions in Poland. To this aim, a survey questionnaire was administered to experienced academics at a higher education institution between January and February 2016. The questionnaires was anonymous, and 60 of them were include in the analysis (Kożuch and Lenart-Gansiniec 2017). Of the respondents, 35.8% worked at public universities and 64.2% worked at private schools in Poland (private schools constituted 3.16% of private higher education institutions in Poland). The survey was completed by professors (38.3%), adjuncts (38.3%), doctoral students (11.7%), and assistant lecturers (11.7%). The majority of respondents were between 34 and 50 years of age. The sample does not enable us to generalize our conclusions for a larger population; however, it does illustrate the analyzed processes.

5.3.2 Evaluation of the Impact of Trust on Interorganisational Learning and Knowledge Creation

The research evaluated the influence of trust on interorganizational learning and knowledge creation. One of the goals of the research was to understand the respondents' opinions on the influence of trust on interorganizational learning and the creation of new knowledge. It appeared from the literature review that knowledge management is not possible without trust in an organization. Trust leads to an increase of knowledge resources (Nahapiet and Goshal 1998). Moreover, trust must be mutual and omnipresent (Paliszkiewicz 2012). Research questions focused on the values highlighted by the respondents, which are oriented on behavior and relations that build a climate of trust (Table 5.1).

The respondents indicated that the most important value is appreciation of the employees' abilities to create valuable ideas. The consistency between the acts of the managerial staff and their words was evaluated on a similar level. The lowest evaluation was awarded to the employees' fulfil-

Table 5.1 Behavior and relations that build organizational trust

Organizational values	*Survey responses (n)*		
	Low	*Moderate*	*High*
Employees of the organizational unit act honestly even when they compete with each other.	25	20	15
Employees of the organizational unit have possibilities for open and honest expression of their opinions.	35	10	15
Employees of the organizational unit always realize actions that they have committed to perform.	40	5	15
Managers of the organizational unit prove their words with deeds: the valid rule and values are confirmed.	5	20	35
Employees in the organizational unit always keep their promises and meet their obligations.	35	25	0
In the organizational unit, the employee's abilities to create valuable ideas are prized.	22	2	40
Employees have the autonomy and resources necessary for realizing organizational goals.	28	20	12
In the organizational unit, managers of a higher level are open and available to the employees.	20	14	26
The ideas of the employees are openly and willingly discussed by the collaborators, even if they are not connected with current work.	28	20	12
Employees of the organizational unit admit to mistakes they made without fear of unfavorable (or unfair) consequences for them.	25	15	20
In the organizational unit, the employees have consideration for mistakes and they learn using their example.	38	10	12

Source: Own elaboration

ment of their actions, from which they also learned from mistakes. It should be emphasized that, in the subject literature, relations between trust and involvement were observed (Bugdol 2006), as well as those between learning from mistakes and organizational learning (Senge 2012).

The last analyzed aspects were the relationships, which dominate in the studied organizational units of higher education institutions. It should be emphasized that relationships constitute a specific bond and basis for the creation of intangible resources; they also make possible the transfer of knowledge in the organizations (Lenart 2014). First, knowledge is rooted in relations. Second, knowledge creation is a collective process, which is dependent on social interactions.

The highest evaluation was given to the relationship of individual rivalry, followed by partner, casual cooperation, and business relationships. The respondents least valued nepotic, entrepreneurial rivalry, and team rivalry relationships. A neutral attitude was demonstrated by the respondents to friendly and social relationships. It seems that the most important factor in appraising an employee was her or his productivity, followed by limited contact between employees, hierarchy, differences in age, low communication skills, and a pragmatic attitude toward work (Leja 2013). Furthermore, literature analysis has shown that there are dependencies between knowledge and relationships. They facilitate the transfer and absorption of knowledge (Lenart 2014) and learning (Scott et al. 2008), especially relationships based on trust and common learning and not individual rivalry (Scott et al. 2008).

Based on this part of our research, one may ascertain that an appreciation of an employee's ability to create valuable ideas and the consistency of the managerial staff's actions with their words are of the biggest significance in organizational behavior and relationships. When it comes to the nature of relations in the examined organizational units of higher education institutions, most often they are of an individual rivalry nature, which does not favor the strengthening of knowledge management and organizational learning.

The next stage of empirical research was statistical verification of the hypothesis regarding the dependency between trust and interorganizational learning, knowledge creation, and relationships in the organization (Fig. 5.1). First, the statistical significance was analyzed. The p value indicates the decreasing credibility ratio of the result: the higher the p value, the less sure the researcher may be that the relationship observed in the sample is credible for the measured figures in the whole population. The p value conforms to the probability of mistaking the obtained result as true (i.e., representative for the population). For the level of trust, adjustments are shown in Fig. 5.1a.

For the level of trust, the p value was 0.00005, which is less than the significance level of <0.05. Therefore, an adjustment resulted in a chi-square distribution with an increasing number of degrees of freedom. In this case, the distribution is normal. The components of the level of trust are a sum of a factor; thus, regardless of the distribution of each of these factors, the distribution of the level of trust will be similar to a normal one. The density function is symmetric versus the mean value of distribution.

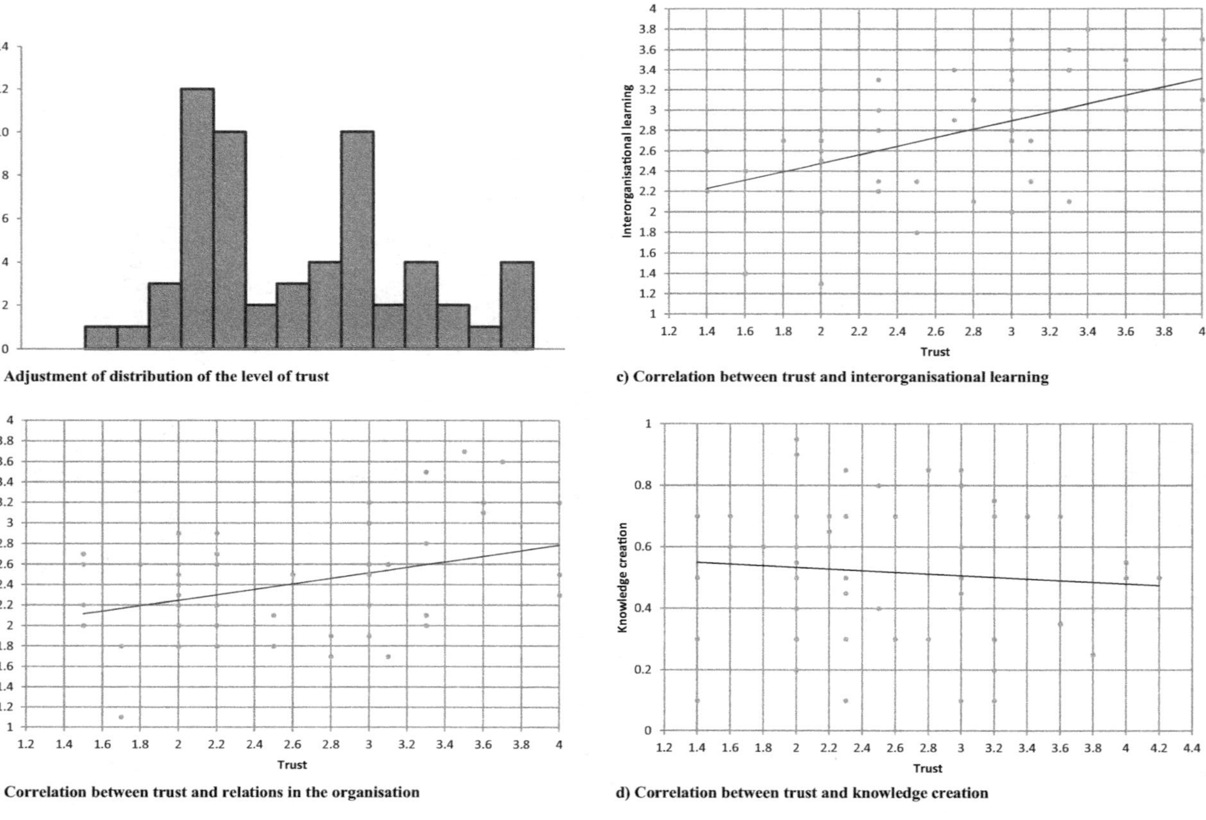

Fig. 5.1   Research results (Source: own elaboration)

Taking into account the complex hypotheses, the dependency between each level of trust and relationships in the organization, interorganizational learning, and knowledge creation were examined. An analysis of the correlation between the studied features began with the preparation of a scatter diagram to illustrate the relationship between the variables. Evaluation of the correlation based on the diagram helps to define the strength and type of the dependency. The points reflect each value of the features, creating a correlation diagram of the scatter. The configuration in the diagram is composed of many marked points lying more or less along a specific curve (Fig. 5.1b).

The correlation scatter diagram shows the strength and type of dependencies. It seldom happens that the marked points lie exactly on a straight line. The more frequently observed configuration is composed of many marked points lying more or less along a straight line. For the influence of the level of trust on relationships in the organization, the points are scattered, which happens when there is a weaker correlation. Furthermore, the dependence between the level of trust and the level of interorganizational learning was verified. Compared with the previous correlation, the points are more scattered for interorganizational learning. When the correlation becomes weaker, then the points start to scatter and move (Fig. 5.1c). For knowledge creation, one may observe a negative dependency; thus, an increase in the results for one variable is accompanied by a decrease in the results for the other variable (Fig. 5.1d).

To establish how the level of trust impacts relationships in the organization, interorganizational learning, and knowledge creation, Spearman's rank correlation coefficient was used to evaluate the dependency between the variables when they are expressed at least on an ordinal scale. Correlation means the existence of a cause-and-effect dependency, with the relationships, interorganizational learning, and knowledge creation being statistically significant. The results for the variables were as follows: relationships in the organization, 0.347160; interorganizational learning, 0.505850; and knowledge creation, −0.287688. The indicated correlation coefficients are significant if p is <0.05000.

The correlation analysis has shown that the strongest correlation exists for interorganizational learning. Therefore, there is a strong dependency between the level of trust and interorganizational learning. In the case of relationships in the organization, one may ascertain that dependency exists to a slight degree. The correlation coefficient that evaluates the level of trust and knowledge creation indicates an inversely proportional dependency; thus, if the value of trust increases, then knowledge creation decreases.

5.4   Chapter Summary

This chapter presented the results of our research on the scope of the relationships between organizational trust and organizational learning in academic institutions. The analysis of the obtained results indicates that trust impacts the level of relations, which in turn determines the possibilities for organizational learning. Taking this into account, one cannot deny the existence of a positive correlation between these two factors. Furthermore, a two-sided relationship exists between them, with a positive experience in the scope of organizational learning and knowledge creation building trust. These findings are in line with the results of research by Bo Bernhard and Sabina Nielsen, who reported that the ability to learn depends on the quality of relationships built on trust (Nielsen and Nielsen 2009). A similar opinion was expressed by Lane et al. (2001), who found a positive dependency between trust and learning. In addition, Murphy-Graham and Lample defined trust "as an essential goal of education from a capabilities perspective" (Murphy-Graham and Lample 2014). A positive impact of trust on learning processes results above all from positive expectations related to collaborating entities, openness between the parties, and a conviction about mutuality. These factors show that each unit is convinced about the sincerity of the relations connecting them with their partners. For this reason, it is easier for them to share the knowledge they possess. However, deeper analyses indicate that, although organizational trust and learning are desirable factors in relations in academic institutions, it is not always easy to achieve them. Our research indicated the following:

1. Trust in academic institutions is built above all by direct communication, which is the principal method of knowledge sharing in these organizations. The most common forms of knowledge sharing in higher education institutions are official meetings, informal meetings during work, project teams, and groups acting within the organizational unit.

2. The respondents gave low ratings to the levels of learning and knowledge sharing in their academic institutions. In general, there are no procedures or solutions that foster organizational learning. In practice, it is realized spontaneously and in an unstructured way. Moreover, individual actions outweigh collective actions to an important degree.

3. The level of trust in academic institutions was also rated low by respondents. These results can be attributed to the specifics of work in organizational units of an academic institution, the individualization of work, and relatively low possibilities of teamwork.
4. There was a strong dependency between the level of trust and interorganizational learning. At the same time, an inversely proportional dependency between trust and knowledge creation was found.

Our results are not free from limitations, including a small sample size, which mean that the analyses are mainly of a survey nature. However, future research on the impact of trust on organizational learning in academic institutions is planned on a larger scale, both in Poland and abroad.

REFERENCES

Blind, P. K. (2006). *Building trust in government in the twenty-first Century: Review of literature and emerging.* 7th Global Forum on Reinventing Government, United Nations, Vienna, June Issues. 3–8.

Boateng, R. (2011). Do organizations learn when employees learn: The link between individual and organizational learning. *Development and Learning in Organizations: An International Journal, 25*(6), 6–9.

Bugdol, M. (2006). *Wartości organizacyjne: szkice z teorii organizacji i zarządzania* [Organizational values: Sketches from the theory on organization and management]. Kraków: Wydawnictwo Uniwersytetu Jagiellońskiego.

Casimir, G., Lee, K., & Loon, M. (2012). Knowledge sharing: Influences of trust, commitment and cost. *Journal of Knowledge Management, 16*(5), 740–753.

Chenhall, R., & Smith, L. (2003). Performance measurement and reward systems, trust and strategic change. *Journal of Management Accounting Research, 15,* 117–143.

Crossan, M. M., Lane, H. W., & White, R. E. (1999). An organizational learning framework: From intuition to institution. *The Academy of Management Review, 24*(3), 522–537.

Czerska, M. (2003). *Zmiana kulturowa w organizacji. Wyzwania współczesnego menedżera* [Cultural change in the organization. Challenges for the contemporary manager]. Warszawa: Diffin.

Daft, R. L., & Weick, K. E. (1984). Toward a model of organizations as interpretation systems. *Academy of Management Review, 9,* 284–295.

Dovey, K. (2009). The role of trust in innovation. *The Learning Organization, 16*(4), 311–325.

Elangovan, A. R., Auer-Rizzi, W., & Szabo, E. (2007). Why don't I trust you now? An attributional approach to erosion of trust. *Journal of Managerial Psychology, 22*(1), 4–24.

Faulkner, P. (2007). A genealogy of trust. *Episteme, 4*(3), 305–321.

Ferres, N., Connell, J., & Travaglione, A. (2005). The effect of future redeployment on organization trust. *Strategic Change, 14*(2), 77–91.

Fiol, C., & Lyles, M. (1985). Organizational learning. *Academy of Management Review, 10*(4), 803–813.

Frost-Arnold, F. (2014). The cognitive attitude of rational trust. *Synthese: An International Journal for Epistemology, Methodology and Philosophy of Science, 191*(9), 1957–1974.

Gammelgaard, J., McDonald, F., Tüselmann, H., Dörrenbächer, C., & Stephan, A. (2011). Effective autonomy, organisational relationships and skilled jobs in subsidiaries. *Management Research Review, 34*(4), 366–385.

Holste, J. S., & Fields, D. (2010). Trust and tacit knowledge sharing and use. *Journal of Knowledge Management, 14*(1), 128–140.

Huotari, M. L., & Iivonen, M. (2004). Managing knowledge based organizations through trust. In M. L. Huotari & M. Iivonen (Eds.), *Trust in knowledge management and systems in organization*. Hershey: Idea Group.

Jashapara, A. (2006). *Zarządzanie wiedzą* [Knowledge management]. Warszawa: PWE.

Kastberg, G. (2016). Trust and control in network relations: A study of a public sector setting. *Financial Accountability & Management, 32*, 33–56.

Keele, L. (2007). Social capital and the dynamics of trust in government. *American Journal of Political Science, 51*(2), 241–254.

Kostova, T. (1999). Transnational transfer of strategic organizational practices: A contextual perspective. *Academy of Management Review, 24*, 308–324.

Kożuch, B., & Dobrowolski, Z. (2014). *Creating public trust. An organisational perspective* (Series: New Horizons in management sciences, Vol. 3). Frankfurt am Main/Berlin/Bern/Bruxelles/New York/Oxford/Wien: Peter Lang.

Kożuch, B., & Lenart-Gansiniec, R. (2017). Trust and knowledge sharing. In: J. Liebowitz, J Paliszkiewicz, & Gołuchowski J. (Eds), *Intuition, trust, and analytics*. Routledge, CRC Press Taylor & Francis Group.

Kożuch, B., Sienkiewicz-Małyjurek, K., & Luty, L. (2015). Rational and relational bases of public managers' new profiles in the context of trust research. *Journal of Intercultural Management, 7*(2), 31–47.

Lane, P., Salk, J., & Lyles, M. A. (2001). Knowledge acquisition and performance in transitional economy international joint ventures. *Strategic Management Journal, 22*, 1139–1162.

Leja, K. (2013). *Zarządzanie uczelnią. Koncepcje i współczesne wyzwania* [University management. Concepts and contemporary challenges]. Warszawa: Oficyna Wolters Kluwe.

Lenart, R. (2014). *Zarządzanie wiedzą w tworzeniu konkurencyjności szkoły* [Knowledge management in the school competitiveness]. Warszawa: Wolters Kluwer.

Li, L. (2005). The effects of trust and shared vision on inward knowledge transfer in subsidiaries' intra- and inter-organizational relationships. *International Business Review, 14*(1), 77–95.

Makhija, M. V., & Ganesh, U. (1997). The relationship between control and partner learning related joint ventures. *Organization Science, 8*, 508–527.

Manu, E., Ankrah, N., Chinyio, E., & Proverbs, D. (2015). Trust influencing factors in main contractor and subcontractor relationships during projects. *International Journal of Project Management, 33*(7), 1495–1508.

McEvily, B., Perrone, V., & Zaheer, A. (2003). Trust as an organizing principle. *Organization Science, 14*(1), 91–103.

Mikuła, B. (2005). Wiedza organizacji i jej rozwój [Organization knowledge and its development]. In A. Stabryła (Ed.), *Innowacyjność we współczesnych organizacjach* [Innovation in contemporary organizations] (pp. 369–368). Kraków: Akademia Ekonomiczna w Krakowie.

Molina-Morales, F. X., Martínez-Fernández, M. T., & Torlò, V. J. (2011). The dark side of trust: The benefits, costs and optimal levels of trust for innovation performance. *Long Range Planning, 44*(2), 118–133.

Murphy-Graham, E., & Lample, J. (2014). Learning to trust: Examining the connections between trust and capabilities friendly pedagogy through case studies from Honduras and Uganda. *International Journal of Educational Development, 36*, 51–62.

Nahapiet, J., & Ghoshal, S. (1998). Social capital, intellectual capital, and the organizational advantage. *Academy of Management Review, 23*(2), 242–266.

Nielsen, B. B., & Nielsen, S. (2009). Learning and innovation in international strategic alliances: An empirical test of the role of trust and tacitness. *Journal of Management Studies, 46*, 1031–1056.

Paliszkiewicz, J. (2012). Zaufanie a zarządzanie wiedzą – przegląd literatury [Trust and knowledge management – a literature review]. In R. Knosala (Ed.), *Innowacje w zarządzaniu i inżynierii produkcji [Innovation in management and production engineering]* (pp. 548–561). Opole: Oficyna Wydawnicza Polskiego Towarzystwa Zarządzania Produkcją.

Pate, J., Beaumont, P., & Stewart, S. (2007). Trust in senior management in the public sector. *Employee Relations, 29*(5), 458–468.

Pedersen, N. J. L. L., Ahlström-Vij, K., & Kappel, K. (2014). Rational trust. *Synthese: An International Journal for Epistemology, Methodology and Philosophy of Science, 191*(9), 1953–1955.

Rahman, M. S., Osmangani, A. M., Daud, N. M., Chowdhury, A. H., & Hassan, H. (2015). Trust and work place spirituality on knowledge sharing behaviour:

Perspective from non-academic staff of higher learning institutions. *The Learning Organization, 22*(6), 317–332.

Rashman, L., Withers, E., & Hartley, J. (2009). Organizational learning and knowledge in public service organizations: A systematic review of the literature. *International Journal of Management Reviews, 11*, 463–494.

Ritter, T. (2000). A framework for analyzing interconnectedness of relationships. *Industrial Marketing Management, 29*(4), 317–326.

Rokita, J. (2005). *Zarządzanie strategiczne. Tworzenie i utrzymywanie przewagi konkurencyjnej* [Strategic management. Creating and maintaining a competitive advantage]. Warszawa: PWE.

Scott, D., Scofield, P., Hunter, C., & Fletcher, D. (2008). Decline of sooty shearwaters Puffinus griseus on The Snares, New Zealand. *Papers and Proceedings of the Royal Society of Tasmania, 142*, 185–196.

Senge, P. (2012). *Piąta dyscyplina. Teoria i praktyka organizacji uczących się* [The fifth discipline: The art and practice of the learning organization]. Warszawa: Wolters Kluwer.

Swift, P. E., & Hwang, A. (2013). The impact of affective and cognitive trust on knowledge sharing and organizational learning. *The Learning Organization, 20*(1), 20–37.

Tabak, F., & Smith, W. P. (2005). Privacy and electronic monitoring in the workplace: A model of managerial cognition and relational trust development. *Employee Responsibilities and Rights Journal, 17*(3), 173–189.

Thomas, C. W. (1998). Maintaining and restoring public trust in government agencies and their employees. *Administration and Society, 30*(2), 166–193.

Wang, C. L., & Ahmed, P. K. (2003). Organisational learning: A critical review. *The Learning Organization, 10*(1), 8–17.

Watkins, K., & Marsick, V. (1999). Sculpting the learning community. *NASSP Bulletin, 83*(604), 78–87.

Wong, A., & Tjosvold, D. (2006). Collectivist values for learning in organizational relationships in China: The role of trust and vertical coordination. *Asia Pacific Journal of Management, 23*(3), 299–317.

CHAPTER 6

The Role and Importance of Trust in the Processes of Human Resource Management

Marek Bugdol

6.1 Introduction

In considering the notion of public motivation, we can refer to external evaluation—that is, whether stakeholders (or more broadly speaking, "the public") trust the organization. Such trust is influenced by a large number of factors, such as analyzing the performance of companies listed on stock exchanges; it is mainly information communicated to the public. However, using the metaphor of an organization as some kind of theater, we can also talk about internal public trust. In this case, the public comprises employees, customers, suppliers, and external entities, among others.

Both internal and external public trust depends to a considerable degree on how the management copes with human resource management processes. This management may strengthen or weaken social capital, productivity, effectiveness, efficiency, and other economic and organizational factors. Furthermore, employees are the best judges and spokespeople of their organizations.

M. Bugdol (✉)
Jagiellonian University, Kraków, Poland

B. Kożuch et al. (eds.), *Managing Public Trust*,
https://doi.org/10.1007/978-3-319-70485-2_6

This chapter will focus on the importance and role of trust in the selected human resource (HR) processes such as recruitment, training, assessment, and motivation. The author will show how these processes can strengthen trust or destroy it.

6.2   TRUST IN THE PROCESS OF SELECTION AND RECRUITMENT

The process of selection and recruitment is of great significance for public trust. Information on how organizations recruit and assess candidates for employment or present their expectations and requirements concerning competences is frequently publicly available; therefore, it is subject to external evaluation. Also, candidates for employment and employees themselves share their opinions with other people, future employees, relatives, and colleagues, among other.

Selection and recruitment constitute the beginning of the process of establishing social ties between the candidates—between future employees and the organization. It should strengthen the organization's image as an institution that is thoroughly professional and socially responsible. It should be also kept in mind that the recruitment process is the beginning of the development of a psychological contract between the employee and the management and the building of organizational values, particularly procedural fairness and trust.

In the processes of recruitment and subsequently selection, the issue of trust depends on a few factors. Firstly, it is the problem of employers' believing that information provided by candidates is true. Such doubts concerning the provision of true information are fully justified. Many researchers (George and Marett 2004; Cullen 2006; Brockett 2006) have proven that candidates provide false information concerning their education, duration of previous employment, salaries, held positions, professional titles, or scopes of duties. Other studies conducted by the Risk Advisory Group (Hodge 2008) showed that lies, omissions, oversights, or exaggerations can be found in half of all curricula vitae (CVs). Information on criminal history or financial may be withheld. Candidates lie mainly during the following two stages: when they prepare documents required in the recruitment process and when they answer questions at interviews. According to one theory (Hodge 2008), lies are told when candidates for employment are afraid of losing their reputation; however, it is impossible to rule out deliberate lies which, in the opinion of those providing false information, could turn out to be beneficial. For this reason, some organizations apply very complex selection techniques. They carefully check the whole documentation, conduct community interviews, or hire detectives to verify the reliability of CVs. Organizations try to ensure that their recruitment processes are perceived in the categories of fairness and reliability. They introduce strict selection procedures that include guidelines for identifying skills, fighting discrimination and biases, conducting particular stages of selection, and maintaining cooperation with other employees or departments in the recruitment process.

Secondly, if organizations use the services provided by recruitment firms, there may be a problem of trust in their integrity and reliability (Pollock 1997). To fulfill an order as soon as possible, some organizations may provide their customers with false or unconfirmed information about candidates for employment. Thirdly, the method of conducting recruitment and selection influences the level of trust in an organization (Bugdol 2010).

The research conducted so far on the relationships between trust and recruitment processes does not exhaust all interesting issues. The following questions could also be addressed:

- Does the use of a large number of recruitment and selection techniques and methods cause a trust trap?
- Does trust in an organization erode as a consequence of frequent recruitments? If so, to what extent?
- How is trust in an organization influenced by the fact that it buys services from an external recruitment agency?

As has already been mentioned, organizations that attempt to protect themselves against hiring dishonest people implement more and more complex methods of verifying candidates' credibility. They conduct detailed examinations of documents (including kindergarten completion diplomas) and thorough community interviews (similar to those used in military organizations). Modern technologies, such as video conferences or interviews over the Internet, are being used more frequently in the recruitment process. Some companies hire "CV detectives"—individuals and agencies specializing in checking employees or candidates for employment. They use situational tests corresponding to particular roles in an organization. Self-report questionnaires are used to assess ambition, reliability, and emotional intelligence. Organizations are also experimenting with nontraditional methods of conducting interviews, such as video chats, group sessions, and panels. However, these measures are in fact a manifestation of the lack of trust in all candidates for employment. Verification procedures are applied to both credible candidates and those who are trying to hide something.

Frequently conducted hiring and dismissal procedures (in other words, a culture of just-in-time hiring) are not good for the building of a positive image of an organization. They cause a situation in which candidates for employment do not believe that the organization is able to provide them with job security. This is a complex problem because there are various reasons for high employee turnover rates. Some organizations find it difficult to balance their production potential or develop very quickly, whereas others look for new forms of activities or are focused exclusively on achieving short-term objectives.

Using services provided by an external recruitment agency may be a necessity, especially if an organization initiates business activities in a new country and does not have sufficient knowledge of the quality of its human resources. However, this option eliminates the possibility of establishing direct contact with future employees; thus, trust has to be developed later in the processes of adaptation and socialization.

The very manner of conducting selection may favor the building of trust or reduce it considerably. The formulation of promises during job interviews is a frequently occurring problem. Such promises concern promotion and development opportunities, among others. If they cannot be kept, then the previously earned trust is lost. However, what happens when promises are being fulfilled? To what extent are employees' expectations consistent with reality? These and many other questions remain unanswered.

6.3   Trust in the Process of Adaptation and Socialization

The recruitment process is strongly connected with the subsequent HR processes—that is, adaptation and socialization. It is believed that the first contacts that occur within the scope of recruitment influence employees' initial expectations. The degree to which such expectations are fulfilled influences the effectiveness of adaptation and socialization (Anderson and

Cunningham-Snell 2003, p. 85). The research conducted so far indicates that socialization is one element of a personnel policy that favors the building of trust (Six and Sorge 2008). Socialization consists of employees' mutual learning from one another, adopting the values and standards effective in a given organization. Through socialization, employees become rightful members of a group or organization. Socialization is a process in which employees assimilate the various standards (ethical, instrumental, autotelic, and other), values, and models of behavior fostered in a particular organization. Adaptation, on the other hand, is identified with the stage of introducing an employee into an organization. During the adaptation process, an employee usually becomes familiar with organizational regulations, has the opportunity to participate in the operations of various organizational units, gets to know new people, and acquires particular skills necessary for further work.

Adaptation has two dimensions: the professional dimension, which indicates adjustment to assigned duties, and the social dimension, which comprises "the company level (the acceptance of an organization's goals, mission and fundamental values) and the team level (the acceptance of a given team's standards and rules, the management style used by superiors, the rules of social contacts and the work atmosphere)" (Pocztowski 2003, p. 171). The professional dimension of adaptation also includes technological adaptation—that is, the process of acquiring competences in the use of modern technologies applied in a particular organization. Many studies indicate an indirect role of the adaptation process in the strengthening of trust. For example, studies conducted in industrial enterprises have shown that adaptation plays a primary role in improving work safety (Gembalska-Kwiecień and Żurakowski 2016).

The development of trust in the initial period of employment depends to a considerable extent on organizational support, communication processes, organizational values and rules, and psychological empowerment (Eberl et al. 2012). What is of primary importance during the initial period of employment is support provided by the management, which usually decreases in the subsequent periods. Such support has a considerable impact on perceived satisfaction (Jokisaari and Nurmi 2009). It is also believed that "organizational trust is important for successful socialization, cooperation and effective teamworking and in the long run helps to minimize risks and decrease operating costs" (Läms and Pučėtait 2006). Thus, during socialization, trust may be strengthened or eroded depending on the general level of organizational and interpersonal trust, whether and to what extent employees receive adequate support, how they assimilate the existing values, and the operating principles of their organization.

In practice, making decisions about what fosters trust is difficult. The factors presented in Table 6.1 are limited exclusively to the variables that have been taken into consideration in the existing research. It should be remembered that the factors are fully dependent on one another. For example, trust in superiors has a considerable impact on the development of empowerment, which, in turn, fosters citizenship behavior in organizations (Huang et al. 2010). Values held by employees influence how superiors' credibility is assessed (Shamir and Lapidot 2003).

In the initial period of employment, some employees follow specially developed adaptation programs or work under the supervision of special advisers. By taking care of new employees, these advisers can play a great role in the development of both organizational and interpersonal trust. Quality-oriented organizations are aware of this and frequently appoint experienced and knowledgeable employees as advisers to trainees.

Another interesting issue is the process of employee assessment and classification. Psychology indicates that first results determine how a person is assessed. Furthermore, superiors' expectations concerning their employees develop on the basis of their experiences and beliefs. However, employees' knowledge, education, social and ethnic origin, etc., should not be ignored. The classification of employees into good and bad employees influences feedback. If a person is classified as a bad employee, they may receive no feedback, have no opportunity for improving their behavior, and consequently the growth of trust is very unlikely.

It is not only superiors that have expectations regarding employees—there are expectations on both sides. New employees have concrete expectations regarding the organization as well as their managers and colleagues. It should be noted that such expectations are influenced by future employees' knowledge about organizations. Unfortunately, such knowledge is frequently limited, based on the skimming of Internet websites or talks with current employees. If such expectations are not confirmed in practice, the levels of motivation and trust may decrease. In the process of adaptation and socialization, an important role is played by public trust created by organizations themselves.

Table 6.1 The key factors in the process of socialization

Factors influencing trust	Definition	Comments
Organizational support	The notion of organizational support was introduced into the literature in the 1980s (Eisenberger et al. 1986). Organizational support is a term referring to how an organization appreciates its employees' commitment (effort, contribution to organizational development and achievement of objectives) and takes care of their well-being (DeConinck and Johnson 2009).	The development of trust in the initial period of employment depends to a large degree on organizational support (Eberl et al. 2012).
Managerial support	Managerial support indicates the degree to which employees have a general idea about how managers appreciate their work, take care of their well-being (the quality of life at a workplace), and provide them with necessary support (cf. Eisenberger et al. 2002).	It is traditionally believed that managerial support leads to organizational support, although it has been also observed that this relationship may be reverse—that is, organizational support causes employees to experience also support provided by the management (Eisenberger et al. 2002).
Communication process	Communication is a process aimed at changing the awareness of the recipient of information in accordance with the intention of the sender (www1).	The processes of social communication are of key importance for the development and maintenance of trust (Brenkert 1998; Albrecht and Travaglione 2003; Burton 2006). Communication skills favor the development of trust (Willemyns et al. 2003). Communication is a carrier of either trust or distrust.

(continued)

Table 6.1   (continued)

Factors influencing trust	Definition	Comments
Psychological empowerment	Empowerment is a manifestation of increasing trust in employees; a means of motivating employees for better work; behavior on the part of managers who intend to provide their subordinates with more authority; a genuine conviction that it is a good idea to use employees' potential; a psychological process of distancing oneself from tasks and duties which have been delegated to others; a type of a social contract (a psychological agreement between managers and subordinates); and an idea of resource management aiming to increase employees' factual influence on the functioning of their organization (Conger and Kanungo 1988; Lee and Koh 2001; Lincoln et al. 2002).	Empowerment has a positive impact on employees' trust in their managers and decreases the costs of internal and external control as well as transaction costs (Moye and Henkin 2006). What is important in the processes of adaptation and socialization is the existence of a strong relationship between psychological empowerment and cognitive trust (Ergeneli et al. 2007).
Values	A value is "something that is an object of relatively permanent desires, that constitutes good in itself" (Stoner et al. 2001, p. 630).	Trust is strongly dependent on the other organizational values, mainly fairness. Trust influences values; values, in turn, influence social trust and cooperation (Siegrist et al. 2003).
Principles	Principles are laws governing some processes or phenomena; formulas explaining such laws; norms of conduct established on the basis of a regulation or custom; and a manner of conduct in particular circumstances (www2). In management sciences, we can distinguish, for example, Fayol's principles of quality or crisis management principles, etc.	All principles occurring in an organization have a hypothetical influence on trust because they determine the manners of conduct in particular situations, thus influencing the sense of psychological security.

Source: The author's own work based on the specified literature

6.4   Trust in the Process of Training

Trust is an important factor in the process of training (Gainey and Klaas 2005; Kahane 2006; Gill 2013). In particular, ethical training concerning organizational culture and values may be a useful tool in restoring public trust (cf. Dando and Bradshaw 2013). The research conducted so far indicates the following:

- There are interrelationships between training and trust, which means that training strengthens and maintains trust (McCauley and Kuhnert 1992; Reade 2003; Reinke 2003; Hemdi and Nasurdin 2006; Six and Sorge 2008).
- Trust in a person conducting training determines its effectiveness, but the sense of community and the integration skills of a trainer are also important (Kahane 2006).
- Social and result-oriented trust play very important roles in cooperation between organizations and entities conducting training (Gainey and Klaas 2005).
- The level of trust depends on how an organization perceives the competences, consequences, and clarity of motives of a training service provider (Leimbach 2005).
- Superiors' trust in new employees may depend on the intensity of training and preferred management styles (cf. Atuahene-Gima and Li 2006).
- Employee training should contribute to increased trust, loyalty, and motivation (Six and Sorge 2008).
- Training may be a factor that fosters trust in an organization and a tool for restoring trust among top management members (Reade 2003).
- Training may strengthen trust in certain human resource management processes, such as an employee assessment system (Reinke 2003).
- Employees who are satisfied with training programs reciprocate with trust in the top management (McCauley and Kuhnert 1992).
- The lack of certain skills in superiors, such as skills related to the manifestation of trust, may be the reason for failures in ethical training (Thornton 2009).
- Well-organized training increases employees' trust in modern technologies (Payre et al. 2017).

- Training teaches mutual respect and trust, which is important in the processes aiming to reduce unethical behavior (Burt 2016).

The major goal of training should be to increase competence and trust. Employees express this trust, taking into consideration their own and other people's assessments of competences and skills as well as their use in various situations. This type of trust occurs in various configurations and is not reduced, as we tend to believe, to trust placed by employees in their bosses and/or experts. We trust someone because we know that they possess knowledge and experience that may be useful for us and/or the whole organization (Bugdol 2010, p. 25).

One of the manifestations of trust is the idea of an educational voucher. According to this idea, all employees receive an equal amount of funds to be spent for educational purposes (e.g., they may purchase a training course, computer software, or pay tuition for postgraduate studies). It is the employee who decides how the voucher will be used. The idea of an educational voucher is based on the reasonable assumption that the employee knows their needs the best. Furthermore, relative freedom in the use of financial resources teaches independence and thrift, facilitates integration (e.g., employees form training groups to save money), and allows quick elimination of a knowledge deficit (e.g., with respect to foreign language skills; Bugdol 2010, pp. 219–220).

It is not only training that influences trust. The level of trust in a given organization exerts an enormous impact on the effectiveness of training activities. This is the case because people trusting each other cooperate better. Thus, HR trainers develop trust in training and development environments (Gill 2013). In many organizations, the level of trust is determined by a training policy or the lack thereof. There are no established rules concerning employees' participation in postgraduate programs or training courses or their financing. The lack of transparent rules favors subjectivity and the sense of unfairness, which, as is generally known, leads to a decrease in trust. Thus, it should be remembered that one of the methods of shaping trust is to ensure procedural and distributional fairness.

We do not know to what extent a training event aimed at increasing trust can be effective. This is not because of a lack of the reliable methods for measuring such effectiveness, but rather because such training programs are not organized. Games and workshops for developing interpersonal skills are a poor substitute for such training. Their major weakness is that they are frequently conducted in artificial conditions, not natural environments.

Training may be one of the methods of restoring and maintaining public trust. It is important for the image of an organization and its customers' trust in it. Even if ethical training is not completely effective, it strengthens organizational values, allows the improvement of an organization's image or the quality of provided services, and thus maintains public trust.

6.5   Trust in Employee Evaluations

Employee evaluations and their quality have a substantial influence on public trust. Firstly, organizations that are unethical and unfair in their employee evaluations take into consideration the results of work only, ignoring the process of achieving such results. They do not treat employee evaluations as a tool for employee development, motivation, and promotion, but rather as a means of increasing productivity and maintaining discipline. Thus, they destroy their own image and undermine the trust of both their employees and customers. Although many factors influence the effectiveness of an evaluation system (e.g., adequate training, the duration of evaluations, the degree of complexity, the understanding of the purpose of evaluations), it is trust that plays the major role (Reinke 2003). What influences trust and satisfaction with evaluations is fairness. A fair evaluation is indispensable for the maintenance of trust (Mani 2002; Hemdi and Nasurdin 2006; Steensma and Visser 2007). If an evaluation system is perceived as unfair, this decreases the level of employees' satisfaction and trust in the management (Mani 2002). The sense of fairness that should accompany evaluations is just a preliminary condition for an employee's trust in the evaluation system itself. Such trust influences modifications of behavior, particularly the elimination of identified weaknesses (Dobbins et al. 1993). The greater the acceptance and reliability of an evaluation system, the higher the level of trust (Mayer and Davis 1999).

There is no doubt that both trust and fairness are values that become particularly evident in the processes of change, such as restructuring or downsizing. As early as the 1990s, it was shown that trust was of great importance in evaluation processes conducted in periods of change (Mishra and Spreitzer 1998).

In practice, formal evaluation systems have both supporters and opponents. Many studies indicate that formal employee evaluation systems are harmful for trust and creativity (Hassan 2007). Improperly functioning evaluation systems cause stress, dissatisfaction, and professional burnout (Gabris and Ihrke 2001). Edward Deming observed that employee evaluations were connected with negative emotions and caused fear; he regarded periodic employee evaluation systems as "one of the seven deadly diseases of management." However, objective and fair employee evaluations provide valuable feedback and fulfill an important educational function. Furthermore, evaluation systems may encourage employees to promote trust (Schraeder et al. 2007). A fair employee evaluation system may have a favorable impact on employees' commitment and satisfaction (Miah et al. 2012; Gupta and Kumar 2013), motivation (Selvarajan and Cloninger 2012), and productivity (Flint 1999).

When analyzing the usefulness of employee evaluations, it is necessary to remember that many other factors accompanying evaluations can influence trust and other organizational values, such as the attitudes and opinions of people conducting evaluations, the quality of feedback, the scope of managerial support, the acceptance of evaluations, and the possibility of exercising control over an evaluation system.

6.6   Trust in Employee Motivation

The research shows that trust influences employees' motivation (Heavey et al. 2017; Casse and Konstandian 2017). This is so because trust is accompanied by a sense of security; furthermore, a high level of trust fosters the sharing of knowledge, which in turn may contribute to the development of innovative products (Ullah et al. 2017; Ozlati 2015).

When new products are being created, project management tools are being implemented, tasks and goals are being established, and people responsible for their achievement are being appointed. If motivational systems are to contribute to the shaping of trust, they require an adequate methodology for establishing goals as well as reliable behavior. Firstly, in accordance with Locke's theory (1968, quoted from Foster 2003, p. 344), "difficult goals lead to higher performance than easy goals." The execution of successive tasks and the achievement of successive goals increase the level of competence trust. Secondly, in the shaping of trust and motivation, an important role is played by the reliable behavior of leaders—that is, the people responsible for managing organizations (Grant and Sumanth 2009).

As is generally known, trust depends to a considerable degree on a sense of fairness. Fairness is regarded as a superior value; therefore, it constitutes a basis for trust. If the relationships between trust and fairness are so strong, it is possible to conclude that for motivational systems to strengthen, shape, and maintain trust, they have to be fair. Similarly, it is worth referring to motivational ideas that are related directly to a sense of fairness. One of the most popular theories of motivation is the theory of fairness formulated by Adams (Foster 2003). According to this theory, people compare their efforts and rewards in an organization to those of others (so-called important people). However, to better understand how employees assess fairness, we should refer to the theory of equity (Makin et al. 2000). We can find its basic elements in the theory by Adams; it was subsequently developed extensively by Makin et al. (2000) on the basis of works on fairness and represents the philosophy of morality. The theory of equity assumes that there are three main categories of assessing fairness: contributions, equalities and needs. To understand the theory of equity, it is necessary to take into consideration the components of the following categories:

(a) Contributions constitute an individual's efforts as well as everything they bring to a group or organization (e.g., education, experience, responsibilities).
(b) Equalities concern the fact that everyone receives the same, irrespective of contributions or needs.
(c) Needs determine remuneration (following the rule that we pay according to needs) (Bugdol 2014).

In practice, however, it is rather difficult to assess what others do and receive in return because there is no easy access to information and opinions are formed on the basis of unverified data, among other reasons. What is important is not only employees' assessments but also their individual expectations: "Employees have to be convinced that their efforts will bring about good effects and good effect will bring them rewards" (Lundy and Cowling 2000, p. 302).

Thus, trust plays an important role in both the implementation and modification of motivational systems. It is the value that causes motivational systems to acquire sense. However, despite the increasing knowledge on motivation, we still know little about how to motivate people. Some organizations have even concluded that the best motivation is a lack of motivation or that all external rewards cause people to focus on acquiring such rewards, not on solving concrete problems. It is not always possible to know how much effort particular people put in the performance of their duties. It is easy to make mistakes in such assessments. Hence, it is easy to destroy both trust and fairness.

6.7   CONTROL AND TRUST

Control has a considerable influence on trust, which can be strengthened or irretrievably destroyed. Meanwhile, the level of trust itself exerts a significant impact on control, and more precisely on its scope, frequency and method of exercise. The research conducted so far indicates the following:

- Control and trust are complementary and strengthen each other (Kalkman and de Waard 2017).
- When there is a high level of trust and a low level of risk, then there is usually little control (Şngün and Wasti 2007, pp. 430–464).
- Various types of control and trust depend on each other. For example, calculative trust has strong effects on outcome-based and behavior control, whereas relational trust affects on social control (Jiang and Lu 2017).
- Process control may strengthen trust in people exercising supervision after supervised employees have undergone intensive training and the market is changeable and demanding (Atuahene-Gima and Li 2006, pp. 342–358).
- Control is positively related to employees' trust in their organization. This relationship is mediated by procedural fairness and organizational prestige (Weibel et al. 2016).
- A high level of trust increases employees' commitment when the level of control is low (Neves and Caetano 2006, pp. 351–364).
- Mutual learning processes play the main role in the shaping of trust and proper control (Inkpen and Currall 2004, pp. 586–599).
- The levels of control and trust influence the effectiveness of knowledge management (Yang and Farn 2009, pp. 210–218).
- The alternate expression of trust and exercise of control may lead to a loss of loyalty (Kusari et al. 2005, pp. D1–D6).

Positive relationships between trust and control may result from the very simple fact that control allows supervisors to correct mistakes and constitutes a regular process by which elements of a system become predictable in the pursuit of required objectives (Leifer and Mills 1996; Robbins and Decenzo 2002). According to some researchers (Coletti et al. 2005, pp. 477–500), control inclines people to cooperate, reduces relational risk, and thus has a positive impact on trust. For this to take place, however, a proper environment is necessary. Employees must have the possibility to observe cooperative behavior.

When analyzing relationships between trust and control, one should keep in mind that there are many different types of trust and control. For example, the control of financial resources included in financial plans or preliminary estimates is one of the methods of checking whether such resources are being spent correctly. If they are positive and publicly available, the results of such control may increase public trust.

There are various research approaches to control, such as the humanist approach, the accidentality approach, the rational approach, the approach consistent with the trend of interpersonal relationships, and the normative approach (Bacharach et al. 2002). All of them refer indirectly to the relationships between control and trust. For example, in the humanist approach, control is a manifestation of the lack of trust in employees and limits their autonomy. The accidentality approach assumes that the effectiveness of control depends on the context (on how employees perceive supervision and the principles of fairness). Thus, the level of trust depends on the adoption of fair principles of control (e.g., on the principle of universality) and the dimensions of trust, such as the credibility and competences of the management.

According to the rational approach, employees display counterproductive behavior because the principles, roles, and policies effective in their organizations are unclear to them. Counterproductive behavior is the enemy of trust. A lack of the knowledge about rules and principles indicates a lack of communication and employee participation—and thus indirectly, a low level of trust. An approach consistent with the trend of interpersonal relationships assumes that employees may behave improperly because various organizational conflicts and tensions occur in their workplace. The normative approach assumes that employees sometimes behave improperly because the integration of standards does not take place or collective and common standards are not developed, which may be caused, among other things, by a low level of trust in the organization. Shaping trust successfully requires knowledge of why people behave improperly. It is important to identify the sources of such behavior. Control itself fulfills the securing and corrective functions, but frequently focuses on irregularities instead of identifying their underlying reasons.

The manner of conducting control activities is also important. Strict control undermines the level of work safety and may be the cause of perceived danger or the lack of safety (Vander Elst et al. 2014, pp. 671–693). Improperly exercised control destroys trust and/or limits its development, which can happen as follows:

- Control is exercised selectively (only with respect to particular employees or groups of employees).
- Control is carried out suddenly and unexpectedly (e.g., for the single purpose of acquiring evidence necessary to dismiss an employee).
- Control turns into a critical assessment of an individual employee (e.g., of their traits of character).
- Control causes an unfavorable change in employees' status (Bugdol 2010).

An organization's social system is full of tension and, like all systems, is characterized by relationships among its elements. Therefore, there are no simple relations between control and trust. For example, in the past it was believed that control exercised within a supply chain undermined trust. At present, it is assumed that "control systems do not necessarily undermine trust. Whether they do so depends on at least six factors: the nature and stage of the inter-firm relationship, the general types of control used by managers, the specific control tools used, their purpose, who participates in designing control systems, and how these systems are designed and implemented" (Sanchez et al. 2012).

A new research problem is the study of relationships occurring between trust and technical control. It turns out that trust is a value that may be of key importance in the application of modern technologies (Van den Berg and Keymolen 2017). For example, the less trust there is in employees, the more sophisticated are the means of technical control.

6.8 Layoffs and Trust

As an integral component of HR management, the employee dismissal process is very important for trust, although it is frequently ignored. Layoffs violate employees' sense of security. People who are losing their sense of security may adopt untypical behavior, make numerous mistakes, or manifest low productivity. After layoffs, particularly group layoffs, it is necessary to rebuild trust (Johnston 2011) by communicating clearly the factual reasons for dismissals and involving employees in decision-making processes. Dismissals, particularly those perceived by employees as unfair, may lead to sabotage, theft of property and knowledge, financial fraud, stalking, and many other types of unethical or even criminal behavior.

The termination of employment is a key moment for personal security and thus for trust. Organizations use various methods for preventing theft of knowledge, acts of sabotage, or vandalism. Such methods usually consist of blocking access to the Internet (before the proper dismissal), conducting talks about layoffs on neutral ground, and preventing dismissed employees from removing any equipment from company premises. The problem is that protecting knowledge or restricting access to information is also a manifestation of a lack of trust. Restricting access to databases does not foster the development of either knowledge or trust. In practice, it is important to determine unambiguously who has access to which resources of knowledge and which knowledge should be regarded as tacit knowledge.

A loss of trust occurs mainly in the case of unfair dismissals. Dismissal for an unjustified reason takes place when the employer is not able to prove that the dismissal has a valid basis or does not comply with a procedure for reducing excessive workforce (Armstrong 2000). To prevent unjust dismissals, some companies try to diagnose the factual reasons for layoffs; the most popular tool for this is a survey questionnaire. It is believed that well-prepared dismissals may increase productivity because worst employees should be laid off, which has a positive influence on competition among employees. In practice, however, when dismissals are carried out, decision makers apply various (not always objective) criteria. Naturally, a lack of objectivity causes a decrease in trust.

It should be also noted that refraining from layoffs may be a means of increasing an organization's credibility and consequently public trust. Some companies are willing to do a lot to prevent dismissals. A case in point is the company Hyperthem Inc., which did not lay off a single full-time employee during a period of 40 years (Tuna 2009).

6.9 Conditions for the Growth and Development of Trust

Many conditions determine the development of trust. In the case of HR management, the shaping of trust has to take into consideration its types and dimensions. A very important role in the organization of trust is played by dimensions such as credibility, reliability, and competences. They can be shaped to a greater degree than, for example, predictability or kindliness (Bugdol 2010).

Credibility is based on the ability of a partner of an interaction to keep their promises (Ganesan and Hess 1997). Behavior that is consistent with made promises is already regarded as credible, even if it does not maximize benefits (Francois and Zabojnik 2005). Employees trust those whom they believe will not let anyone down, especially in situations involving threats, risks, or changes. Reliability does not consist of the absence of any errors or omissions. A reliable person is not without faults, but they can overcome their faults in key situations requiring reliable behavior (e.g., in the event of a defective product, conflict, or dispute) (Bugdol 2010). Competences are the key factor influencing trust. Integrity and honesty lead to the development of moral trust, whereas competences contribute to the development of practical trust, which is expected by managers. Competences allow the transformation of ideas into valuable products (Kanter 1997) and influence the development of trust. In the practice of management, an important role is played by competence management programs. There are definitely more opportunities for competence management than for ensuring credibility and reliability.

It is important to pursue procedural, informational, and distributional fairness from the very beginning. In shaping trust, one must consider the fact that trust is just one of many organizational values. It is impossible to prepare a trust development program without allowing for satisfaction, commitment, or solidarity. Ethical values constitute a foundation for trust (Bugdol 2010).

6.10 Chapter Summary

This chapter discusses only a few selected aspects of the shaping of trust. The problem is that organizational values participate in the creation of organizational culture and are included in everyday interactions—the symbolism of an organization and its processes. Therefore, in practice, taking care of values cannot be limited to ensuring adequate HR methods. In the practice of management, it is assumed that all HR management processes can either destroy organizational values or strengthen and maintain them. Therefore, it is important for organizations, particularly large ones, to create their own trust development programs.

A diagnosis of organizational values is also important. Training activities that develop interpersonal skills are of particular significance for trust. However, it should be emphasized that they have both supporters (e.g. Palo and Padhi 2003) and opponents (e.g. Mayer et al. 1987). The most controversial opinions concern the role of employee evaluation systems in the shaping of organizational values. Evaluation systems are frequently perceived as unfair; this perception decreases employees' satisfaction and trust in the management (Mani 2002). Further, much depends on how superiors deal with employee promotions and individual development policies. If promotions are regarded as fair, they can foster employee commitment, job satisfaction, and productivity (Wan et al. 2012).

How organizations cope with the management of employees not only influences their productivity and economic results, but it also indirectly shapes their images. Therefore, HR management influences public trust, which is of key importance for every organization in both the public and private sectors.

References

Albrecht, S., & Travaglione, A. (2003). Trust in public-sector senior management. *The International Journal of Human Resource Management, 14*(1), 76–92.

Anderson, N., & Cunningham-Snell, N. (2003). Selekcja pracowników [Selection of workers]. In N. Chmiel (Ed.), *Psychologia pracy i organizacji*. Gdańsk: GWP.

Armstrong, M. (2000). *Zarządzanie Zasobami Ludzkimi*. Kraków: ABC.

Atuahene-Gima, K., & Li, H. (2006). The effects of formal controls on supervisee trust in the manager in new product selling: Evidence from young and inexperienced salespeople in China. *Journal of Product Innovation Management, 23*(4), 342–358.

Bacharach, S. B., Bamberger, P. A., & Sonnenstuhl, W. J. (2002). Driven to drink: Managerial control, work-related risk factors, and employee problem drinking. *Academy of Management Journal, 45*(4), 637–658.

Brenkert, G. G. (1998). Trust, business and business ethics: An introduction. *Business Ethics Quarterly, 8*(2), 195–203.

Brockett, J. (2006). The truth about job interview lies. *People Management, 11*(12), 11.

Bugdol, M. (2010). *Wymiary i problemy zarządzania organizacją opartą na zaufaniu.* [Dimensions and problems of trust-based organization management]. Wyd. Kraków: UJ.

Bugdol, M. (2014). *Znaczenie sprawiedliwości w zarządzaniu ludźmi. Dlaczego warto być sprawiedliwym* [The importance of justice in managing people. Why should you be fair]. Wyd. Warszawa: Difin.

Burt, E. (2016, August). Is violence at work out of control. *People Management, 2016,* 44–45.

Burton, S. K. (2006). Without trust, you have nobody: Effective employee communications for today and tomorrow. *Public Relations Strategist, 12*(2), 32–36.

Casse, P., & Konstandian, A. (2017, June). The art of motivating. *Training Journal, 2017,* 32–34.

Coletti, A. L., Sedatole, K. L., & Towry, K. L. (2005). The effect of control systems on trust and cooperation in collaborative environments. *Accounting Review, 80*(2), 477–500.

Conger, J. A., & Kanungo, R. N. (1988). The empowerment process: Integrating theory and practice. *Academy of Management Review, 13*(3), 471–482.

Cullen, L. T. (2006). Getting wise to lies. *Time, 167*(18), 59.

Dando, N., & Bradshaw, K. (2013, May). Rebuilding trust: The role for L&D. *Training Journal, 2013,* 23–27.

DeConinck, J. B., & Johnson, J. T. (2009). The effects of perceived supervisor support, perceived organizational support, and organizational justice on turnover among salespeople. *Journal of Personal Selling & Sales Management, 29*(4), 333–350.

Dobbins, G. H., Platz, S. J., & Houston, J. (1993). Relationship between trust inappraisal and appraisal effectiveness: A field study. *Journal of Business & Psychology, 7*(3), 309–322.

Eberl, P., Clement, U., & Möller, H. (2012). Socialising employees' trust in the organisation: An exploration of apprentices' socialisation in two highly trusted companies. *Human Resource Management Journal, 22*(4), 343–359.

Eisenberger, R., Huntington, R., Hutchison, S., & Sowa, D. (1986). Perceived organizational support. *Journal of Applied Psychology, 71*(3), 500–507.

Eisenberger, R., Stinglhamer, F., Vandenberghe, C., Sucharski, I., & Rhoades, L. (2002). Perceived supervisor support: Contributions to perceived organizational support and employee retention. *Journal of Applied Psychology, 87*(3), 565–573.

Ergeneli, A., Ari, G. S., & Metin, S. (2007). Psychological empowerment and its relationship to trust in immediate managers. *Journal of Business Research, 60*(1), 41–49.

Flint, D. H. (1999). The role of organizational justice in multi-source performance appraisal: Theory-based applications and directions for research. *Human Resource Management Review, 9*(1), 1–20.

Foster, J. J. (2003). Motywacja w miejscu pracy [Motivation in workplace]. In N. Chmiel (Ed.), *Psychologia pracy i organizacji.* Gdańsk: GWP.

Francois, P., & Zabojnik, J. (2005). Trust, social capital, and economics development. *Journal of the European Economic Association, 3*(1), 51–94.

Gabris, G. T., & Ihrke, D. M. (2001). Does performance appraisal contribute to heightened levels of employee burnout? *Public Personnel Management, 30*(2), 157–172.

Gainey, T. W., & Klaas, B. S. (2005). Outsourcing relationships between firms and their training providers: The role of trust. *Human Resource Development Quarterly, 16*(1), 7–25.

Ganesan, S., & Hess, R. (1997). Dimensions and levels of trust: Implications for commitment to a relationship. *Marketing Letters, 8*(4), 439–448.

Gembalska-Kwiecień, A., & Żurakowski, Z. (2016). *The system of training and adaptation of employees in achieving the improvement of work safety in the mine.* Scientific Papers of Silesian University of Technology. Organization & Management / Zeszyty Naukowe Politechniki Śląskiej. Seria Organizacji i Zarządzanie, Issue 92, p. 85–94.

George, J., & Marett, K. (2004). The truth about lies. *HR Magazine, 4*(44), 87–91.

Gill, L. (2013). Developing trust in training and development environments. *Human Resources Magazine, 18*(4), 35.

Grant, A. M., & Sumanth, J. J. (2009). Mission possible? The performance of prosocially motivated employees depends on manager trustworthiness. *Journal of Applied Psychology, 94*(4), 927–944.

Gupta, V., & Kumar, S. (2013). Impact of performance appraisal justice on employee engagement: A study of Indian professionals. *Employee Relations, 35*(1), 61–78.

Hassan, A. (2007). Human resource development and organizational values. *Journal of European Industrial Training, 31*(6), 435–448.

Heavey, C., Halliday, S. V., Gilbert, D., & Murphy, E. (2017). Enhancing performance: Bringing trust, commitment and motivation together in organisations. *Journal of General Management, 36*(3), 1–18.

Hemdi, M. A., & Nasurdin, A. M. (2006). Predicting turnover intentions of hotel employees: The influence of employee development human resource management practices and trust in organization. *Gadjah Mada International Journal of Business, 8*(1), 21–42.

Hodge, P. (2008). Lies, damn lies and CVs. *Director (00123242), 61*(10), 64–66.

Huang, X., Iun, J., Liu, A., & Gong, Y. (2010). Does participative leadership enhance work performance by inducing empowerment or trust? The differential effects on managerial and non-managerial subordinates. *Journal of Organizational Behavior, 31*(1), 122–143.

Inkpen, A. C., & Currall, S. C. (2004). The coevolution of trust, control, and learning in joint ventures. *Organization Science, 15*(5), 586–599.

Jiang, W., & Lu, Y. (2017). Influence of initial trust on control from client perspective: Construction industry in China. *Engineering Construction & Architectural Management, 24*(2), 326–345.

Johnston, M. (2011). In practice rebuilding trust after layoffs. *Chief Learning Officer, 10*(12), 29.

Jokisaari, M., & Nurmi, J.-E. (2009). Change in newcomers' supervisor support and socialization outcomes after organizational entry. *Academy of Management Journal, 52*(3), 527–544.

Kahane, E. (2006). Trust and powerful learning. *T+D, 60*(7), 51–53.

Kalkman, J. P., & de Waard, E. J. (2017). Inter-organizational disaster management projects: Finding the middle way between trust and control. *International Journal of Project Management, 35*(5), 889–899.

Kanter, R. M. (1997). *The frontiers of management.* Boston: Harvard Business School Press.

Kusari, S., Cohen, D., Singh, J., & Marinova, D. (2005). Trust and control mechanisms in organizational boundary spanners' cognitions and behaviors. *Academy of Management Proceedings, 8*, D1–D6.

Läms, A.-M., & Pučėtait, R. (2006). Development of organizational trust among employees from a contextual perspective. *Business Ethics: A European Review, 15*(2), 130–1410.

Lee, M., & Koh, J. (2001). Is empowerment really a new concept? *Human Resources Management, 12*(4), 684–695.

Leifer, R., & Mills, P. K. (1996). An information processing approach for deciding upon control strategies and reducing control loss in emerging organizations. *Journal of Management, 22*(1), 113–137.

Leimbach, M. P. (2005). Invited reaction: Outsourcing relationships between firms and their training providers: The role of trust. *Human Resource Development Quarterly, 16*(1), 27–32.

Lincoln, N. D., Travers, C., Ackers, P., & Wilkinson, A. (2002). The meaning of empowerment: The interdisciplinary etymology of a new management concept. *International Journal of Management Review, 4*(3), 271–290.

Lundy, O., & Cowling, A. (2000). *Strategiczne zarządzanie zasobami ludzkimi* [Strategic human resources management]. Kraków: ABC.

Makin, P., Cooper, C., & Cox, Ch. (2000). *Kontrakt psychologiczny. Zarządzanie ludźmi w pracy.* [Organizations and psychological contract]. Warszawa: PWN.

Mani, B. G. (2002). Performance appraisal systems, productivity, and motivation: A case study. *Public Personnel Management, 31*(2), 141–160.

Mayer, R. C., & Davis, J. H. (1999). The effect of the performance appraisal system on trust for management: A field Quasi-Experiment. *Journal of Applied Psychology, 84*(1), 123–136.

Mayer, S. J., Russell, J. S., & James, S. (1987). Behavior modeling training in organizations: Concerns and conclusions. *Journal of Management, 13*(1), 21–41.

McCauley, D. P., & Kuhnert, K. W. (1992). A theoretical review and empirical investigation of employee trust in management. *Public Administration Quarterly, 16*(2), 265–285.

Miah, D., & Mominul Haque Talukder, A. K. M. (2012). The effects of employees' perceptions of performance appraisal process of readymade garments industries in Bangladesh: An empirical study. *IBA Business Review, 7*(1), 94–105.

Mishra, A. K., & Spreitzer, G. M. (1998). Explaining how survivors respond to downsizing: The roles of trust, empowerment, justice, and work redesign. *Academy of Management Review, 23*(3), 567–588.

Moye, M. J., & Henkin, A. B. (2006). Exploring associations between employee empowerment and interpersonal trust in managers. *Journal of Management Development, 25*(2), 101–117.

Neves, P., & Caetano, A. (2006). Social exchange processes in organizational change: The roles of trust and control. *Journal of Change Management, 6*(4), 351–364.

Ozlati, S. (2015). The moderating effect of trust on the relationship between autonomy and knowledge sharing: A national multi-industry survey of knowledge workers. *Knowledge & Process Management, 22*(3), 191–205.

Palo, S., & Padhi, N. (2003). Measuring effectiveness of TQM training: An Indian study. *International Journal of Training & Development, 7*(3), 203–216.

Payre, W., Cestac, J., Dang, N-T., Vienne, F., & Delhomme, P. (2017, April). Impact of training and in-vehicle task performance on manual control recovery in an automated car. *Transportation Research: Part F, Part A. 46*, 216–227.

Pocztowski, A. (2003). *Zarządzanie zasobami ludzkimi* [Human Resource Management]. Warszawa: PWE.

Pollock, A. (1997). Will UK NHS trust be only recruitment agencies? *Lancet, 350*, 125.

Reade, Q. (2003). Top-level training helps cola giant rebuild trust and cut staff turnover. *Personnel Today, 5*(27), 9.

Reinke, S. J. (2003). Does the form really matter?: Leadership, trust and acceptance of the performance appraisal process. *Review of Public Personnel Administration, 23*(1), 23–37.

Robbins, S. P., & DeCenzo, D. A. (2002). *Podstawy zarządzania* [The foundations of management]. Warszawa: Polskie Wydawnictwo Ekonomiczne.

Sanchez, J. M., Velez, M., & Araujo, P. (2012). Six key factors for balancing control and trust. *International Management Review, 8*(1), 32–36.

Schraeder, M., Becton, J. B., & Portis, R. (2007). A critical examination of performance appraisals. *Journal for Quality & Participation, 30*(1), 20–25.

Selvarajan, T. T., & Cloninger, P. A. (2012). Can performance appraisals motivate employees to improve performance? *A Mexican study International Journal of Human Resource Management, 23*(15), 3063–3084.

Shamir, B., & Lapidot, Y. (2003). Trust in organizational superiors: Systematic and collective consideration. *Organization Studies, 24*(3), 463–491.

Siegrist, M., Earle, T. C., & Gutscher, H. (2003). Test of trust and confidence model in the applied context of electromagnetic field (EFM) risk. *An International Journal, 4,* 705–716.

Six, F., & Sorge, A. (2008). Creating a high-trust organizations an exploration into organizational policies that stimulate interpersonal trust building. *Journal of Management Studies, 45*(5), 857–884.

Şngün, A. E., & Wasti, S. N. (2007). Trust, control, and risk: A test of Das and Teng's conceptual framework for pharmaceutical buyer-supplier relationships. *Group & Organization Management, 32*(4), 430–464.

Steensma, H., & Visser, E. (2007). Procedural justice and supervisors' personal power bases: Effects on employees perceptions of performance appraisal sessions, commitment, and motivation. *Journal of Collective Negotiations, 31*(2), 101–118.

Stoner, J., Freeman, E., & Gilbert, D. (2001). *Kierowanie* [Management]. Warszawa: PWE.

Thornton, L. F. (2009). Leadership ethics training why is it so hard to get it right? *T+D, 63*(9), 58–61.

Tuna, C. (2009). *Są firmy, które tną koszty, nie zwalniając personelu* [There are companies that cut costs without releasing staff]. Dziennik Finansowy, 08.01.

Ullah, M. I., Hamid, K. B. A., Shahzad, A., & Mahmood, Z. (2017). Enhancing the innovation capability in dairy farms through knowledge sharing. *Pakistan Journal of Commerce & Social Sciences, 11*(1), 89–104.

Van den Berg, B., & Keymolen, E. (2017). Regulating security on the Internet: Control versus trust. *International Review of Law, Computers & Technology., 31*(2), 188–205.

Vander Elst, T., Van den Broeck, A., De Cuyper, N., & De Witte, H. (2014). On the reciprocal relationship between job insecurity and employee well-being: Mediation by perceived control? *Journal of Occupational & Organizational Psychology, 87*(4), 671–693.

Wan, H. L., Sulaiman, M., & Omar, A. (2012). Procedural justice in promotion decisions of managerial staff in Malaysia. *Asia Pacific Business Review, 18*(1), 99–121.

Weibel, A., Den Hartog, D. N., Gillespie, N., Searle, R., Six, F., & Skinner, D. (2016). How do controls impact employee trust in the employer? *Human Resource Management, 55*(3), 437–462.

Willemyns, M., Gallois, C., & Callan, V. J. (2003). Trust me, I'm your boss: Trust and power in supervisor-supervisee communication. *International Journal of Human Resource Management, 14*(1), 117–127.

Yang, S.-C., & Farn, C.-K. (2009). Social capital, behavioral control and tacit knowledge sharing – Multi-informant design. *International Journal of Information Management, 29*(3), 210–218.

(www1) https://mfiles.pl/pl/index.php/Komunikacja. Accessed 15 July 2017.

(www2) https://sjp.pwn.pl/slowniki/zasada.html

CHAPTER 7

Cultural Factors of Trust in a Public Organization as a Workplace

Michał Chmielecki and Łukasz Sułkowski

7.1 Introduction

Perry and Mankin (2007) have discovered that a lot of employees hold increasingly negative views of their organizations. Four out of five employees are suspicious of their management (Lazarus and Salem 2005). A similar appraisal was offered by Reina and Reina (1999), who suggested that organizational trust has been at its lowest level since the construct has been measured. Most of the increasing distrust in organizations can be traced to some highly visible scandals that have affected both the public and private sectors in recent years (Tzafrir 2005). In the private sector, occurrences that involved Worldcom, Tyco, Enron, and Arthur Andersen serve as a reminder of the types of events and institutions necessary for the widely circulated dissolution of trust among the general public (Pillmore 2003; Gledhill 2003; Zekany et al. 2004; Conroy and Emerson 2006). Hayden (2008) stated that some scandals have happened in higher education institutions where degradation in the level of trusts has been recorded. From the perspective of an internal organization, similar research has insinuated that some variables related to an employee's view of a work

M. Chmielecki (✉)
University of Social Sciences, Warszawa, Poland

Ł. Sułkowski
Jagiellonian University, Kraków, Poland

B. Kożuch et al. (eds.), *Managing Public Trust*,
https://doi.org/10.1007/978-3-319-70485-2_7

environment could affect the employee's perception of trust in the organization's research (Williams 2005; Hubbell and Chory-Assad 2005; Ellis and Shockley-Zalabak 2001).

This chapter evaluates organizational trust in the context of culture with many of the following variables: interpersonal conflict, resistance to change, empowerment, demographics, and support for innovation, as noted in the literature.

7.2   Public Trust Within Social Systems

Fukuyama (1995) opined that trust within socials systems is a very important source of social capital—and therefore, a fundamental element of social functioning. Using the lens of social capital to view trust has led to the production of three main points of analysis that have very serious implications for organizations. Three streams have examined how trust as a form of social capital was associated with reducing the cost of transactions in organizations, increasing the spontaneous sociability among members of an organization, and facilitating the right forms of compliance to authority in an organization. Trust in an organization has been viewed as a choice behavior and a psychological state. Lewis and Weigert (1985a) defined trust as the attempt of a precarious action with the confidence that everyone involved in the course of action will act dutifully and competently. This definition is in terms of a psychological state.

Across disciplines, the definition of trust is different. However, almost all definitions of trust contain the element of vulnerability or risk (Rousseau et al. 1998). Generally, trust exists when different parties are disposed to make themselves liable to the actions of another party based on positive notions about the other party's behavior and/or motivation (Mayer et al. 1995; Yang et al. 2002; Ferrell et al. 2010).

If the discipline of organizational science is examined, it will be found that the perspective of logical choice is the most influential theory necessary for understanding trust and all its implications. The perspective of logical choice borrows a lot from the economic theory of Williamson (1993), the sociological theory of Coleman (1990), and the political theory of Hardin (1992). From this perspective, every decision about trust can be seen as the same with every other form of choice that involve risk taking. This is because people are assumed to have the motivation to make logical and effective choices. According to Schelling (1960), the motivation of choice is a conscious calculation of advantages. This calculation is based on an internally consistent and explicit value system.

7.3 SYSTEM TRUST AS A SUBSTITUTE FOR ORGANIZATIONAL TRUST

System trust was defined by Luhmann and his colleagues (1970) as a substitute for organizational trust with the appearance that all is working fine and in good order. This trust is very important for monetary exchange and political power to function (Lewis and Weigert 1985b). The absence of the trust of the public and their confidence in the effectiveness, reliability, and legitimacy of cultural symbols such as laws and money will cause the crashing of modern social institutions (Lewis and Weigert 1985b). Furthermore, system trust supports interpersonal trust Durkheim (2008). It is expected that individuals could lose the trust of others with a gradual reduction of trust in institutions. This basis for understanding the concept of system trust in society is very useful for understanding system trust in an organization.

According to Sztompka (1999), the relationship between interpersonal trust and system-level trust cannot be easily trusted. Sztompka wrote that there are many major targets of trust. The most basic ones are the other people that we interact with. The trust that we show people is defined as interpersonal trust. Sztompka (1999) also discovered that various authors categorized some other types of trust under social trust, including system trust. Giddens (1990) opined that interpersonal trust usually involves face-to-face communication, whereas system trust is usually geared towards social objects and is faceless. However, Sztompka (1999) argued that there are some people behind other social objects, no matter how complex they are, and that it is people that that we endow with trust. Sometimes, we are familiar with them; however, we could also imagine them, have some information about them, or obtain testimony about them secondhand.

Sztompka (1999) explained when he trusts Lufthansa airlines and decides to fly with them to Tokyo, it implies that they trust their cabin crew, the pilots, the ground personnel, supervisors, controllers, technicians, and so on. "He does not need to meet all of them in person to have some image of them, drawn from various sources (stereotypes of German efficiency and precision, including their suggestive commercials, references from friends, etc.)" (p. 41–42). This is a very good example of why Sztompka argued that the differences between system level and interpersonal trust are not that clear. Sztompka (1999) elaborated on this blurry difference between system-level and interpersonal trust and defined another level of social trust, where objects are furnished with trust as are technological systems.

According to Giddens (1990), systems of professional expertise or technical achievement make up a large proportion of the social environment and material that we live in today. These systems include water and power, air traffic control, telecommunications, financial markets, transportation, and computer networks. Sztompka (1999) opined that the techniques of operation for these systems are not clear to the general public. The author also argued that the concept of trust in these systems is now an essential aspect of everyday life.

Sztompka (1999) wrote that the topic of systemic trust is quite close to legitimacy. Following the distinctions of Weber, it could be said that legitimacy presupposes personal trust (or as it could be called, virtual personal trust). This is seen in the emotional ties with people who are not close to us and the presumed intimacy. Legal intimacy presumes institutional or procedural trust. Sztompka (1999) postulated that trust in two dozen people was at the base of all types of trust, including system trust. Even while exhibiting system-level trust, an individual expects actions that are beneficial from another, such as the agents of various organizations and institutions.

According to Culbert and McDonough (1986), confusion and misunderstanding occurs as a result of the centrality and importance of trust as a way of determining organizational efficiency. This is because very few managers identify how much a smoothly running system is dependent on the ability of members to internalize a predefined and restricted set of assumptions, values, and goals. Culbert and McDonough (1985) also labeled the internalization process as a way of committing to the dominant reality of a system. An attempt to get the commitment of an employee in the context of an organization can be seen as asking the employee to internalize the predominant reality of the system. Culbert and McDonough (1986) also viewed this process of internalization as a process that is needed for the long-term success of the organization. They opined that internalization helps members to act decisively and impulsively without stopping to debate the consequences of an action. The authors explain this process as being very similar to what one experiences when driving on an expressway: making very complex decisions and performing necessary complex actions without stopping to think of each step.

Culbert and McDonough (1986) focused their attention on internalization because they believed it was very important for making decisions as to whether to trust or not. They believed that employees who choose to trust an organization will internalize the values, goals, and assumptions of the organization and its systems. Employees who do not trust an organization are believed not to have undergone the process of internalization. Culbert and McDonough (1986) stated that employees will be afraid to internalize a system that favors management as opposed to a system that recognizes the unique input of subordinates in the organization. They thereby defined trust as the willingness of an individual to internalize a view of a system as one that will protect them ultimately and recognize their contributions to that organization.

Culbert and McDonough (1986) stated that employees believe that the systems of their organizations will reduce perceived vulnerability by reducing performance to only the areas that can be appraised without bias. The authors reported that there are other ways to reduce vulnerability, such as viewing participation as a game, acting as a partisan to the organization, and following the example of those who wield power in the organization. Empowerment was determined to be the major building block of understanding the concept of trust in an organization. They believed that employees in an organization would not internalize a system unless the system empowers them professionally and personally. This idea supports the inclusion of empowerment in a study model theoretically.

7.4   Public Trust and Culture

Trust shows the willingness of one person/party to be vulnerable to another as a result of a belief in the party's ability, fairness, competence, good intent, capacity, and reliability. Many logical calculations emphasize the concept of trust. Individuals usually consider the personal disposition, background, and culture of another when determining if they are to be trusted or not. Culture is the reflection of the habits and assumptions of a society; it has a very important role in establishing the level of trust. This is why cross-cultural interactions often involve embarrassment, misunderstandings, very little self-efficacy, and even psychological distress (Molinsky 2007). Many authors agree that behavior is majorly influenced by industry, nationality, religion, and professional or corporate culture.

Culture is composed of implicit and explicit patterns of behavior. This behavior is transmitted and acquired by symbols that constitute the unique achievements of human groups (Sułkowski 2002). This includes their embodiments in artifacts and the major component of culture, which consists of traditional ideas and the values that are attached (Sułkowski 2012). Hofstede (1980) defined culture as the collective programming of the mind that separates a category of people or the members of a group from another one.

According to Schein (1999), there are three levels of culture: artifacts, values, and basic assumptions. Artifacts are the manifestations of culture that are observable. Observers have the ability to smell, see, touch, taste, and hear them. In the context of an organization, these include furnishings and physical buildings, styles of interactions, company logos, communication methods, styles of dressing, and language (Schneider and Barsoux 2003). Values show the creed of a group about how everything should be done (Doney and Cannon 1997). According to Rokeach (1973), values are enduring beliefs that a select mode of conduct or a particular mode of existence has more social standing than a different end state of existence or mode of conduct. Basic assumptions make up the third and deepest level of culture. According to Schneider and Barsoux (2003), basic assumptions are the unconscious beliefs that classify some actions as good, correct, or normal. Schein (1999) saw these assumptions as the best source of cultural behavior and value. Assumptions are learned at an early age alongside values. They are strengthened for the duration of an individual's socialization into culture such that they are rarely questioned and usually taken for granted.

People from various cultures differ in their willingness to trust each other (Inglehart et al. 1998; Johnson and Cullen 2002). Many scholars claim that Westerners (e.g., Western Europeans, North Americans) are wont to make a fast assumption of trust across many interpersonal interactions. This swift assumption of trust is that other people deserve to be trusted until they prove otherwise (Dirks et al. 2009; Weber and Malhotra Murnighan 2005). On the other hand, Easterners (e.g., South and East Asians) trust less than Westerners (Delhey and Newton 2005; Yamagishi and Yamagishi 1994).

One other useful basis for the explanation is looseness clarification and cultural tightness. Yamagishi et al. (1998) and Takahashi et al. (2008) suggested that low- and high-trust cultures have various structures for behavior control. Tight cultures (cultures in which social norms are defined clearly and imposed reliably) usually enforce behavioral expectations through sanctioning (institutional mechanisms) and monitoring. In comparison, loose cultures (cultures where social norms are informal or flexible) usually propose expectations but allow individuals to define a range of acceptable behavior within which they can exercise or show their preferences (Gelfand et al. 2010). The definition of loose and tight cultures was proposed by Gelfand, Nishii, and Raver in 2006. In loose cultures, enforcement is left to interpersonal mechanisms rather than law. The research by Yamagishi states the implications for trust in negotiations. Due to the fact that behavior in tight cultures is governed by institutional mechanisms, individuals from tight cultures tend to rely on institutional trust in contracts and laws more than interpersonal trust for controlling sanction deviance and behavior. Interpersonal mechanisms govern behaviors in loose cultures, so the opposite of what happens in tight cultures will happen there (Takahashi et al. 2008; Yamagishi et al. 1998; Yamagishi and Yamagishi 1994).

7.5   Trust and Organizational Performance

Trust has been recognized as a major component of organizational success by Schoorman et al. (2007). It has been proven that trust can facilitate effective business transactions (Williams et al. 1988), boost employee commitment and motivation, and increase the satisfaction of customers (Doney and Cannon 1997). In general, trust is a good promoter of collaborative behavior between organizational stakeholder groups (Gulati 1995; Uzzi 1997) and in organizations (Dirks and Ferrin 2001; Williams 2001). This is because it cultivates innovation, creativity, knowledge transfer (Edmondson 1999), and commitment. By reinforcing the bond between a firm and its stakeholders (e.g., investors, customers, employees), trust could be a source of competitive advantage for an organization.

Trust is very important for individuals who are in positions of authority. According to Tyler and Degoey (1996), the ability of authorities to effectively manage would suffer terribly if they needed to constantly justify or explain their actions. Furthermore, it is too impractical and costly to monitor employees' performance. Not every act of indiscipline can be seen or punished by managers. They can neither praise nor recognize every act. Therefore, employees must be ready to follow organizational rules and regulations, respect authorities in an organization, and accept the procedures and outcome of resolutions before an organization can operate effectively and efficiently.

Tyler (1994) showed that individuals in an organization will accept the outcomes of an organization more if they trust the motives and intentions of authority. This held true even when outcomes for individuals were not favorable in any manner. Joseph and Winston (2005) examined associations between an employee's perception of servant leadership and trust in organizational leaders. Using the Organizational Trust Inventory, Nyhan and Marlowe (1997) found a positive and strong relationship between levels of organizational trust and the general perceptions of organizational servant leadership. The employees of organizations that are servant-led showed a higher level of organizational trust than employees who worked in places where the management practiced a non-servant style of leadership. The study was entrenched in trust theory, which inculcates the importance of leadership behavior in the development of the trust of employees in leaders (Dirks and Ferrin 2001). This study added some empirical support for models that are theoretical, suggesting that servant leadership is specific and can elicit trust. Greenleaf (1977) determined that servant leadership comes from and is a precursor to trust in organizations and leaders because this increases the perceptions of trustworthiness in leaders. According to Zolin et. al (2004), this perception of trustworthiness in leaders should have a reciprocal relationship to trust of leadership.

According to Dirks and Ferrin (2001), organizational trust is gaining substantiation. This has led to an ever-growing body of literature that focuses on recognizing the reasons for organizational trust (Kramer 1999). Recent literature has taken the perspective that involves positive expectations regarding the intention and behavior of another party as a point of departure (e.g., Rousseau et al. 1998). All of these expectations are based on the trust or attributes of the party that is trusted.

A lack of trust will cause an organization to have negative attitudes, a decreased ability to make profit, impaired decision making and thinking, a damaged reputation, and a reduced ability to breed creativity and innovation (Bibb and Kourdi 2004, pp. 30–34). A lack of trust will seriously reduce the ability of an organization to grow and achieve its full potential (Chmielecki 2012). Is there a relationship between the fallen trust level of our country and the condition of our country's innovation and economy? Currently, organizations are making very tough decisions and experiencing very poor yields or profits in a declining economy.

The advantages of a trust-based culture are efficiency, capacity, meaning, self-regulation by working together, inspired performance, and competitive advantage (Ciancutti and Steding 2001). For this and other reasons, the theory of organizational trust is the major focus of organizational sciences. Trust is the key that removes a lack of performance in an organization and help to build or rebuild a constructive or strong culture that performs well (Chmielecki 2013). It is very important to build trust because trust is inspiring, improves mutual understanding and communication, leads to greater risk-taking, delivers greater efficiency and reduced costs, and provides more effective and credible leadership (Bibb and Kourdi 2004, pp. 16–17).

De Cremer et al. (2001) reported that trust increases contributions within an organization. Some of the trending things that occur in an organization or workforce are increased implementation of work teams, diversity, and participative style of management. Yamagishi and Midori (1994) reported that distrust creates more distrust and prevents individuals from partaking in opportunities that will develop social intelligence (i.e., the ability to behave wisely). If people are unable to act wisely, then poor decisions will be made. Bachmann and Zaheer (2006, p. 280) stated that trust within an organization was well related to increased performance and reduced transaction costs (Chmielecki 2015).

If social capital is considered according to the positive theory, there is a concept called "positive social capital." This is a case of social capital that increases the creative or generative potential of individuals and groups. Social capital has elements that are mutual and trust bonds. It also contains acts of generosity, gratitude, practices that gives joy, openness to new ideas, and acts of decency (Baker and Dutton 2007). According to the thesis of the positive theory, organizational development is possible due to conditions that breed mutual understanding of interest and needs and the setting and achievement of personal goals in an environment of friendship and harmony. Before these kinds of conditions can appear, every member of the team must like and rely on each other. The relevance of trust and sympathy has been known for a long time through management studies.

Two attitudes are the most important factors that contribute to the integrity of a team. Integrity is defined as the social dimension of the effectiveness of a team; it fulfills objectives or conditions its productivity. Integrity (sympathy and mutual trust) is not enough in this particular case (the expectations of co-workers of achieving goals together). Without integrity, the productivity of a team will be mediocre at best, even with the most skillful employees. Sympathy is a very basic tool of mutual influence—that is, the more you like some people, the more likely you will be to help them, be convinced by them, or indulge them. However, trust is a value that that is one of the most important foundations of social capital. It sets the conditions of many important attitudes in the field of achieving goals in an organization. The importance of trust has created numerous key attitudes that are important in the field of achieving goals in an organization. The relevance of trust has created numerous studies in this subject at the beginning of the century (Levin and Cross 2004). Some of the important attitudes that result from relationships with mutual trust are sharing of one's knowledge with co-workers, loyalty, the relation of individual interest to the interest of an organization, honesty, and openness (Glinska- Neweś 2007).

It is very important for leaders to understand culture because it can be seen by stakeholders (e.g., investors, customers, employees). If it can be seen and felt, it will have an impact on the effectiveness of an employee, leader, and ultimately the effectiveness of the firm. Those that have travelled to other countries or held jobs with different employers will understand these concepts. For anyone who has a deep belief or assumption that has brought success, alternate assumptions, strategies, and beliefs may be considered undiscussable, disconcerting, or unreasonable. Organizations such as IBM, Apple, Procter & Gamble, DEC, Acme Insurance, and Atari all have stories of how culture has played a major force in their success and/or failures (Schein 1999, p. 4).

Schein (1999) opined that an unmanaged culture will instead manage you, and you will not be aware of the level at which it is happening (p. 185). Argyris (1985) suggested that there will be better organizational effectiveness when there is agreement between an organization's adopted values and actual organizational practices than when there are internal contradictions between actual practices and adopted philosophies (Smart and St. John 1996, p. 223). Schein (1985) emphasized the importance of examining cultural issues at the levels of an organization so as to understand what happens in organizations, how to run them, and how to improve them (p. 30).

Chatman and Eunyoung Cha (2003) observed that strong cultures are based on two characteristics: high agreement levels among employees or subordinates on what is valued and high intensity levels about these values (p. 23). The authors further observed that strong cultures boost the performance of an organization in two ways. Firstly, they improve the performance of an organization by energizing the employees, appealing to their higher values and ideas, and rallying them around a set of unified and meaningful goals. Secondly, cultures that are strong augment performance by coordinating and shaping the behavior of employees (p. 21). Argyris (1985), Chatman and Eunyoung Cha (2003), and Robbins and Judge (2008) all expressed that strong values have relationships between what they work toward and what they value; these cultures will achieve much more and be more effective. Finally, Denison (1990) claimed that organizational values and beliefs must match organizational procedures and policies in order for the organization to attain excellence (p. 10).

7.6   Chapter Summary

Organizational culture is the structure that directs the behavior of people and helps to filter information. Culture is a stabilizer, prioritizer, and reality generator. Leaders need to discern and have an understanding of the current culture and identify what cultures will help them in achieving their goal, accomplishing their designated mission, and fulfilling the potential of the organization to be as great as it can be.

O'Toole and Bennis (2009) opined that, moving forward, the new standard for measuring organizational leadership will be closer to the level at which executives create organizations that are ethically, socially, and economically stable (p. 55). Organizational culture will affect the process of decision making in today's globally connected economy. What are the values, assumptions, structures, beliefs, and processes that an organization should adopt to compete globally? What kind of culture will give a business the opportunity to compete globally and still adapt to our rapidly changing world?

No specific organizational culture has been proven to be the most effective or the best in any situation. Culture is always right as long as it succeeds; however, when an organization starts to fail, the elements of culture have started to fail and the culture must change (Schein 1999, p. 187). No leader should start with the ideology that culture needs to change, but they must analyze and comprehend the culture of an organization and determine if the culture is consistently aligned with the values and strategic mission of a company. The culture must also align with the members' assumptions, organizational conditions, and realities that they face daily.

Culture is an entity that is alive; it evolves daily based on the reality that is perceived. Organizations and their employees are more frequently entangled in complex interdependencies that cut across professional, organizational, and national borders, which pose a challenge for people from various cultures to manage unfamiliar relationships with unfamiliar parties. Long-lasting relationships require, among other things, a mutual trust that one's vulnerabilities and weaknesses will not be exploited in a given exchange. Just like individuals, organizations enter into relationships with other organizations and individuals for mutual benefits that involve mutual trust.

Inequality among workers, reduction of diversity, and low power distance benefits sharing of knowledge and cooperation.[1] When control over workers is increased, their commitment to work is reduced; this weakens the acquisition of knowledge, the pursuit of creative solutions, and the willingness to share existing or new knowledge. Poland is dealing with high uncertainty avoidance, and evidence indicates that a formal organizational structure has no positive effects on the management of knowledge. Effective organizations allow knowledge to flow, no matter the role or function of an employee.

Notes

1. Power distance refers to the way in which power is distributed and the extent to which the less powerful accept that power is distributed unequally. Put simply, people in some cultures accept a higher degree of unequally distributed power than do people in other cultures, so low pdi means there are less barriers in terms of hierarchy etc. that allow higher levels of knowledge sharing and cooperation.

References

Argyris, C. (1985). *Strategy, change and defensive routines.* London: Pitman Publishing.

Bachmann, R., & Zaheer, S. (2006). *Handbook of trust research.* Northhampton: Edward Elgar Publishing Limited.

Baker, W., & Dutton, J. E. (2007). Enabling positive social capital in organizations. In J. E. Dutton & B. R. Ragins (Eds.), *Exploring positive relationships at work: Building a theoretical and research foundation* (pp. 325–345). Mahwah: Erlbaum.

Bibb, S., & Kourdi, J. (2004). *Trust matters for organizational and personal success.* New York: Palgrave Macmillan.

Chatman, J. A., & Cha, S. E. (2003). Leading by leveraging culture. *California Management Review, 45*(4), 20–34.

Chmielecki, M. (2012). Cultural barriers of knowledge management-a case of Poland. *Journal of Intercultural Management, 4*(2), 100–110.

Chmielecki, M. (2013). Knowledge sharing among faculty–Qualitative research findings from Polish universities. *International Journal of Contemporary Management, 12*(3), 93–102.

Chmielecki, M. (2015). Factors influencing effectiveness of internal communication. *Management and Business Administration, 23*(2), 24–38.

Ciancutti, A., & Steding, T. L. (2001). *Built on trust: Gaining competitive advantage in any organization.* Chicago: Contemporary Books.

Coleman, J. S. (1990). Commentary: Social institutions and social theory. *American Sociological Review, 55*(3), 333–339.

Conroy, S., & Emerson, T. (2006). Changing ethical attitudes: The case of Enron and ImClone scandals. *Social Science Quarterly, 87*, 395–410.

Culbert, S. A., & McDonough, J. J. (1985). *Radical management: Power politics and the pursuit of trust.* New York: Simon and Schuster.

Culbert, S. A., & McDonough, J. J. (1986). The politics of trust and organization empowerment. *Public Administration Quarterly, 10*(2), 171–188.

De Cremer, D., Snyder, M., & Dewitte, S. (2001). The less I trust, the less I contribute (or not)? The effects of trust, accountability and self-monitoring in social dilemmas. *Journal of Social Psychology, 31*(1), 93–107.

Delhey, J., & Newton, K. (2005). Predicting cross-national levels of social trust: Global pattern or Nordic exceptionalism? *European Sociological Review, 21*(4), 311–327.

Denison, D. R. (1990). *Corporate culture and organizational effectiveness.* New York: John Wiley.

Dirks, K. T., & Ferrin, D. L. (2001). The role of trust in organizational settings. *Organization Science, 12*(4), 450–467.

Dirks, K. T., & Ferrin, D. L. (2002). Trust in leadership: Meta-analytic findings and implications for research and practice. *Journal of Applied Psychology, 87*(4), 611.

Dirks, K. T., Lewicki, R. J., & Zaheer, A. (2009). Repairing relationships within and between organizations: Building a conceptual foundation. *Academy of Management Review, 34*(1), 68–84.

Doney, P. M., & Cannon, J. P. (1997). An examination of the nature of trust in buyer-seller relationships. *The Journal of Marketing, 61*(2), 35–51.

Durkheim, E. (2008). *Contributions to L'Année sociologique.* New York: Simon and Schuster.

Edmondson, A. (1999). Psychological safety and learning behavior in work teams. *Administrative Science Quarterly, 44*(2), 350–383.

Ellis, K., & Shockley-Zalabak, P. (2001). Trust in top management and immediate supervisor: The relationship to satisfaction, perceived organizational effectiveness, and information receiving. *Communication Quarterly, 49*(4), 382–398.

Ferrell, O. C., Gonzalez-Padron, T. L., Hult, G. T. M., & Maignan, I. (2010). From market orientation to stakeholder orientation. *Journal of Public Policy & Marketing, 29*(1), 93–96.

Fukuyama, F. (1995). *Trust*. New York: Simon and Schuster.

Gelfand, A. E., Diggle, P., Guttorp, P., & Fuentes, M. (Eds.). (2010). *Handbook of spatial statistics*. Boca Raton: CRC Press.

Gelfand, M. J., Nishii, L. H., & Raver, J. L. (2006). On the nature and importance of cultural tightness-looseness. *Journal of Applied Psychology, 91*(6), 1225–1244.

Giddens, A. (1990). The consequences of modernity (Cambridge). *Polity, 53*(83), 245–260.

Gledhill, J. (2003). The Enron scandal: Global corporatism against society. *Social Analysis, 47*, 130–135.

Glińska-Neweś, A. (2007). Kulturowe uwarunkowania zarządzania wiedzą w przedsiębiorstwie. Towarzystwo Naukowe Organizacji i Kierownictwa. Stowarzyszenie Wyższej Użyteczności "Dom Organizatora".

Greenleaf, R. K. (1977). *Servant leadership. A journey into the nature of legitimate power and greatness*. New York: Paulist Press.

Gulati, R. (1995). Does familiarity breed trust? The implications of repeated ties for contractual choice in alliances. *Academy of Management Journal, 38*(1), 85–112.

Hardin, R. (1992). The street-level epistemology of trust. *Analyse & Kritik, 14*(2), 152–176.

Hayden, E. (2008). Designer debacle: A high-profile scientist, a graduate student, and two major retractions. *Nature, 453*(May), 275–278.

Hofstede, G. (1980). *Culture's consequences: Comparing values, behaviors, institutions,and organizations across nations* (2nd ed.). Thousand Oaks: Sage.

Hubbell, A., & Chory-Assad, R. (2005). Motivating factors: Perceptions of justice and their relationship with managerial and organizational trust. *Communication Studies, 56*, 47–70.

Inglehart, R., Basáñez, M., & Menéndez Moreno, A. (1998). *Human values and beliefs: A cross-cultural sourcebook: Political, religious, sexual, and economic norms in 43 societies; findings from the 1990–1993 World Values Survey*. Ann Arbor: University of Michigan Press.

Johnson, J. L., & Cullen, J. B. (2002). Trust in cross-cultural relationships. In J. L. Johnson & J. B. Cullen (Eds.), *The blackwell handbook of cross-cultural management* (pp. 335–360). Oxford: Blackwell.

Joseph, E. E., & Winston, B. E. (2005). A correlation of servant leadership, leader trust, and organizational trust. *Leadership & Organization Development Journal, 26*(1), 6–22.

Kramer, R. M. (1999). Trust and distrust in organizations: Emerging perspectives, enduring questions. *Annual Review of Psychology, 50*(1), 569–598.

Lazarus, H., & Salem, M. (2005). Trust, distrust, and their implications for decision making and profit. In J. P. Cangemi, C. J. Kowalski, R. L. Miller, & T. W. Hollopteter (Eds.), *Developing trust in organizations* (pp. 45–50). Boston: McGraw-Hill.

Levin, D. Z., & Cross, R. (2004). The strength of weak ties you can trust: The mediating role of trust in effective knowledge transfer. *Management Science, 50*(11), 1477–1490.

Lewis, J. D., & Weigert, A. J. (1985a). Social atomism, holism, and trust. *The Sociological Quarterly, 26*(4), 455–471.

Lewis, J. D., & Weigert, A. (1985b). Trust as a social reality. *Social Forces, 63*(4), 967–985.

Mayer, R. C., Davis, J. H., & Schoorman, F. D. (1995). An integrative model of organizational trust. *Academy of Management Review, 20*(3), 709–734.

Molinsky, A. (2007). Cross-cultural code-switching: The psychological challenges of adapting behavior in foreign cultural interactions. *Academy of Management Review, 32*(2), 622–640.

Nyhan, R. C., & Marlowe, H. A. (1997). Development and psychometric properties of the organizational trust inventory. *Evaluation Review, 21*(5), 614–635.

O'Toole, J., & Bennis, W. (2009, June). What's needed next: A culture of candor. *Harvard Business Review, 87*(6), 54–61.

Perry, R., & Mankin, L. (2007). Organizational trust, trust in the chief executive and work satisfaction. *Public Personnel Management, 36*, 165–179.

Pillmore, R. (2003). How we're fixing up Tyco. *Harvard Business Review, 81*(December), 96–103.

Reina, D., & Reina, M. (1999). *Trust and betrayal in the workplace: Building effective relationships in your organization.* San Francisco: Berrett-Koehler.

Robbins, S. P., & Judge, T. A. (2008). *Essentials of organizational behavior.* Upper Saddle River: Pearson Prentice Hall.

Rokeach, M. (1973). *The nature of human values* (Vol. 438). New York: Free Press.

Rousseau, D. M., Sitkin, S. B., Burt, R. S., & Camerer, C. (1998). Not so different after all: A cross-discipline view of trust. *Academy of Management Review, 23*(3), 393–404.

Schein, E. H. (1985). *Organizational culture and leadership.* San Fransisco: Jossey-Bass.

Schein, E. H. (1999). *The corporation culture survival guide.* San Franscisco: Jossey-Bass.

Schelling, T. C. (1960). *The strategy of conflict.* Cambridge, MA: Harvard University Press.

Schneider, S. C., Barsoux J.-L. (2003). *Managing across cultures.* London: Pearson Education.

Schoorman, F. D., Mayer, R. C., & Davis, J. H. (2007). An integrative model of organizational trust: Past, present, and future. *Academy of Management Review, 32*(2), 344–354.

Smart, J. C., & St. John, E. P. (1996). Organizational culture and effectiveness in higher education: A test of the "culture type" and "strong culture" hypotheses. *Educational Evaluation and Policy Analysis, 18*(3), 219–241.

Sułkowski, Ł. (2002). *Kulturowa zmienność organizacji*. Warszawa: Polskie Wydawnictwo Ekonomiczne.

Sułkowski, Ł. (2012). *Kulturowe procesy zarządzania*. Warszawa: Difin.

Sztompka, P. (1999). *Trust: A sociological theory*. Cambridge: Cambridge University Press.

Takahashi, C., Yamagishi, T., Liu, J. H., Wang, F. X., Lin, Y. C., & Yu, S. (2008). The intercultural trust paradigm: Studying joint cultural interaction and social exchange in real time over the Internet. *International Journal of Intercultural Relations, 32*(3), 215–228.

Tyler, T. R. (1994). Psychological models of the justice motive: Antecedents of distributive and procedural justice. *Journal of Personality and Social Psychology, 67*(5), 850.

Tyler, T. R., & Degoey, P. (1996). Trust in organizational authorities. In *Trust in organizations: Frontiers of theory and research* (pp. 331–356). Thousand Oaks/London/New Delhi: Sage.

Tzafrir, S. (2005). The relationship between trust, HRM practices and firm performance. *International Journal of Human Resource Management, 16,* 1600–1622.

Uzzi, B. (1997). Social structure and competition in interfirm networks: The paradox of embeddedness. *Administrative Science Quarterly, 42,* 35–67.

Weber, J. M., Malhotra, D., & Murnighan, J. K. (2005). Normal acts of irrational trust: Motivated attributions and the trust development process. *Research in Organizational Behavior: An Annual Series of Analytical Essays and Critical Reviews, 26,* 75–101.

Williams, C. C. (2005). Trust diffusion: The effect of interpersonal trust on structure, function, and organizational transparency. *Business & Society, 44*(3), 357–368.

Williams, M. (2001). In whom we trust: Group membership as an affective context for trust development. *Academy of Management Review, 26*(3), 377–396.

Williams, B., Bateson, P., Good, D., Dasgupta, P., Dunn, J., Luhmann, N., et al. (1988). *Trust: Making and breaking cooperative relations*. New York: Blackwell.

Williamson, O. E. (1993). Calculativeness, trust, and economic organization. *The Journal of Law and Economics, 36*(1, Part 2), 453–486.

Yamagishi, T., & Yamagishi, M. (1994). Trust and commitment in the United States and Japan. *Motivation and Emotion, 18*(2), 129–166.

Yamagishi, T., Cook, K. S., & Watabe, M. (1998). Uncertainty, trust, and commitment formation in the United States and Japan. *American Journal of Sociology, 104*(1), 165–194.

Yang, H., Shankar, M., Buirchell, B., Sweetingham, M., Caminero, C., & Smith, P. (2002). Development of molecular markers using MFLP linked to a gene conferring resistance to Diaporthe toxica in narrow-leafed lupin (Lupinus angustifolius L.) *TAG Theoretical and Applied Genetics, 105*(2), 265–270.

Zekany, K., Braun, L., & Warder, Z. (2004). Behind closed doors at WorldCom: 2001. *Issues in Accounting Education, 19,* 101–117.

CHAPTER 8

Trust and Strategic Partnerships: Barriers to Developing Dynamic Capabilities in a Public Organization

Jaakko Sivusuo and Josu Takala

8.1 Introduction

Many industries and marketplaces have been faced with great change due to rapid technology development and globalization (Sivusuo and Takala 2016). Digitalization is also a huge driver of dynamics. If organizations want to survive competition in a dynamic environment, they must have dynamic capabilities (Helfat et al. 2007; Teece et al. 1997). A dynamic environment forces organizations to concentrate on and sometimes change their core functions. Outsourcing is one way of concentrating on the core; in addition, competencies can be brought into the organization. Both of these approaches require the ability to network—that is, to conduct business together with other companies and partners. Networking is also referred to as a *partnership*, which may be viewed as strategic in some contexts (Ståhl and Laento 2000).

Pressure from globalization and technology development forces organizations to think about how to survive in competition. An organization's competences play a huge role in building and sustaining a competitive advantage. There are many different ways to gain and build competences

J. Sivusuo (✉) • J. Takala
University of Vaasa, Vaasa, Finland

B. Kożuch et al. (eds.), *Managing Public Trust*,
https://doi.org/10.1007/978-3-319-70485-2_8

115

in organization. A partnership allows an organization to obtain complementary assets from partner organizations. As a result, organizations can gain critical competences and assets for sustaining a competitive advantage through competition (Helfat et al. 2007).

Today, organizations must make strategic decisions as part of planning for the future. Decisions about operational processes can be seen as a part of strategic decisions. Operational processes produce an organization's offerings for customers. These basic decisions about operational processes can be divided into three types: self-produce, ally, or buy from the market. An alliance can be seen as a partnership or an even deeper strategic partnership (Ståhl and Laento 2000).

Organizations often conduct business through official partnership agreements. The aim of these agreements is to clarify the roles and responsibilities between partner organizations. Partnership can also be conducted without official agreements. Either way, trust plays a large part in a partnership. It can be said that a partnership is trust, and everything else is built on it. Trust is also a word that can be heard often in an organization's speeches and official statements. However, how trust actually occurs in real-life business dealings between partners remains unclear.

The research presented in this chapter is based on a case study of organizations that work under partnerships with their customers. Some of these organizations have official partnership agreements; between other customers, the partnership may be verbal in nature. The study focuses how official partnerships support dynamic capabilities generation in organizations. In other words, we explore how partnerships help an organization to secure and develop a sustainable competitive advantage. We also define a partnership and clarify its causes and consequences.

Cooperation between customers and suppliers is classified as three types in this study: strategic partnerships, normal partnerships, and suppliers. This study mainly concentrates on partnerships and strategic partnerships, with supplier cooperation given less consideration.

8.2   Case Organizations

This study concentrates on three case organizations, which have between 300 and 1000 employees. All case organizations can be classified as large corporations. Table 8.1 provides a comparison of the case organizations in this study.

Table 8.1 Comparison of the case organizations

Organization	Organization A	Organization B	Organization C
Number of employees	300	800	1100
Number of normal partnerships	20	5	0
Number of strategic partnerships	1	1	1
Main offerings for customers	Products and services	Services	Products and services
Main business model	Project business	Service business	Service business

The business models of these organizations are based on the service and product industries. Official strategic partnerships are constructed around the service industry. All strategic partnerships in this study are national partnerships. The number of strategic partnerships is the same for all case organizations. International partnerships are classified under the category of normal partnerships.

The organization designated as Organizatoin A has more than one partnership model in its businesses: one official strategic partnership and many so-called normal partnerships. The strategic partnership has lasted many decades and evolved over time. Organization A's business model is not based only on partnerships. It also produces services and products for customers without any kind of partnership agreements. The normal partnerships are much smaller than the strategic partnerships. Also, the business conducted under normal partnerships has lasted a much shorter time than the strategic partnership. Normal partnerships are also time-limited, which is one of the biggest differences from strategic partnerships. Organization A's business model is based on the products that it sells to customers, but they also have services in their portfolio. In short, it can be said that Organization A's business model covers both service and product businesses.

A strategic partnership makes up 70% of Organization B's operations. This strategic partnership has been formalized over the last decade, but the roots of the partnership go back several more decades. Organization B also has another side to its operations, in which it sells services to customers without any partnership elements.

Organization C is the youngest organization included in this study. Its operation model was built around a strategic partnership from the start. The organization also experienced some major changes throughout its lifecycle.

In general, the framework for strategic partnerships is long-term with local agreements between organizations. In this context, "local" means that both organizations are operating in the same country; thus, their cultures also have the same characteristics. Normal partnerships may be global in nature and thus have different aspects, such as nationality or culture. Organization A had the most global operations in this study.

8.2.1   Research Process and Methods

A case study can be implemented in many different ways. Quantitative and/or qualitative methods can be used for collecting data, along with field studies, interviews, archive materials and other methods (Yin 1981; Eisenhardt 1989). This research is based on a case study. Semi-structured interviews were used for data collection, with the same questions used in each interview. Interviewees were unaware of how the other participants answered the questions to minimize the chances of leading in the answers.

The number of interviewees ranged between 1 and 5 per case organization. Every person interviewed was a member of the board in their organization. Thus, they were able to build and maintain partnerships. An organization's board and management team play a major role in building dynamic capabilities in their organizations. For that reason, the target group of interviewees consisted of individuals on the management team.

8.2.2   Research Problem and Questions

The aim of this study was to explore the dynamic capabilities in an operation model based on partnership. Dynamic capabilities have been researched more frequently in recent years. This trend indicates that organizations and researchers are interested in this subject. The term "partnership" is also heard frequently in many speeches, mission statements, and official communications. However, not many studies have explored the association between dynamic capabilities and partnership.

The research problem is built around the challenges that are typical in dynamic business markets. An organization's agility and its ability to sense and react are typical features that are stressed in the theory of dynamic capabilities. However, through partnerships, organizations are trying to find stability in their businesses by attempting to stabilize market dynamics. Thus, dynamic capability and partnership can be viewed as conflicting states because one stresses transformation and the other focuses on stability.

Our research questions were as follows:

- What factors drive organizations in a partnership-based operating model?
- How does a strategic partnership support evolving dynamic capabilities?
- What kind of problems are associated with a partnership-based operating model in terms of dynamic capability?

Plenty of research can be found in the field of dynamic capabilities. There are also some studies focusing on defined markets, such as in the electronics industry (Koskinen 2014). Our study will enrich the dynamic capabilities theory from the strategic partnership viewpoint. Strategic partnerships for dynamic capabilities is a largely unexplored area in the literature.

8.3   Literature Review: Dynamic Capabilities, Strategic Partnership, and Trust

Organizations today often operate in turbulent markets where rapid changes are common. To obtain and maintain a competitive advantage, an organization must react faster and more effectively than its competitors. In the past century, many economies have faced major changes, and traditional earning logic has also changed. Many market segments have turned from local to global. Organizations will not survive competition if they use outdated strategies; rather, they must focus on what their competitors are doing and why. An organization's limited resources and time also add to the overall complexity.

The roots of the theory of dynamic capabilities can be found in a resource-based view (Wang and Pervaiz 2007). With a resource-based view, an organization is able to achieve competitive advantage if its resources are valuable, rare, inimitable, and non-substitutable (Penrose 1959; Barney 1991). In the 1990s, markets became more dynamic. Because the resource-based view was developed for static markets, there was need for something else if an organization was to sustain a competitive advantage (Landroguez et al. 2011). Thus, the theory of dynamic capabilities was created, taking the resource-based view and extending it to dynamic markets (Eisenhardt and Martin 2000).

Teece was one of the first authors to explore dynamic capabilities. In his definition, the framework of dynamic capabilities fills the gap between a resource-based view and dynamic markets. This framework also highlights the role of rapid technology development. Teece defined dynamic capabilities as repeatable processes inside the organization. These processes develop within the organization itself. However, dynamic capabilities are path dependent (Teece et al. 1997); they also are not single or ad-hoc actions, but are learned routines inside an organization (Winter 2003). Dynamic capabilities can be transformed and developed over time (Zollo and Winter 2002). Agility can be viewed as an aspect of dynamic capabilities (Vázquez-Bustelo et al. 2007) and may include proactive and effective responses, rapidity, and agile resource allocation. One of the most important things related to agility is an organization's ability to build partnerships (Doz and Kosonen 2008).

8.3.1   Partnership and Dynamic Capabilities

The theory of dynamic capabilities can be seen in many real-life examples. Some of them are sector specific, whereas others extend into different business markets. This chapter explores the relationship between dynamic capabilities and partnership. Relational capabilities and alliances are identified as examples of dynamic capabilities. From the strategic management point of view, the theory of dynamic capability is relatively new. This is one of the reasons why there are so many different definitions for dynamic capabilities (Czakon 2009) and relational capabilities. Helfat et al. (2007) defined relational capabilities as an organization's ability to generate, expand, or change its resource base via alliances or partnerships. Dyer and Harbir (1998) stressed an organization's willingness to develop its operations and capabilities through partnership. Thus, to achieve dynamic capabilities via partnerships, an organization must understand what it is doing and why; in addition, it must want to operate in a partnership-based relationship.

When discussing partnership-based dynamic capabilities, we can also talk about relational capabilities. Dynamic capabilities are an organization's ability to renew a resource base (Teece et al. 1997; Danneels 2008), whereas relational capabilities are focused on how organizations are able to renewal their resource bases via partnerships (Helfat et al. 2007). With regard to dynamic capabilities, relational capabilities are based on learning and making use of a partner's capabilities. An organization's learning mechanisms play a major role in gaining a competitive advantage from a partnership-based operating model. Organizations must have learning mechanisms for building relational capabilities. Relational capabilities alone will not provide any benefits to the organization. The organization must include relational capabilities in their operational routines to achieve any benefits. However, although learning is one of the reasons to form a partnership, learning alone will not help organizations. Both organizations in partnership must be able to exploit the things they learn in their operations (Zollo and Winter 2002).

In summary, it can be said that a partnership-based operation model includes a definition of dynamic capabilities. Partnerships can be approached from many different angles, and relational capabilities can be implemented in many different ways. Examples include partnerships, strategic partnerships, alliances, and networks.

8.3.2 Partnership and Trust

As mentioned previously, there are many different definitions for partnership; this chapter introduces several of them, including the definition used in the study. A partnership can be viewed and implemented in many different ways, including by outsourcing. In practice, outsourcing exploits an aspect of another organization, such as knowledge. One starting point for outsourcing is to study an organization's production chain. Basically, an organization has two options for every section of the production chain—service or product—which can be undertaken by the organization itself or acquired from an outside organization. The same situation applied to knowledge—it can be built inside the organization or acquired externally (Kämäri 2010).

Hyötyläinen and Nuutinen (2010) defined five types of partnerships: basic supplier, solution supplier, joint supplier, value network supplier, and value partner. These types differ in their maturity stages of collaboration between the supplier and customer. The deeper the relationship is between the organizations, the greater is the knowledge that is shared between them. Knowledge is mainly tacit in a basic supplier relationship, and increases in the other types.

Ståhl and Laento (2000) classified three types of partnerships: operative partnerships, tactical partnerships, and strategic partnerships. An operative partnership is the closest to traditional trading, in which one party is the buyer and the other is the seller. An operative partnership also carries the least risk. However, an operative partnership is a temporary and usually short-term contract between organizations. Both organizations usually have their own interests and goals in an operative partnership. One typical element of an operative partnership model is a low and strictly limited exchange of information. The main goal for an operative partnership is usually cost-effectiveness.

The outcome of tactical partnership is not predefined. Practically, in addition to the contract, organizations in a tactical partnership compound processes, eliminate overlapping functions, and learn from each other. A successful tactical partnership results in cost-effectiveness and also new knowledge for organizations. A tactical partnership is the first partnership form that includes the term *trust*. Not all activities can be instructed or described in a tactical partnership, so the role of trust is important. Both partners must understand each other's needs, which requires an integration of knowledge capital. This integration of knowledge capital will not succeed without trust (Ståhl and Laento 2000).

In a strategic partnership, an organization's scope of cooperation is so deep that it can almost be described as a fusion between them. A strategic partnership differs from tactical and operational partnerships in that both parties usually have equally strong roles. A strategic partnership has the biggest potential and also the biggest risk. Therefore, selection of the right partner is a crucial factor for success (Ståhl and Laento 2000).

As mentioned, a partnership can be described and classified in many different ways. In our study, a partnership is classified as one of three types: a strategic partnership, a normal partnership, or operation without any kind of partnership. These classifications are used to clarify and explore research problems in this study.

8.4   RESEARCH STUDY

8.4.1   *Trust and Strategic Partnership*

This case study investigated the relationship between trust and strategic partnership in three organizations. The main task was to clarify the role between trust and strategic partnership. The research question was how organizations perceive the role of trust in strategic partnership.

8.4.1.1 Organization A

Trust is seen as one of the most important things in a successful partnership. It can be said that trust is a prerequisite for building a successful partnership. Organization A perceives trust as a result of cooperation. Both parties must be involved in building trust. Organization A also highlighted that trust is always built from scratch. It is also an output from a partnership, which must be earned again and again.

Organization A has normal partnerships as part of its operations. These are usually short-term agreements (e.g., delivering a project for a customer). A successful normal partnership needs knowledge transfer from one organization to another, but it focuses only on a project or another bounded entity. This, it is a short-term partnership.

Organization A also has strategic partnerships. In a strategic partnership, trust is much deeper than in a normal partnership. The same goes for knowledge transfer, which is focused much further in the future. Thus, it is not limited only to the project being delivered but extends to future work as well.

8.4.1.2 Organization B

Organization B has one long-term strategic partnership. This strategic partnership lasted even as Organization B's services, products, and capabilities have changed over time. This shows that there is not any particular skill or competence on which the partnership is built.

Trust has also played a major role in building and maintaining strategic partnerships in Organization B's operations, which is seen as an interaction between individuals. The trust is built between individuals inside an organization, not between organizations. Organization B also has normal partnerships; however, the trust is not as deep in normal partnerships as it is in the strategic partnership. Organization B stated that trust is more like a spice in normal partnerships—it can certainly help, but it is not obligatory.

The role of an organization is seen as building and maintaining opportunities and processes. Thus, the organization has to create operating models in a way that interactions between individuals are going to happen. The development of operations in a strategic partnership happens through cooperation. In a normal partnership, the development of operations either does not exist or both parties develop operations independently.

8.4.1.3 Organization C

Organization C's operation model was built from the start for strategic partnerships. Organization C focuses on individuals and their relationships for developing partnerships. This also plays a major role in building trust.

When Organization C was starting its business and operational construction, providing recognition to the right individuals was a crucial task. The aim was to find individuals who were able to commit over the long term to build the organization. Their task was also to build a strategic partnership-based business model. The long-term commitment was needed because building trust and partnerships takes a great deal of time—years or even a decade.

One of the most important aspects in the individual selection is that individuals' thoughts are aligned with those of the organizations. This includes the vision about the organization and also the main drivers for the business model. Organization C also expands and shares their thoughts for every successful strategic partnership. If an organization and its individuals have different views about the future, success will not be achieved.

8.4.1.4 Summary

Every organization in this case study highlighted the importance of trust in a successful partnership. The deeper the partnership is between organizations, the deeper the trust must be. Interviews also indicated that trust is built between individuals, not organizations. Trust must be cherished and rebuilt all the time because an organization's individuals will change as time passes. Therefore, organization must have processes and methods for building trust in place, even when individuals leave the organization. Trust is also a prerequisite for being successful in a strategic partnership. It can be said that there is no real partnership without trust. Of course, there are organizations under strategic partnership agreements that operate without trust; however, these partnership could be considered so-called shotgun marriages.

Figure 8.1 shows the relationship between an individual and an organization in terms of dynamic capabilities. To achieve a sustainable competitive advantage, an organization's and an individual's strategic frameworks must be in balance. In this context, the strategic framework is a vision for

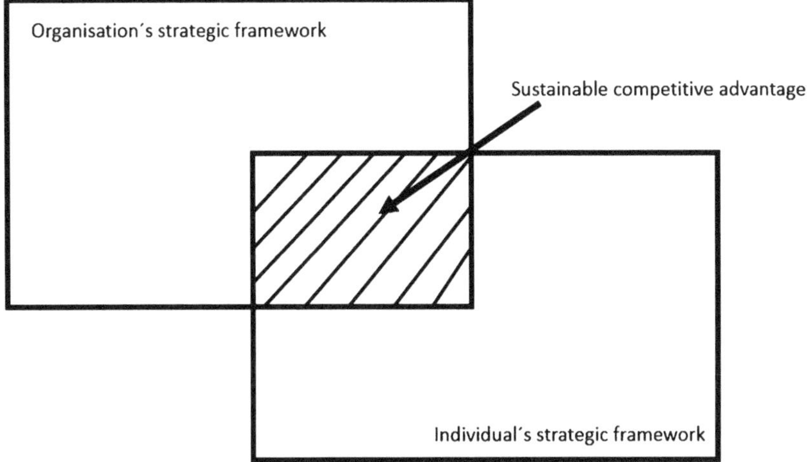

Fig. 8.1 Strategic framework of an organization and an individual

the future. It contains a variety of things, such as developing a business model, building partnerships, expanding capabilities, and reacting to weak signals from the market.

Trust and its related attributes are not easy to explain. Trust is built around individuals; however, there is no clear pattern or process to describe how it works. We do know that trust can be built between individuals and their interactions. Organizational processes and management models must provide opportunities for these interactions; these opportunities can be described.

8.4.2 Drivers and Reasons for Strategic Partnership

This section defines the drivers and reasons for establishing a strategic partnership. Results from the case studies are presented. Our main question focused on why case organizations operate some parts of their businesses under a strategic partnership and the main benefits gained from it. We also present the results of our literature review, specifically in terms of the drivers for establishing a strategic partnership.

8.4.2.1 Organization A

Organization A stated that their biggest reason for having partnerships was securing and ensuring knowledge. Through partnerships, an organization is able to leverage partners' capabilities. However, these capabilities will not necessary be bought inside the organization. This kind of capability or knowledge "renting" requires the same mindset of both partners. These kinds of partnerships may be temporary and last for the duration of a single project. When the project is finished, the knowledge from the partnership is no longer needed.

A strategic partnership is the result of a long-term normal partnership. Over time, the partnership and cooperation between the organization deepens. When asked about the biggest drivers for a strategic partnership, organization A named time, trust, and cooperation. Organization A's partner also participates in the strategy process. Thus, knowledge transfer and knowledge capital are open between both organizations. Organization A was the only organization in this study that allowed strategic partners to participate in their own strategy process.

8.4.2.2 Organization B

Organization B's long-term normal partnership was extended to a strategic partnership that operated with an official agreement. Both organizations drifted into a strategic partnership through fusion. Thus, the operating model requires both parties to be successful. Organization B also highlighted knowledge transfer and trust as drivers for the strategic partnership.

The main reason for Organization B's strategic partnership was stabilize a dynamic environment. Thus, both partners in the strategic partnership are able to concentrate on building businesses together. This is possible through long-term contracts. Even through Organization B has long-term contracts, they highlighted that they have to develop operations and partnership regardless. Some day in the future, the contract will end and competitors may change.

This strategic partnership also binds the customer to the supplier, which is one reason to form a partnership. Organization B also noted the need to recognize whether the customer is willing to partner at an early stage. A partnership-based business model is a conscious choice of an organization and will not be made by mistake.

8.4.2.3 Organization C

Organization C was built around a strategic partnership from its start. This situation is quite rare when examining the different partnerships. Organization C chose this model because it allowed the company and its partner to succeed in their businesses. Both organizations recognized the need for partnering. This is one crucial aspect for having a good partnership relationship. Organization C was able to select its partner in advance. This is also a very important task for management when selecting suitable partners for long-term contracts. The organization must understand what they want from a partnership. If the organization is not able to answer why and what they are searching for from a partnership, the partner selection will likely fail.

8.4.2.4 Summary

One major driver for forming a partnership is business need. All case organizations are operating in areas where partnering is a typical way of doing business. Case organizations also recognize that they cannot operates in the market without partnering. It can be said that strategic partnering is a prerequisite for competitiveness. A strategic partnership itself will not guarantee success for organizations; however, it is a very good platform for building competitive advantage.

Knowledge is another driver and reason for partnering. Through partnering, organizations are able to obtain knowledge without acquiring it inside the organization. This finding contributes to relational capabilities. The role of knowledge increases greatly when an organization is operating on project business. Projects are usually short term and the knowledge is used for a short while. This kind of knowledge is something that organizations can either buy inside or obtain from partners.

8.4.3 Dynamic Capabilities and Their Role in Strategic Partnership

Discussions about dynamic capabilities focus on speed, quick decisions, and turbulent environments, whereas strategic partnership discussions highlight words such as stability, long-term, and continuity. At first glance, these two conditions are fighting each other. However, all case organizations were trying to stabilize their environments through strategic partnerships. This provides great opportunities to concentrate on developing and maintaining dynamic capabilities. Organizations understand that the competitive advantage obtained from a strategic partnership is temporary; they also understand that dynamic capabilities must be maintained so that the organizations are difficult to beat in competition.

A strategic partnership provides great opportunities for building dynamic capabilities. Usually, dynamic capabilities are based on the relational capabilities in a strategic partnership. This can be seen as a global trend. Many organizations today are consolidating with other companies, mainly for capabilities and knowledge. Turbulent environments make it difficult for an organization to develop capabilities internally. It is faster to find good partner with the right capabilities.

A partnership-based operation model does not always support dynamic capabilities. The following sections highlight some problems that can result from a strategic partnership. These problems may prevent organizations from achieving a sustainable competitive advantage. However, organizations can prevent these pitfalls with the following advice.

8.5   Pitfalls

8.5.1   *Fat and Lazy Syndrome*

Every organization in this study recognized the same problem, which we call the "fat and lazy syndrome"—that is, a collapse of dynamic capabilities because of a strategic partnership. A strategic partnership can guarantee very long contracts, which are protected from competition. This arrangement also provides great opportunities for sensing and seizing from the customer interface. The customer's needs come before the supplier.

Through this model, an organization's external pressure for sustaining a competitive advantage may decrease or even disappear. However, organizations must be aware that a competitive advantage gained from a strategic partnership is only temporary. When competition changes, both partners in a strategic partnership can be in trouble. It is difficult to react if an organization has not maintained its dynamic capabilities. Dynamic capabilities must be maintained, even when the external environment does not require it.

How can an organization prevent this syndrome in their operations? An organization's management can properly allocate resources. Organization C stated that an organization must change its resource base periodically, even if there is no clear reason to do so. In this way, dynamic capabilities inside the organization can be maintained, even if the external environment does not require it. This might be costly for an organization, but maintaining dynamic capabilities inside an organization is typically not free.

8.5.2   *Unbalanced Equilibrium*

In the development of a strategic partnership, it is very important for both parties to understand each other's roles, tasks, goals, and positions in the partnership. Both organizations must understand these entities in the same way. Only then can both partners be in an equal position with each other.

The level and quality of dynamic capability is defined by the inferior organization in a strategic partnership. Basically, the speed of renovation and resource allocations can only be put in place as fast as the slower partner is able. Issues may result when either partner lacks any dynamic capabilities. In such a case, building and maintaining dynamic capabilities in a strategic partnership may be impossible.

8.6   Chapter Summary

The role of dynamic capabilities is continually increasing while competition and development move forward. Organizations have had to create new operating and business models to sustain a competitive advantage. This study describes several organizations that have built a competitive advantage around partnerships. These organizations have developed their operating models and business approach with their partners.

This study provided an overview of relational capabilities via case studies. Relational capabilities are seen as one form of dynamic capabilities; these are also common dynamic capabilities from partnerships. Normal or strategic partnerships do not guarantee that organizations can build dynamic capabilities between them. The "fat and lazy syndrome" and unbalanced equilibrium are examples of pitfalls in a strategic partnership. These problems might arise when organization has reached a temporary competitive advantage through a strategic partnership. All of these problems can be avoided with the proper decisions and contributions from management. An organization's management either allows or blocks the dynamic capabilities in an organization. Building and maintaining dynamic capabilities require time and resources. In a static mode, it may seem unnecessary to build dynamic capabilities; however, when competition or change arise, the organization must act. At that point, there is no time to start building those capabilities in an organization.

There are a few reasons why organizations are driving themselves toward strategic partnerships. The first reason is capabilities or knowledge. Through a partnership, an organization has access to knowledge that it does not need to own. Organizations can rent knowledge from each other in a partnership. This kind of knowledge transfer needs both organizations to participate. Otherwise, it will not happen. The type of partnership also defines the kind of knowledge transfer between organizations. In a strategic partnership, the knowledge transfer between organizations is the widest and the deepest. In normal partnerships, the knowledge is focused on a particular entity, such as a project.

Another driver for a strategic partnership is a long-term normal partnership. Usually, when normal partnerships last long enough, they transform into strategic partnerships. Long-term partnerships are also good platforms for building trust. Trust can be seen as a prerequisite for a successful partnership—and perhaps one of the most important things related to a successful partnership. An interesting finding of our study is that trust builds between individuals from organizations, not between organizations themselves. This is a very important thing for an organization to understand when its operating model is based on a strategic partnership. Fortunately, organizations are able to create opportunities for trust building. An organization should also be able to secure trust through processes, even if individuals leave the organization.

Finally, it is worth noting how many strategic partnerships our case organizations had: Each organization had only one strategic partnership. This raises a question: If an organization has a very deep partnership that is like a strategic partnership, then the number of partners is approaching the number one. This finding could be an interesting area for future research.

References

Barney, J. (1991). Firm resources and sustained competitive advantage. *Journal of Management, 17*(1), 99–120.

Czakon, W. (2009). Relational capability of organizations: Theoretical advances. *Journal of Economics & Management, 5,* 48–65.

Danneels, E. (2008). Organizational antecedents of second-order competences. *Strategic Management Journal, 29*(5), 519–543.

Doz, Y. L., & Kosonen, M. (2008). The dynamics of strategic agility: Nokia's rollercoaster experience. *California Management Review, 50*(3), 95–118.

Dyer, J. H., & Harbir, S. (1998). The relational view: Cooperative strategy and sources of interorganizational competitive advantage. *Academy of Management Review, 23*(4), 660–679.

Eisenhardt, K. M. (1989). Building theories from case study research. *Academy of Management Review, 14*(4), 532–550.

Eisenhardt, K. M., & Martin, J. A. (2000). Dynamic capabilities: What are they? *Strategic Management Journal, 21*(10–11), 1105–1121.

Helfat, C. E., Sydney, F., Will, M., Peteraf, M. A., Singh, H., Teece, D. J., & Winter, S. G. (2007). Dynamic capabilities: Understanding strategic change in organizations. *Strategic Management Journal, 18,* 1–147.

Hyötyläinen, R., & Nuutinen, M. (2010). *Mahdollisuuksien Kenttä, Palveluliiketoiminta Ja Vuorovaikutteinen Johtaminen.* Helsinki: Teknologiateollisuus ry.

Kämäri, V. (2010). *The strategic management of a partnership programme: A multiple-case study in the finnish defence administration.* Lappeenranta: Lappeenranta University of Technology.

Koskinen, J. (2014). *A dynamic business model for high-tech industry in a global environment – The origin of operational patterns by means of social selection.* Vaasa: University of Vaasa.

Landroguez, S. M., Barroso Castro, C., & Cepeda-Carrión, G. (2011). Creating dynamic capabilities to increase customer value. *Management Decision, 49*(7), 1141–1159.

Penrose, E. (1959). *Theory of the growth of the firm.* Oxford: Blackwell.

Sivusuo, J., & Takala, J. (2016). Management changes in MRO business through product lifecycle. *Management and Production Engineering Review, 7*(3), 87–93.

Ståhl, P., & Laento, K. (2000). *Strateginen kumppanuus–Avain Uudistumiskykyyn Ja Ylivoimaan.* Helsinki: WSOY.

Teece, D. J., Pisano, G., & Shuen, A. (1997). Dynamic capabilities and strategic management. *Strategic Management Journal, 18*(7), 509–533.

Vázquez-Bustelo, D., Avella, L., & Esteban, F. (2007). Agility drivers, enablers and outcomes: Empirical test of an integrated agile manufacturing model. *International Journal of Operations & Production Management, 27*(12), 1303–1332.

Wang, C. L., & Pervaiz, K. A. (2007). Dynamic capabilities: A review and research agenda. *International Journal of Management Reviews, 9*(1), 31–51.

Winter, S. G. (2003). Understanding dynamic capabilities. *Strategic Management Journal, 24*(10), 991–995.

Yin, R. K. (1981). The case study crisis: Some answers. *Administrative Science Quarterly, 26*(1), 58–65.

Zollo, M., & Winter, S. G. (2002). Deliberate learning and the evolution of dynamic capabilities. *Organization Science, 13*(3), 339–351.

PART III

The Development of Public Trust

CHAPTER 9

Building Public Trust in Social Media

Dorota Marquardt, Barbara Filipczyk, Jerzy Gołuchowski,
and Joanna Paliszkiewicz

9.1   Introduction

Communication, interactions, and cooperation are increasingly becoming computer-mediated. The existence of trust between the sender of message and its recipients is necessary within the processes of communication in the public sphere, which is shaped using social media. A tool that is often used for such communication is Twitter.

Twitter is used to share information, opinions, and knowledge in the form of tweets and retweets. Studying the processes of building social trust using social media is, understandably, a difficult task due to the fact that the trust-building process itself is complex and time consuming. It engages at least two parties—the trustee and the trustor. The role of the medium is also not without significance because its usage may enhance or diminish trust development. Building trust toward public institutions and their representatives in the social media takes place on several levels (e.g., Gołuchowski et al. 2017a).

To determine the most commonly used and efficient mechanisms, this chapter analyzes the methods of communication of the City Halls of

D. Marquardt (✉) • B. Filipczyk • J. Gołuchowski
University of Economics in Katowice, Katowice, Poland

J. Paliszkiewicz
Warsaw University of Life Sciences, Warszawa, Poland

B. Kożuch et al. (eds.), *Managing Public Trust*,
https://doi.org/10.1007/978-3-319-70485-2_9

voivodship capitals in Poland and/or their presidents on Twitter, focusing on the subject of the participatory budget.

9.2   Impact of Social Media on the Development of Public Trust

Social media has revolutionized communication in the modern world by creating a new communication sphere (Hynan et al. 2014; Tench and Jones 2015; Hadzialic 2016). Social media forms a plane for creating one's own image, seeking social support, organizing social campaigns, and undertaking political activities. Numerous institutions and companies entered the world of social media and use it to share information and establish contact with their clients. The profiles of companies and well-known brands are willingly added by social media users to their friend lists due to their interest in the offered products. Many users consider the information obtained by means of social media portals or blogs as being more important[1] than information shared by traditional means of communication. Social media outlets have thus become tools for both cooperation and expressing opinions and arguments.

Studies on the impact of social media on public trust have been conducted for some time. Public trust has been very important in public administration and political science, and many scholars have focused on this topic (Miller and Listhaug 1990; Carnevale 1995; Fukuyama 1995; Putnam 1995; Sztompka 1996; Harisalo and Stenvall 2004; Kim 2005; Bouckaert 2012; Llewellyn et al. 2013; Kożuch and Dobrowolski 2014). The subject is important for supporting the development and implementation of public policies and, subsequently, for effective and cooperative compliance (Fard et al. 2007).

Social media is being increasingly used by local governments (Mainka et al. 2014; Madestam and Falkman 2017). Through these new media, citizens and politicians can meet and interact in a new way (Coleman and Blumler 2009; Parmelee and Bichard 2012). According to the research presented by Hong (2013), this communication increases public trust in the government. Utz (2009) and Parmelee and Bichard's (2012) confirmed that politicians who are more interactive on social media are more favored. Social media has the potential to engage stakeholders in future e-participation projects (Effing et al. 2011) and encourages dialogue between the citizens and the government (Yi et al. 2013). In addition,

Kruikemeier et al. (2013) revealed that interactive and personalized online communication by politicians affect citizens' political involvement. According to the research presented by Lee and Oh (2012), the public's reaction was more positive in response to politicians who use Twitter in a personalized way.

Nevertheless, social media-based public trust building is uncharted territory. Government agencies generally lack experience and knowledge about implementing social media (Lee and Kwak 2012). As found in studies of Park and Reber (2008), Bortree and Seltzer (2009), Rybalko and Seltzer (2010), and Hatun (2016), the potential of websites and social media has not been fully used to build public trust. Previous research also fails to explain how stakeholders use social media to impact decision-making rather than for opinion expression and discussion (Ferro et al. 2013). The role of social media needs to be further examined to understand its influence on people and online deliberation (Criado et al. 2013), as well as to understand the opportunity to build public trust and redesign stakeholders' roles and responsibilities by using social media (Susha and Grönlund 2014).

Other scholars contest this view, pointing to the Internet as a medium where the public sphere is very much alive and functioning (Dahlgren 2005; Gimmler 2001; Papacharissi 2002; Poster 1997). Studies of political participation indicate that Internet use has led to an increase in the public's political interest (Gibson et al. 2005). Therefore, it is claimed that the public sphere of today is no longer a physical space. Rather, it is found in the media and in networks and acts as the "cultural/informational repository of the ideas and projects that feed public debate" (Castells 2008, p. 79). However, the gaps that were noticed in our review of the state-of-the-art research draw attention to the theoretical, methodological, and technological barriers of the research on public trust.

9.3   Analysis of Public Trust Building in Participatory Budget Consultation

One aim of the participatory budget is to increase the engagement of citizens in the social life in the region (see e.g. Gilman 2016; Czarnecki 2014; Łukomska-Szarek 2014; Tybuchowska-Hartlińska 2016). Therefore, the process results not only in the realization of the given project, which is significant to a given society, but also increased social participation in an activity. Undertaking an activity associated with the local society usually requires great effort; therefore, it is connected with a necessity to trust the ones who encourage such behavior.

To examine the way in which such trust is built by Polish institutions, we analyzed the Twitter accounts of the City Halls of voivodship capitals that have participatory budgets[2] and their presidents in Poland. Some of the City Halls created separate channels devoted to this subject (see Table 9.1).

Participatory budgets represent are one example within the set of participatory innovations that empower citizens to be more active participants in the governance of their communities and the connected decision-making. Research has convincingly demonstrated that participatory budgets have enhanced the quality of democracy, improved governance, and empowered citizens (Gilman 2016; Sintomer et al. 2008).

Original campaigns are undertaken to involve citizens in the building of budgets. The organization of a campaign requires efficient communication that uses specialized applications and social media. Traditional media also support these campaigns. Undoubtedly, an important aspect of these campaigns is the creation of the necessary level of public confidence in local authorities and projects, as well as the proposed innovations. Twitter has also become a campaign tool. This is depicted by the characteristics of Twitter discussions on the development of participatory budgets in the voivodship cities in Poland (Table 9.2).

In our study, the tweets associated with the subject of the participatory budget (see Table 9.2) underwent a detailed analysis. The analysis of social media messages is becoming increasingly important because of the engagement in civic activities through these media. The analysis allowed us to investigate trust mechanisms on Twitter by identifying the linguistic patterns used by the local government units. The patterns of trust building were distinguished by the three basic foundations of trust (benevolence, integrity, and competence) and the measures that were appropriately attributed to them (cf. Paliszkiewicz 2013; Gołuchowski et al. 2017a). The theoretical, methodological, and technological barriers associated with the analysis of trust and proposals to overcome these barriers are illustrated in the analysis of Twitter communications about the participatory budgets in voivodship cities in Poland.

Table 9.1 Social media use by the voivodship capitals in Poland

Voivodship	Voivodship capital City Hall and its president	Twitter	Facebook
Silesia	Katowice	X	X
	Marcin Krupa	X	X
Lower Silesia	Wrocław	X	X
	Rafał Dutkiewicz	X	X
Kuyavia-Pomerania	Bydgoszcz	X	–
	Rafał Bruski	X	X
Kuyavia-Pomerania	Toruń	X	X
	Michał Zaleski	–	–
Lublin	Lublin	X	X
	Krzysztof Żuk	X	X
Lubusz	Gorzów Wielkopolski	–	–
	Jacek Wójcicki	X (restricted access)	X
Lubusz	Zielona Góra	X	–
	Janusz Kubicki	–	X
Łódź	Łódź	X	–
	Hanna Zdanowska	X	X
Lesser Poland	Kraków	X	X
	Jacek Majchrowski[a]	X	X
Masovia	Warszawa	X	X
	Hanna Gronkiewicz-Waltz	X	X
Opole	Opole	–	–
	Arkadiusz Wiśniewski	X	X
Subcarpathia	Rzeszów	X	X
	Tadeusz Ferenc	–	–
Podlaskie	Białystok	X	–
	Tadeusz Truskolaski	X	–
Pomerania	Gdańsk	X	X
	Paweł Adamowicz	X	–
Świętokrzyskie	Kielce	X	–
	Wojciech Lubawski	–	–
Warmia-Masuria	Olsztyn	–	X
	Piotr Grzymowicz	X	X
Greater Poland	Poznań	X[b]	X
	Jacek Jaśkowiak	–	X
West Pomeranian	Szczecin	X	–
	Piotr Krzystek	–	–

X, City Hall and/or the president has an account in the given medium
–, No account in the given medium
[a]No posts were present in March 2017
[b]Latest entry was 9 February 2016

Table 9.2 Characteristics of the study material from the Twitter portal

Voivodship capital City Hall and its president	Number of original posts in March 2017	Number of posts associated with the participatory budget subject	Voivodship capital City Hall and its president	Number of original posts in March 2017	Number of posts associated with the participatory budget subject
Katowice	143[a]	5	Warszawa	65	0
Marcin Krupa	11	1	Hanna Gronkiewicz-Waltz	27	0
Wrocław	103	0	Opole	–	–
Rafał Dutkiewicz	11	0	Arkadiusz Wiśniewski	–	–
Bydgoszcz	83	0	Rzeszów	17	0
Rafał Bruski	7	0	Tadeusz Ferenc	–	–
Toruń	20	1	Białystok	105	1
Michał Zaleski	–	–	Tadeusz Truskolaski	37	0
Lublin	20	0	Gdańsk	321	6
Krzysztof Żuk	11	0	Paweł Adamowicz	44	2
Gorzów Wielkopolski	–	–	Kielce	0	0
Jacek Wójcicki	–	–	Wojciech Lubawski	–	–
Zielona Góra	36	0	Olsztyn	–	–
Janusz Kubicki	–	–	Piotr Grzymowicz	9	1
Łódź	64	3	Poznań	0	0
Hanna Zdanowska	20	0	Jacek Jaśkowiak	–	–
Kraków	160	7	Szczecin	90	1
Jacek Majchrowski[b]	0	0	Piotr Krzystek	–	–

[a]Katowice city's latest post was 10 December 2016 (account has existed since 2010), with a total of 327 tweets. However, the account of the City Hall press office was created in January 2016 and has been taken into consideration. Furthermore, there is an account associated with the participatory budget (@BOKatowice)

[b]No posts were present in March 2017

9.4   Research Methodology

Our approach aimed to develop a method of supporting trust analysis in social media in a manner that was as automated as possible. The foundations of the relationship, in which a significant role is played by the sender's credibility, are sometimes difficult to capture; however, they shape the final level of the recipient's trust towards the sender and the message itself. Metaphorically speaking, the sender sells the content; then, through acceptance and acquisition (by making it "theirs"), the readers become the buyers. Therefore, it is significant to capture the signals included in the content and its context. These signals are decoded by the person granting trust to the sender. In the last stage, based on these signals and other conditions (i.e., on the identified/measured psychological inclination to trust), the person attributes a given trust level to the trustee (Doligalski 2009).

To eliminate or at least diminish the inconveniences of the manual approach, we aimed to create tools that facilitate the analysis of the building and development of trust with the use of information technology. The creation of such tools is associated with several obstacles resulting not only from the limited possibilities of automatic natural language processing, but also from the specificity of the Twitter posts (including the use of abbreviations and hashtags, which often determine context and recipients of message, and the appearance of language errors).

Trust is understood and analyzed as a relationship based on three basic foundations: benevolence, integrity and predictability, and competence (for more information, see Paliszkiewicz and Koohang 2016). A theoretical model of trust building on Twitter is presented in Table 9.3.

Benevolence is an indication of interest and recognition of individual needs and accessibility. Interest manifestation is indicated by participation in the dialogue or by answers to the posed questions; the recognition of individual needs can be deduced from the dialogue content, if such takes place, whereas accessibility can be assessed by the level of the text's obscurity. Integrity can be determined by the consistency of both activities and the adopted values that are communicated by means of the materials related to the tweets. Competence consists of, above all, knowledge and professionalism. Sharing knowledge is significant when it comes to building trust. (In the case of the participatory budgets, this knowledge will be associated with the process of creating projects and the realization

Table 9.3 Theoretical model of public trust building on Twitter

Trust foundation	Feature	Feature description
Benevolence	Interest indication	Ensuring the ability to reply to a report proves interest in the stakeholders and their opinions. Interest in the stakeholders' remarks and response to their comments are proof that the organization takes into account the opinions of the individuals interested/engaged in its activity.
	Individual needs recognition	Information on the consultations conducted with the stakeholders in relation to the given areas is an indication of the recognition of the given stakeholder group's needs.
	Accessibility	The selection of an appropriate text genre, communication means, and low text complexity level are signs of respect toward the stakeholders and minimize the time needed to understand the message.
Integrity	Organizational values and ethical behavior	Value declarations and codes of ethics prove that the organization acts transparently and will not conduct any activity to the stakeholders' disadvantage.
	Action consistency and declaration realism	The consistency of the chairpersons' declarations with the actions described on Twitter enhances the organization's credibility and proves its integrity.
Competence	Knowledge	A clear determination of the scope of the organization and the most important areas of its activity determine whether it will be perceived as a professional organization. Expressed knowledge concerning the areas of interest of the given stakeholder groups proves the awareness of the significance of their actions for the benefit of the organization.
	Professionalism	Professionalism is an indicator of the ability to properly function in the market.

Source: Based on Gołuchowski et al. (2017b)

of previous projects.) Professionalism manifests itself through the manner of the knowledge transfer.

Building trust on Twitter takes place by means of the natural language. Io evaluate the trust creation mechanisms, we assumed, in accordance with the weak version of the Sapir-Whorf hypothesis, that language is not neutral to a certain extent (Cf. Burgess 2013). The language was reviewed from a discursive point of view using discourse analysis methods. Discourse analysis is treated here as an eclectic method of text examination, which takes into account the context as well as the situation in which the given message occurs (Gołuchowski et al. 2015).

To indicate the most commonly used and most efficient mechanisms, we analyzed the methods of communication used by the City Halls. Tweets associated with the participatory budget appearing on the accounts of the City Halls or their presidents constituted a small proportion of the posted messages. In March 2017, they amounted to merely 2% of all posts. Therefore, it can be assumed that such tweets do not build trust from the basic level (none of the accounts were created in the researched month), but they increase it. This is especially true because, as mentioned before, the process of participatory budgeting is largely based on trust toward the institution itself.

Most of the analyzed tweets had a similar structure. They usually consisted of two sentences and were accompanied by a photo, video, or link redirecting the reader to external information. However, despite the seeming similarity (which is forced by the platform), several significant differences were noted.

Accessibility, as one of the elements of benevolence, manifested through the complexity of the language used in the published tweets. Alongside other factors, the difficulty level of the texts (determined by means of the Gunning text readability or FOG index[3]) indicates a certain communication strategy. The FOG index was measured automatically by means of a software program that used earlier arrangements developed as part of the Clarin project.[4]

Our research commenced with the corpus gathering, followed by a quantitative analysis that focused on counting the number of tweets and retweets, the number of sentences, and photos and audiovisual material posted in the tweets. Then, with the help of a mixed methodology (quantitative-qualitative: the so-called coding within the limits of the grounded theory), we defined the thematic scope of tweets and retweets.

Later, referring to the three basic dimensions of trust, we defined the following:

(a) Benevolence: We analyzed the user's engagement and complexity of texts (using automatic natural language processing tools).
(b) Integrity: Through qualitative text analysis, we compared these values to the actions described on Twitter and the initiatives taken by the relevant local government unit.
(c) Competence: We examined what knowledge the City Halls shared with the users as well as the style of the language they used.

9.5   Results

The text complexity values for tweets by the Katowice City Hall fit ranged between 19 and 32. The highest values were achieved by tweets that informed about meetings and encouraged the submission of applications. Lower values were associated with tweets about what has been done (which are often connected with expressing emotions). The lowest values were given to messages informing readers about the fact that the city will have a certain budget in the given year (which often include a number).

The messages from Łódź City Hall had a lower text complexity level than Katowice, ranging between 13.7 and 15.7. With minor exceptions for detailed information on the submission of participatory budget applications and acquiring additional data, Kraków tried to simplify their communications by replacing more complex words with pictographs. This resulted in a rather low index of obscurity (beginning at 2.4). All of the lower indices are accompanied by video materials, whereas the higher values had pictures or posters.

Gdańsk[5] did not replace words with pictographs but supplemented the text with them, thus doubling the words deemed as being important. Videos were attached to messages, encouraging readers to submit projects. The text complexity level was also low, with the highest value being 19 and the average being 14.2.

Because the initiative of a participatory budget should be aimed at the widest possible audience, the text complexity level should be low. Most of the tweets we examined met this criterion, thus building trust toward the easy-to-understand message. There is a tendency toward oversimplification of texts accompanied by video materials. A higher FOG index was usually reserved for tweets that provided information about procedures.

An indication of interest, manifesting through engagement in the dialogue, seems to be an inseparable element of communication in social media. On Twitter, users exchange information and opinions and converse with each other (Levinson 2010). Institutions, on the other hand, usually turn to Twitter for one-sided information sharing (e.g., regulation orders, alerts). However, it is difficult to determine a trend on the basis of the analyzed material because citizens did not pose many questions in reply to tweets about the participatory budget (or in reply to tweets posted by the City Halls in general). Although questions were sometimes posted (and received answers from the City Halls) on the accounts devoted entirely to participatory budgeting, this did not occur on the main profiles. The situation is different when it comes to the accounts of the city presidents themselves. Questions are raised there more frequently and the presidents engage in the discussion. This may result from the lower anonymity of the communication, as the identity of the interlocutor is well known.

It was not possible to assess the level of the recognition of individual needs in the analyzed material. Only a few of the city presidents posted messages about the participatory budget, thus resulting in a lack of data. The consistency of both activities and the adopted values associated with the participatory budget can be assessed on the basis of the materials referred to by the tweets. The Katowice City Hall indicated specific project realizations, such as a water playground, but almost every article or video accompanying the tweets referred to the activation and involvement of the local society.[6]

Toruń voivodship prioritized the information campaign. In Łódź, a main focus was on the benefits that the participatory budget delivers for the people who engage in the process. Examples of realizations referred to the happiness caused by projects that are realized due to the participatory budgeting.[7] Kraków voivodship, on the other hand, focused on help for the ones who needed it the most. Materials referred to in the tweets were associated with telephones for the elderly (which send out information on the location of the person should something happen to them), safe pedestrian crossings, free English-language classes, free internet, and historical murals, among others. A separate entry was devoted to helping individuals with disabilities. The video materials often featured elderly people.

In the tweets and materials posted by Gdańsk City Hall, "change" was the most frequently used noun—that is, a change in something that the citizens dislike. Readers are encouraged to take part in the process through tweets such as, "Do you want to change your district or City?

[Chcesz zmienić swoją dzielnicę albo Miasto?]" The Gdańsk City Hall used most of its tweets to inform readers on how to submit an application. Individual entries from Bialystok were usually devoted to encouraging an activity. Olsztyn and Szczecin, on the other hand, placed their focus on involvement in the same process without indicating any particular realizations.

The competences of a given institution are best determined by evaluating the level of knowledge sharing and communication professionalism. The respective City Halls and their presidents prioritize various communication styles. Some of them, such as Łódź, shortened the distance to the recipient by communicating in a way that is typical for social media.[8] Their tweets were not only written in a colloquial style, but they were also riddled with emoticons and pictographs. Other cities, such as Bialystok or Szczecin, communicated using the official Polish language, which includes elements of the legal style. Kraków, Katowice, and Gdańsk used an intermediate style that contained elements of both the official language and the colloquial style.

The greatest amount of information on the matter of the participatory budget was found in the communication channels of Olsztyn and Szczecin. Although all of the institutions and presidents provided informed about the application submission procedure and the associated deadlines, these details dominated the profile of Gdańsk City Hall. The greatest amount of information on the realized budgets was found in tweets from the Katowice, Kraków, and Łódź City Halls.

9.6   Chapter Summary

Social media is an important platform for public discourse, the participants of which consist of not only individual members of social media but also the employees and associates of public organizations. An organization's purpose in leading a discourse is the acquisition and production of credible knowledge that influences the creation of public opinion and citizens' attitudes, such as those expressed during elections by means of voting. Effective building and maintenance as well as an effective analysis of trust in social media are important when conducting a public activity.

This chapter examined trust building on Twitter during the participatory budgeting process of City Halls in Poland. The analysis of public trust on Twitter revealed certain patterns that aim to build and maintain trust toward public institutions. If a local government presents information associated with the submission of budget projects or informs about meeting dates, the text is usually more complex and the language style tends to be more official. The text complexity level is usually connected with the style. For example, the City Halls that communicated in an unofficial manner had a lower FOG index than those that utilized the official style. Most of the City Halls focused on the communication of uniform values. For example, Łódź focused on the resulting happiness from the realized budgets, Kraków focused on helping citizens in need, Gdańsk focused on changing the surroundings, and Katowice focused on the involvement of the local society.

Our analysis also aimed to identify the linguistic mechanisms used by selected City Halls to build trust on Twitter; this allowed us to determine the most commonly used mechanisms by Polish City Halls. To build trust, Polish authorities tried to avoid using the official language, simplify their communication, and add audiovisual material to the textual information. They wanted to be understood by most of the platform's users. However, they did not want to abandon accuracy in transmitting the most important procedural information, which accounts for the appearance, albeit much less often, of messages that were much more complicated but also more precise. Local government units appear to be moving away from the official style in an attempt to shorten the distance between the sender and the receiver by using emoticons and pictograms.

Importantly, the Polish authorities provided coherent communications about their most important values. In 90 percent of the analyzed material, the most important values for the given units could be determined. In summary, the most important linguistic trust-building mechanisms on Twitter were as follows: (1) simplifying communication while ensuring the accuracy of the information being conveyed; (2) improving the linguistic content through the use of audiovisual material, usually illustrating the most important projects (the spoken language used there is usually easier to recognize); (3) departing from the linguistic structures of the official style, which are not always understandable; (4) coherently communicating about the most important values for the City Hall (associated with the civic budgeting process).

The indication of interest (benevolence), as manifested through the engagement in the dialogue, seems to be an inseparable element of communication in social media. Twitter is characterized by the fact that the users exchange information, share opinions, and converse with each other (Levinson 2010). Institutions, on the other hand, often conduct one-sided information sharing (e.g., regulation orders, alerts). The competences of a given institution are best determined by evaluating the level of knowledge sharing and communication professionalism. In this study, the City Halls and their presidents used a variety of communication styles.

The results obtained in this study should be considered as preliminary findings. The dataset needs to be expanded for further investigations. Future studies should focus on an analysis of trust in social media, including an analysis of the dialogue between governments and citizens.

Notes

1. Authors' own study conducted among the students of University of Economics in Katowice (Paliszkiewicz and Koohang 2016).
2. There are 16 voivodships in Poland. However, two of those have two cities indicated as the seats of the voivodship authorities. All of the 18 cities were taken into account.
3. The Gunning text readability index (FOG) is calculated as follows: $0,4*[(LW/LZ) + 100*(LWT/LW)]$, where LW is the number of words in the text, LWT is the number of words containing more than four syllables (adjusted to the Polish language; for more information, see Gołuchowski et al. 2017b), and LZ is the number of sentences.
4. Program created by Tadeusz Marquardt, which split the text into sentences, sentences into words, and words into syllables.
5. The remaining City Halls and presidents published individual tweets; therefore, the analysis excluded such data due to the difficulty in determining the communication tendencies.
6. Exemplary realizations: In the hyperlink to *Dziennik Zachodni*: "Many people are involved in this project and my friends often ask me when it will be opened and how will it all look like. This shows that a local society has established around the issue of the water playground [Wiele osób zaangażowało się w ten projekt, a znajomi często pytają mnie, kiedy nastąpi otwarcie, jak to wszystko będzie wyglądać. To pokazuje, że wokół wodnego placu zabaw zawiązała się nawet lokalna społeczność]." Available at http://www.dziennikzachodni.pl/wiadomosci/katowice/a/wodny-plac-zabaw-w-katowicach-bedzie-gotowy-w-lipcu-wizualizacje,11933286/.

    Marcin Krupa, the President of Katowice, highlighted in a video that the participatory budget is a common initiative: https://twitter.com/BOKatowice/status/847004732292038657.

The posters feature the slogan: "Maybe you already have an idea and you want to discuss it with the neighbors [A może masz już gotowy pomysł i chcesz go omówić z sąsiadami]?" Available at https://twitter.com/BOKatowice/status/846634263122509824.

7. For example, see a video showing children's happiness caused by the opening of a cinema (https://twitter.com/Miasto_Lodz/status/836999745658843138); the projects enumerated on the poster associated with exhibitions, city decorating, popular music, etc. (https://twitter.com/Miasto_Lodz/status/841651370130362369); and jokes (UFO and San Escobar).
8. It is also associated with the blurring of the boundaries between the spoken and the written language; for example, see Crystal 2002.

References

Bortree, D. S., & Seltzer, T. (2009). Dialogic strategies and outcomes: An analysis of environmental advocacy groups' Facebook profiles. *Public Relations Review, 35*, 317–319.

Bouckaert, G. (2012). Trust and public administration. *Administration, 60*(1), 93–94.

Burgess, F. (2013). *The language of corporate governance: A sociological analysis.* Retreived from http://www.lccge.bbk.ac.uk/publications-and-resources/postgraduate-research/docs/130930-Dissertation-Language-of-CorpGov.pdf. Accessed 16 Jan 2017.

Carnevale, D. G. (1995). *Trustworthy government: Leaderships and management strategies for building trust and high performance.* San Francisco: Jossey Bass.

Castells, M. (2008). The new public sphere: Global civil society, communication networks, and global governance. *The Annals of the American Academy of Political and Social Science, 616*(1), 78–93.

Coleman, S., & Blumler, J. G. (2009). *The internet and democratic citizenship: Theory, practice and policy.* Cambridge: Cambridge University Press.

Criado, J. I., Sandoval-Almazan, R., & Gil-Garcia, J. R. (2013). Government innovation through social media. *Government Information Quarterly, 30*(4), 319–326.

Crystal, D. (2002). *Language and the internet.* Cambridge: Cambridge University Press.

Czarnecki, K. (2014). Udział mieszkańców w ustalaniu wydatków budżetu gminy w ramach tzw. budżetu partycypacyjnego (na przykładzie Torunia w latach 2013–2014) [Shares of the inhabitants in determining the community expenditure under the participatory budget (on the example of Toruń, 2013–2014)]. *Prawo Budżetowe Państwa i Samorządu, 2*(1): 125–145.

Dahlgren, P. (2005). The internet, public spheres, and political communication: Dispersion and deliberation. *Political Communication, 22*(2), 147–162.

Doligalski, T. (2009). Budowa wartości klienta z wykorzystaniem Internetu [Building the customer value by using Internet]. In B. Dobiegała-Korona, & T. Doligalski (Ed.), *Zarządzanie wartością klienta* [Managing customer value]. Warszawa: Poltext.

Effing, R., Van Hillegersberg, J., & Huibers, T. (2011). Social media and political participation: Are Facebook, Twitter and YouTube democratizing our political systems? In E. Tambouris, A. Macintosh, & H. De Bruijn (Eds.), *Electronic participation*. Berlin/Heidelberg: Springer.

Fard, H. D., Asghar, A., & Rostamy, A. (2007). Promoting public trust in public organizations: Explaining the role of public accountability. *Public Organization Review, 7*(4), 331–344.

Ferro, E., Loukis, E. N., Charalabidis, Y., & Osella, M. (2013). Policy making 2.0: From theory to practice. *Government Information Quarterly, 30*(4), 359–368.

Fukuyama, F. (1995). *Trust: The social virtue and the creation of prosperity*. New York: Free Press.

Gibson, R. K., Lusoli, W., & Ward, S. (2005). Online participation in the UK: Testing a 'contextualised' model of internet effects. *The British Journal of Politics & International Relations, 7*(1), 561–583.

Gilman, H. (2016). *Engaging citizens: Participatory budgeting and the inclusive governance movement within the United States*. Ash Center occasional papers series, Harvard. http://ash.harvard.edu/files/ash/files/participatory-budgeting-paper.pdf?m=1455295224

Gimmler, A. (2001). Deliberative democracy, the public sphere and the internet. *Philosophy & Social Criticism, 27*(4), 21–39.

Gołuchowski J., Konieczna D., & Losa-Jonczyk A., (2015). Zarys koncepcji dyskursywnego badania blogosfery [Outline of discursive concept of blogosphere research]. In Język a media. *Zjawiska komunikacyjne we współczesnych mediach* [Language and media. Communication phenomena in the modern media] (pp. 13–31). Kraków: Collegium Columbinum.

Gołuchowski, J., Filipczyk, B., Paliszkiewicz, J. (2017a, October 26). Social media and trust. In J. Liebowitz, J. Paliszkiewcz, & J. Gołuchowski (Eds.), *Intuition, trust, and analytics* (Data analytics applications), Auerbach Publications 1st Edition.

Gołuchowski, J., Konieczna, D., & Losa-Jonczyk, A. (2017b, October 26). Building trust in CSR reports. In J. Liebowitz, J. Paiszkiewcz, & J. Gołuchowski (Eds.), *Intuition, trust, and analytics* (Data analytics applications), Auerbach Publications 1st Edition.

Hadzialic, S. (2016). Transformation of the new communication media within the frame of interpersonal interaction. *International Journal on Global Business Management & Research, 5*(2), 116–134.

Harisalo, R., & Stenvall, J. (2004). Citizens' trust in ministers. In M. Huotari & M. Iivonen (Eds.), *Trust in knowledge management and systems in organizations* (pp. 147–117). Hershey: Idea Group Publishing.

Hatun, B. T. (2016). Government public relations in turkey: Social media usage of turkish ministries in relationship building. *Online Journal of Communication and Media Technologies, 6*(1), 48–63.

Hong, H. (2013). Government websites and social media's influence on government-public relationships. *Public Relations Review, 39*(4), 346–356.

Hynan, A., Murray, J., & Goldbart, J. (2014). 'Happy and excited': Perceptions of using digital technology and social media by young people who use augmentative and alternative communication. *Child Language Teaching and Therapy, 30*(2), 175–186.

Kim, S. E. (2005). The role of trust in the modern administrative state. *Administration and Society, 37*(5), 611–635.

Kożuch, B., & Dobrowolski, Z. (2014). *Creating public trust. An organisational perspective.* Frankfurt am Main: Peter Lang GmbH.

Kruikemeier, S., Van Noort, G., Vliegenthart, R., & De Vreese, C. H. (2013). Getting closer: The effects of personalized and interactive online political communication. *European Journal of Communication, 28*(1), 53–66.

Lee, G., & Kwak, Y. H. (2012). An open government maturity model for social media – Based public engagement. *Government Information Quarterly, 29*, 492–503.

Lee, E. J., & Oh, S. Y. (2012). To personalize or depersonalize? When and how politicians' personalized tweets affect the public's reactions. *Journal of Communication, 62*(6), 932–949.

Levinson, P. (2010). *New new media.* Cracow: Penarson.

Llewellyn, S., Brooks, S., & Mahon, A. (2013). *Trust and confidence in government and public services.* New York: Routledge.

Łukomska-Szarek, J. (2014). Budżetowanie partycypacyjne jako instrument współzarządzania sferą publiczną [Participatory budgeting as an instrument for co-management of the public sphere]. *Nierówności Społeczne a Wzrost Gospodarczy, 40*: 137–144.

Madestam, J., & Falkman, L. L. (2017). Rhetorical construction of political leadership in social media. *Journal of Organizational Change Management, 30*(3), 299–311.

Mainka, A., Hartmann, S., Stock, W. G. & Peters, I. (2014). *Government and social media: A case study of 31 informational world cities.* System Sciences (HICSS), 47th Hawaii International Conference on, Hawaii, 6–9 January, pp. 1715–1724.

Miller, A. H., & Listhaug, O. (1990). Political parties and confidence in government: A comparison of Norway, Sweden and the United States. *British Journal of Political Science, 20*(3), 375–386.

Paliszkiewicz, J. (2013). *Zaufanie w zarządzaniu [Trust in management]*. Warsaw: Wydawnictwo Naukowe PWN.

Paliszkiewicz, J., & Koohang, A. (2016). *Social media and trust: A multinational study of university students*. California: Informing Science Press.

Papacharissi, Z. (2002). The virtual sphere: The internet as public sphere. *New Media and Society, 4*(1), 9–27.

Park, H., & Reber, B. H. (2008). Relationship building and the use of web sites: How fortune 500 corporations use their web sites to build relationships. *Public Relations Review, 34*, 409–411.

Parmelee, J. H., & Bichard, S. L. (2012). *Politics and the Twitter revolution: How tweets influence the relationship between political leaders and the public*. Lanham: Lexington Books.

Poster, M. (1997). Cyberdemocracy: The internet and the public sphere. In D. Porter (Ed.), *Internet culture*. New York/London: Routledge.

Putnam, R. (1995). Tuning in, tuning out: The strange disappearance of social capital in America. *Political Science and Politics, 28*(4), 664–683.

Rybalko, S., & Seltzer, T. (2010). Dialogic communication in 140 character or less: How fortune 500 companies engage stakeholders using Twitter. *Public Relations Review, 36*, 336–341.

Sintomer, Y., Herzberg, C., & Röcke, A. (2008). Participatory budgeting in Europe: Potentials and challenges. *International Journal of Urban and Regional Research, 32*(1), 164–178.

Susha, I., & Grönlund, Å. (2014). Context clues for the stall of the citizens' initiative: Lessons for opening up e-participation development practice. *Government Information Quarterly, 31*(3), 454–465.

Sztompka, P. (1996). Trust and emerging democracy. *International Sociology, 11*(1), 37–62.

Tench, R., & Jones, B. (2015). Social media: The wild west of CSR communications. *Social Responsibility Journal, 11*(2), 290–305.

Tybuchowska-Hartlińska, K. (2016). Budżet partycypacyjny–nowe narzędzie w rękach obywateli [Participatory budget-a new tool in the hands of citizens]. *Political Preferences 12*.

Utz, S. (2009). The (potential) benefits of campaigning via social network sites. *Journal of Computer-Mediated Communication, 14*(2), 221–243.

Yi, M., Oh, S. G., & Kim, S. (2013). Comparison of social media use for the US and the Korean governments. *Government Information Quarterly, 30*(3), 310–317.

CHAPTER 10

Public Service Design and Public Trust: Conceptualizing the Sustainability

Adam Jabłoński

10.1 Introduction

The modern environment of public management constantly experiences new interpretations, including classic concepts, new public management ideas, and further interpretations used to develop the field. Concepts related to strategic management that are based on experiences in other sectors—mainly economics and business—are gaining importance. It is important to develop the concept of public service design with regard to trust management mechanisms. The place and role of trust management in public organizations should be identified to fulfill the expectations of stakeholders in public organizations, especially inhabitants and citizens.

At this point, it is worth asking what public service criteria will be important to achieve an acceptable level of trust in public organizations. If we refer to the definition of public management by Kożuch, public values and the public interest become crucial; these can be achieved by building mutual trust. According to Kożuch's definition, public management involves examining the methods and scope of harmonizing activities to ensure that the goals of organizations in the public sphere are properly set; furthermore, the organized actions of individuals that are focused on the creation of public values and the implementation of the public interest

A. Jabłoński (✉)
WSB University in Poznań, Poznań, Poland

153

B. Kożuch et al. (eds.), *Managing Public Trust*,
https://doi.org/10.1007/978-3-319-70485-2_10

should be optimally used (Kożuch 2004, p. 255). In such an approach, it is crucial to ensure the durability of relationships and the sustainability and stable functioning of public organizations using a sustainability concept.

The purpose of this chapter is to present the relationship between public service design and public trust management in the context of ensuring the continuity of public trust-based organizations. It is particularly important to pay attention to the criteria of this continuity with regard to the various interpretations of the sustainability concept. The scope of this chapter includes the principles of building a concept of sustainable management with respect to ethics, economics, and ecology to meet the expectations of stakeholders in public organizations.

10.2   Public Trust and Public Distrust

The concept of trust has been broadly and multidimensionally described in management sciences and other fields for many years. Both in philosophical and sociological terms, the new interpretations of the concept of trust are determined together with the search for mutual cause-and-effect relationships. This unfortunately results in some conceptual chaos, which is not conducive to generating common logical rules for defining the concept of trust. With regard to business and public management, trust is understood in many ways.

Nowadays, trust is becoming one of the essential determinants of building interorganizational relationships, at the level of both business organizations and public organizations. The dimension of trust reduces the uncertainty surrounding the dialogue between organizations and affects the risk of a relationship and its value in itself. The complexity of the issue is so great that it is expressed in the lack of a uniform interpretation of trust, particularly because trust can be regarded as a multidimensional construct shaped by its constituent elements, which include competencies, loyalty, reliability, openness, reputation, honesty, sincerity, transparency, kindness, and commitment.

Trust can be defined as "the belief that others, through their action or inaction, will contribute to my/our well-being and refrain from inflicting damage upon me/us" (Offe 1999, pp. 42–87). According to Six, interpersonal trust is a psychological state comprising the intention to accept vulnerability to the actions of another party, based upon the expectation that the other will perform a particular action that is important to you (Six 2007).

Within organizational settings, the virtues of trust as a social resource have been discussed primarily on three levels. The first major theme has been its constructive effect with respect to reducing transaction costs within organizations. Second, the role that trust plays in spontaneous sociability among organizational members has been explored. Third, there has been appreciation of how trust facilitates appropriate (i.e., adaptive) forms of deference to organizational authorities (Kramer and Cook 2004). Blind believes that democracy requires cooperation, which is the crux of the matter therein (Blind 2007).

A particular type of trust is organizational trust. This specific type of trust is applicable in management sciences. It may refer to relationships inside the organization and may include relationships at the level of many organizations. This may affect communication factors at the individual and group levels. Organizational trust is thus an attribute of the system or network that organizations are embedded in. A specific type of culture is created, namely the culture of trust. This results in the development of the social capital of the organizations between which relationships arise. This is justified also in relationships with public organizations.

The resulting public value in public organizations is an element of exchange and sharing. This exchange and sharing of public values is supported by trust mechanisms. A culture of trust based on common norms, processes, and standards is a platform for mutual interpersonal and inter-organizational dialogue. An individual dimension refers, for example, to relationships with the citizens, inhabitants of a given region, and the group dimension to cause-and-effect relationships between organizations. In this context, we deal with organizational and institutional trust, and this is already a step to public trust. McKnight et al. defined institution-based trust as "the security one feels about a situation because of guarantees, safety nets, or other structures" (McKnight et al. 1998, pp. 473–490).

According to Ferlie, Ashburner, Fitzgerald, and Pettigrew, the efforts of the public sector reform to restore trust are focused on reducing the distance between government and citizens. To achieve this, a new public services mission may be created that is based on high-quality services reflecting the user's concern (Ferlie et al. 1996). Factors supporting public trust include the quality of relationships with stakeholders, resulting in the mutual diffusion of public values. The diffusion of public value through public trust shapes the configuration of stakeholders' expectations and the continuity of mutual positive relationships. In the context of organizational culture, the proper combination of trust and reliability supported by mutual social capital can be formed.

Unfortunately, the negative factor of cultural relationships may be a lack of trust. Kramer (1999) focused on the differences between trust and lack of trust in organizations. This also applies to trust levels. If trust is directed only to compulsory activities related to the control and verification of mutual conduct, there will be no deeper subtext, such as the voluntary shaping of relationships. A lack of trust will result in impeded reliability and increased pressure on social sanctions. It can lead to the dysfunction of trust. Trust dysfunction may lead to the destruction of public values. It may result in negative behavior characterized by distrust, opportunistic behavior, and mutual relationships of unethical conduct, which are opposite to logic. Creating high levels of trust is sometimes simply impossible for government. Distrust in government not only emanates from government or citizen–government interaction but also from social factors (e.g., a tradition of being very critical towards government) (Bouckaert and van de Walle 2003).

Lewicki and Bunker distinguished between three types of trust: calculus-based trust, knowledge-based trust, and identification-based trust (Lewicki and Bunker 1996). "The trust-based paradigm" in the public sector can be supported and harnessed by supportive and effective leadership behaviors, public service oriented and norm-based motives, unbiased organizational incentive and compensation systems, or streamlined hierarchical and lateral communications and transactions among employees, managers, and supervisors (Park 2009). Recent trends in public sector reform see public sectors moving away from command-and-control systems to trust-based steering and collaboration. The desire to lower transaction costs and reduce short-term opportunistic behaviors is at the core of this evolution (Van de Walle 2010).

According to the above, a paradigm based on trust in public management becomes an important factor in creating public value (a crucial element of mutual relationships) and a determinant of meeting the needs of stakeholders in relation to public organizations. This may lead to a shift from a culture of low trust to higher order cultures. The public context of trust can be expressed as a set of values, principles, and standards adequate for the expectations of stakeholders, ensuring the development and provision of public services in line with the competencies, honesty, and transparency of public organizations. It can also be expressed by building the identity of a public organization and strengthening the engagement of stakeholders in shared public services, resulting in co-production.

10.3   Public Service Design Versus Public Trust

In the concept of public service, public interest is the result of social dialogue and indicates the shared values and common interests of citizens (Denhardt and Denhardt 2003). In this interpretation, it is particularly important to skillfully design public services. An appropriate approach to this type of action should take into account stakeholders' participation in this process and the degree to which this participation is confirmed. This participation may be focused on the mechanisms of embedding stakeholders in the process of mutual relationships with public organizations. In such an approach, public service design requires the identification of existing barriers that impede the development of the expected public value, the recipients of which are stakeholders in the public organization. Public service design affects the efficiency of these organizations towards higher-order values, by pursuing higher objectives in harmony with stakeholders.

Osborne and Strokosch argued that the services management literature can add valuable insights into our understanding of co-production, because of the central role that the latter concept plays within the services literature. Consequently, it arguably provides a more accurate starting point for theorizing about public services production. In combination with the public administration literature, it can stretch our understanding of co-production (Osborne and Strokosch 2013).

Pestoff, Osborne, and Brandsen attempted to distinguish between three different roles of the third sector in relation to public services:

- Co-governance: an arrangement in which the third sector participates in the planning and delivery of public services
- Co-management: an arrangement in which the third sector produces services in collaboration with the state
- Co-production: an arrangement in which citizens produce their own services, at least in part

The latter role could also refer to autonomous service delivery by citizens without direct state involvement, but with public financing and regulation (Pestoff et al. 2006).

With reference to the analyzed literature, the concept of coproduction can be defined as cooperation between an individual customer and a provider of public services by providing, in direct interaction, the resources for the production of a service that satisfies the individual needs of the customer and is based on the customer's voluntarism (Petukienė 2010, pp. 137–147).

In public service design, it is important to use the concept of *design thinking*. Design thinking is a research approach to the problems analyzed, including creative thinking processes (Rudkin 2015). An issue of design is reflected in many different business concepts. The following types of design can be distinguished (Rudkin 2015):

- User oriented
- Social, integrated
- Architectural, graphic
- Services

Design thinking can be described as "a discipline that uses the designer's sensibility and methods to match people's needs with what is technologically feasible and what a viable business strategy can convert into customer value and market opportunity" (Brown 2009).

Margolin and Buchanan stressed that, although design thinking must take into account the achievements of many disciplines (e.g., psychology, sociology, anthropology, engineering sciences), the core of design thinking is the ability to conceive, clarify, develop, and present new solutions (Margolin and Buchanan 1995). Nonetheless, recurring strategies have been empirically observed in the design process, such as the following:

1. Illumination of the problem space: In their exploration of a problem space, designers apply an intuitive (not fully verbalized) understanding, mainly by considering exemplary user cases or scenarios, as opposed to formulating general hypotheses or theories regarding the problem.
2. Illumination of the solution space: Designers explore equally a great number of alternative ideas; thus, their method matches the open and multidimensional character of the challenge itself.
3. Iterative alignment of spaces: In frequent iterations, ideas are transformed into tangible representatives (prototypes). These representatives facilitate communication not only within the design team, but

also with users or employers. Thus, designers keep in touch with the problem-relevant environment (Lindberg et al. 2010).

Design thinking applied to business strategy and business transformation is sometimes described as integrative thinking (Cooper et al. 2010).

There are many informative approaches to characterizing design thinking, some of which are now detailed. These characterizations highlight the skills often associated with good designers, namely the ability to tolerate the ambiguity that shows up in viewing design as inquiry or as an iterative loop of divergent-convergent thinking; maintain sight of the big picture by including systems thinking and systems design; handle uncertainty; make decisions; think as part of a team in a social process; and think and communicate in the several languages of design (Dym et al. 2005). Design thinking in the public sector has been described by Seddon and Brand (2008). Design thinking also can be used as a method for intensifying regional development (Szewczykowski et al. 2014).

A process approach using design thinking allows one to determine the interdependence of processes analyzed in the company, as well as criteria for their verification, evaluation, and regular monitoring. In addition, it introduces the possibility of accounting for the necessary corrective measures to achieve the planned results and improve continuously (Wawak n.d.).

An effective tool for understanding the mutual images of an organization is mind mapping. A mind map is a graphical tool that allows users to organize and better visualize ideas and creative conceptions, which can help users to expand their businesses, solve problems, rebuild their sales strategies, build teams, and increase a company's performance on a daily basis (Buzan and Griffiths 2010). Mind mapping enhances the potential of visual thinking, which supports the implementation of design thinking. Visual thinking is the use of visual skills (both real and imaginative visions) to identify ideas that cannot be reached by other means, develop new ideas fast and intuitively, and present the ideas to other people in such a way that they grasp them (Roam 2010). Therefore, the use of mind mapping in the design thinking process allows managers to better understand a strategy they develop and cascade it to lower levels of management. This method is used during the implementation of strategic workshops.

In this perspective, the relationship between public service design and public trust management gains importance. A factor that can be used to describe this relationship and embed it in the structure of interrelations is social sensitivity, which is focused on the creation of socially acceptable public value. Public services are designed so that this sensitivity is noticed by public organization stakeholders. Public trust can then be used to build social justice. At the same time, technology development shapes a new way of designing public services. The speed of access to the service results in stronger relationships and the dynamic process of mutual communication. This has a positive impact on the humanization of the relationship. In addition, knowledge and its sharing in the implementation of public services are particularly important in public service design. Trust supported by knowledge management mechanisms and the development of intellectual capital contributes intensely to building a climate of trust among public organizations, as well as in their relationships with other entities and stakeholders. In addition to trust, knowledge becomes a driver of long-term benefits for stakeholders in public service design.

10.4   Sustainability in Public Organizations Versus Public Trust

The real-world problems of sustainability are characterized by making decisions on behalf of others, as well as by great uncertainty in the consequences of those decisions. Strikingly, much of the economic literature on sustainability has addressed neither concern. As it turns out, the law on trusts necessarily wrestles with them both and provides a ready springboard for inquiry (Scott 1999).

Research has shown that good and frequent distribution of information has a positive effect on the successful implementation of sustainability initiatives. Management needs to ensure that this information is clear and available for employees. In addition to good information and communication, staff training is essential, including information about the procurement function. Bureaucracy can have a paralyzing effect on sustainability initiatives, so small project teams increase the chances for success considerably. Another problem is that the procurement function was found to have a mainly advisory role and therefore had only a limited influence on sustainability. Organizations need to examine the role of their procurement department and make sure it is able to be a driving and motivating actor. Celebrating successful initiatives and communicating successes to all stakeholders are important factors in the continued development of sustainability initiatives (Gelderman et al. 2017).

There are currently three approaches to sustainability:

1. The classic approach is broadly described in literature and well-recognized based on the *triple bottom line* (Elkington 1998). Businesses based on the triple bottom line may be mature companies founded on stakeholders' analysis and corporate social responsibility or young companies working on ecological aspects (e.g., in the field of renewable energy sources). These business models may be referred to as sustainable business models.
2. The second approach is based on assumptions. For example, as Schaltegger and Burritt stated: "The value proposition must provide both ecological or social and economic value through offering products and services [in a] business model for sustainability" (Schaltegger and Burritt 2000, pp. 643–655).
3. In the third approach, new business ventures are based on technological innovations that break the classical economic rules (i.e., profit is not the most important factor). This includes business models based on a sharing economy (e.g., Uber). These companies work with network effects, so it is important to ensure their sustainability through the continuity of business. (The requirements of laws, social needs, ecological rules, labor rules, and others are also very important, as well as the stability and sustainability of these business models.)

A focus on maintaining the system's functioning should, above all, take into account the needs of a public organization's stakeholders. In this approach, trust becomes a factor in stabilizing interorganizational relationships at the level of balancing communication between stakeholders and public organizations. Public trust thus ensures the continuity of interpersonal and interorganizational relationships. The continuity of these relationships is also expressed in building public transactional trust, which results in a reciprocal, bilateral, or multilateral exchange toward a stable relationship. The mechanism of sharing in the so-called sharing economy is a new field for designing public, trust-based services. In the design and implementation of public services, trust is focused on sharing relevant information, reducing control levels, and explaining each other's needs and expectations. Public services include a smaller control package, while ensuring the continuity of public services and mutual relationships. This limited control package should be supported by ethical and pro-social behavior.

10.5   Co-Production Versus Sustainability

Co-production is defined here as an arrangement where both clients and "regular" producers contribute a mix of activities at the point of delivery of public services (Fledderus et al. 2014). According to John Alford, co-production means any active behavior of nonpublic institutions that is undertaken jointly with public institutions (or is at least stimulated by those institutions), is at least partially voluntary, and leads deliberately (although in an unplanned manner) to generating public good (Alford 2009). Elinor Ostrom claimed that public administration is viewed from the perspective of a service provider, and that society is assumed to play a passive role; thus, co-production mechanisms should be implemented (Ostrom 2000).

Pestoff et al. (2006) distinguished the following three concepts:

- *Co-governance*: the involvement of the third sector in planning and providing public services
- *Co-management*: cooperation between the third sector and public administration in providing public services
- *Co-production*: the provision of public services by citizens themselves, at least to a certain extent, or in a state-independent way but with public funding and regulation

According to Brandsen and Honingh's (forthcoming), co-production is viewed as a deliberate action of the service provider to increase users' activities that are aimed at specific outcomes. They identified three basic elements of co-production after a thorough literature review: it is a relationship between the employees of an organization and (groups of) citizens; it demands direct and active inputs from these citizens to the work of the organizations; and the professional is a paid employee of the organization, whereas the citizen receives compensation below market value or no compensation at all. Specifically, the focus in this paper was on participation at the delivery phase. Brandsen and Honingh (2016, pp. 427–435) would say that co-production of an activation program is a form of "co-production in the implementation of core services." This form of co-production represents a situation where citizens are actively involved in the delivery, but not the design, of a service that is at the core of the organization.

Co-production is a participatory (socialized) model of public service provision—an alternative to the statist and market paradigm of these services. Co-production can occur at every stage of the process of providing public services, from organizing and financing the service system through their direct provision to their quality control or availability (Sześciło 2015). Ostrom stated that individual co-production is primarily focused on gaining private value and described the relationship between a single user and a service provider (e.g., the public service organization as a whole, or a single professional) (Ostrom 2000). Collective co-production takes place when a group of users participate in the delivery of a service. It adds complexity with regards to attaining outcomes, as users become dependent on the efforts of fellow users. For example, free-riding behavior might be a source of frustration for other users. Bovaird argued that co-production could take place both at the individual and the collective levels (Bovaird 2007).

Co-production implies that citizens can play an active role in producing public goods and services of consequence to them (Ostrom 1996). According to Fledderus, a user who is actively involved in his or her employment opportunities will be more likely to experience competence and internal control over his or her chances on the labor market (Fledderus et al. 2014). When the user develops a strong belief that there may be a solution for his or her unemployment, the relationship with the service provider is also likely to improve.

Bandura examined individual co-production to build trust. In this approach, users increase their perceptions of control, as they are able to influence the service process through their involvement (Bandura 2001). An important element of perceived control is the feeling of self-efficacy, which refers to the experience of competence. During co-production, people learn particular skills and techniques and are able to apply these qualities. Such enactive mastery is the strongest way to perceive competence.

Rotter argued that repeated experiences lead a person to discovering his or her level of performance capability, whereas repeated success in performing a task increases the perception of one's ability to perform that task (Rotter 1966). Furthermore, having influence over the outcome of a service will decrease feelings that outcomes depend on external factors, such as luck, fate, or religion. This refers to one's locus of control—that is, internal versus external. Co-production is therefore based on seeking synergies between the activities taken by an administration and its citizens (Pestoff 2012). Co-production can also create public innovation; this particular variation is social innovation.

A Bureau of European Policy Advisors (BEPA 2011) report identified three crucial approaches to addressing social innovation, as follows:

- Social demand innovations, in which innovations respond to social needs not previously met by the market or existing institutions. They target vulnerable groups in society and imply a new approach to solving the problems of youth, migrants, the elderly, and the socially excluded, among others.
- Social challenges, in which innovations that are important to society as a whole integrate social, economic, and environmental issues (in line with the principle of sustainable development).
- Systemic change, which is gained in the process of organizational development and changes in the relationship between public institutions and other stakeholders.

An essential challenge in developing public innovations by co-production is to find ways to ensure its sustainability as well as to create conditions for sharing knowledge that all partners have in order to improve the provision of public services (Sienkiewicz-Małyjurek 2016). It is important to focus on synergy and symbiosis between stakeholders creating a service, as part of co-production related to jointly creating services for sustainability. These three sustainability determinants may determine the principles of co-production stability as a basis for achieving the continuity of relationship.

It is therefore increasingly important to link co-production and project service design with ensuring sustainability through the development of mutual public trust between participants in mutual individual and group relationships. This link is expressed in the creation of new public services, which are made credible by trust attributes. They should be supported by the competence of public organizations, where the creation of trust is supported by the intellectual capital of individual stakeholders. Thus, the relational factors at the level of interaction, expectations, and costs of the exchange of value between stakeholders strengthen the overall propensity to trust, which ensures the continuity of public organization management in the relationship with stakeholders.

10.6   Conceptualizing the Sustainability of Public Organizations

When conducting a multidimensional analysis of the key concepts related to public management, it is important to conceptualize sustainability principles in public organizations. These may refer, among other things, to the achievement of strategic objectives of public organizations that are focused on environmental, social, and economic goals and to crucial public values. Public value for sustainability may be focused on smart development, sustainable development, and growth conducive to social inclusion. To preserve synergies, symbiosis, and symmetry with stakeholders through co-production, it is important to identify the graphical model of public organization management. This can be done by applying the rules for public service design.

By conceptualizing and operationalizing public service design for sustainability, the following steps should be followed:

1. Defining the vision of a public organization
2. Defining the essential values of a public organization
3. Dividing key values into their attributes
4. Linking key values with the smart specializations of the region
5. Defining key strategic priorities in relation to key values
6. Relating key values to the strategy and overriding objectives of a public organization
7. Identifying the sources of funding for a public organization to ensure its continuity, taking traditional and alternative sources of strategy funding into account

Through the application of graphical design thinking, the model in Fig. 10.1 presents the relationships between the vision of a public organization, the key values, and their attributes, which shape how they are used in the management of public organizations. A systemic approach to the principles of entrepreneurship and social sensitivity is important for building a mutual dialogue and public trust, whereas the reference to stakeholder activity is related to the implementation of co-production principles. Figure 10.2 explicitly refers to linking key public values with how the strategy of a public organization is implemented. It is expressed by defining strategic priorities supported by overriding objectives within the framework of the strategy of a public organization.

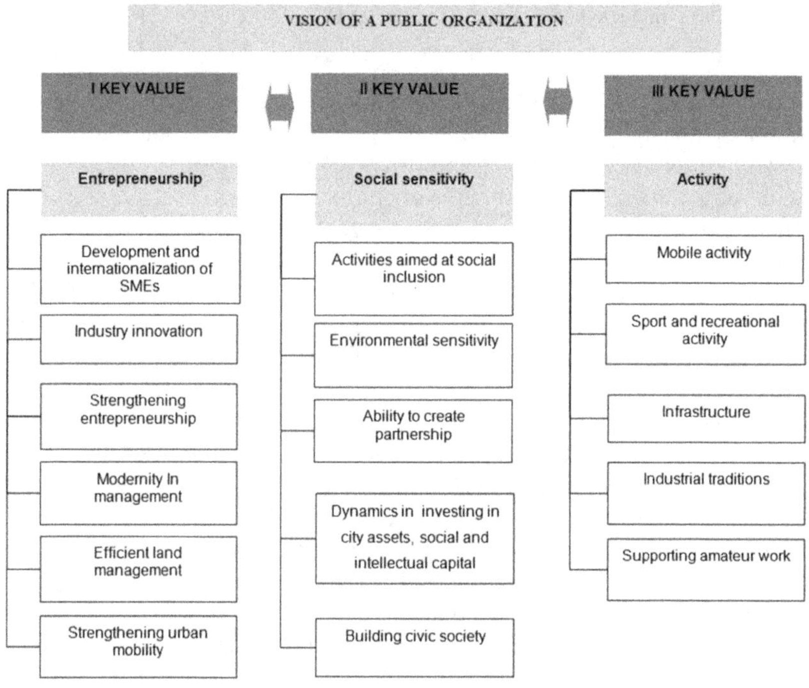

Fig. 10.1 Model that links the vision of a public organization with key public values and their attributes

10.7   DISCUSSION AND LIMITATIONS

When conducting a multidimensional analysis, attention should be paid to the place and role of public trust in building public value by using public service design and co-production. Trust becomes a driver and a factor that is a source of dialogue between individual stakeholders and the recipients of public value. Co-production and public service design determine the development of a new look at public services by creating new needs and a new interpretative dimension of public management. Public trust is then an element of moral standards and values, and a culture of trust directs the behavior in contacts between stakeholders at positive interpersonal and interorganizational relationships. Ethics, which is an important component of trust-based relationships, eliminates the destructive behavior in contacts with the stakeholders of public organizations. This greatly affects

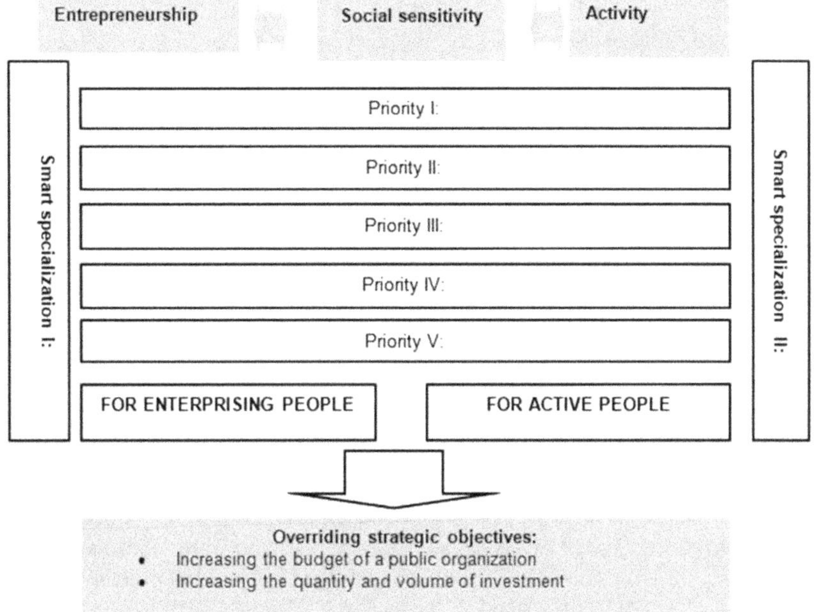

Fig. 10.2 Model of the relationships between key public values and smart specializations, with reference to the priorities and strategic objectives of a public organization

the durability of relationships and the sustainability of public organizations. This implies the harmonization and humanization of mutual social dialogue. Moreover, this determines the balance of expectations and the consistent achievement of goals embedded in the strategy of public organizations.

However, there are also limitations in this context, including the following:

- No uniform look at sustainability in public organizations
- The heterogeneous definition of the concept of public trust in public management
- The importance of lack of trust or low trust in public organizations
- An increasing influence of public service design and co-production in public organization management in the context of the standard mechanisms of public management

Further research perspectives toward the development of the subject include the following:

- The further conceptualization and operationalization of public trust in relation to public service design and co-production
- The broad use of the sustainability concept in public management
- An analysis of public trust management in terms of the sustainability concept

10.8   CHAPTER SUMMARY

The mechanisms of public organization management are now different from those several years ago. Currently, optimal management solutions in public organizations are sought. These solutions should be adequate not only for the needs of stakeholders, but also for those that directly engage them in shared tasks. Mechanisms such as co-production and public service design set new prospects for public management. Co-production, however, plays a special role here. It has a positive influence on relationships with stakeholders, establishes mutual dialogue, and opens new spaces of cooperation. In addition, the transfer of a large center of gravity to citizens creates new ways of communication, resulting in bonds. New co-production services also determine the new fields of public management. This is particularly true of public and social innovations.

A bonding factor is the use of sustainability in public management. For sustainability to achieve the desired effect, it is necessary to build mutual public trust. Public trust is shaped and is, at the same time, the result of positive interpersonal and interorganizational relationships. The joint implementation of co-production and public service design in such an approach determines sustainability in trust-based public organizations.

REFERENCES

Alford, J. (2009). *Engaging public sector clients. From service-delivery to co-production*. Basingstoke: Palgrave Macmillan.

Bandura, A. (2001). Social cognitive theory: An agentic perspective. *Annual Review of Psychology, 52*(1), 1–26.

Blind, P. K. (2007). *Building trust in government in the twenty-first century: Review of literature and emerging issues*. Symposium Conducted at the Meeting of the

7th Global Forum on Reinventing Government Building Trust in Government, Vienna.

Bouckaert, G., & van de Walle, S. (2003). Comparing measures of citizen trust and user satisfaction as indicators of 'good governance': Difficulties in linking trust and satisfaction indicators. *International Review of Administrative Sciences, 69*, 329.

Bovaird, T. (2007). Beyond engagement and participation: User and community coproduction of public services. *Public Administration Review, 67*(5), 846–860.

Brandsen, T., & Honingh, M. (2016). Distinguishing different types of co-production: A conceptual analysis based on the classical definitions. *Public Administration Review, 76*(3), 427–435.

Brown, T. (2009). *Change by design: How design thinking transforms organizations and inspires innovation.* New York: Harper Business.

Buzan, T., & Griffiths, C. (2010). *Maps of thoughts for business.* Łódź: Wydawnictwo JK.

Cooper, R., Junginger, S., & Lockwood, T. (2010). Design thinking and design management: A research and practice perspective. In T. Lockwood (Ed.), *Design thinking: Integrating innovation, customer experience and brand value* (pp. 57–63). New York: Allworth Press.

Denhardt, J. V., & Denhardt, R. B. (2003). *The new public service. Serving not steering.* Armonk: M.E. Sharpe.

Dym, C. L., Agogino, A. M., Eris, O., Frey, D. D., & Leifer, L. J. (2005, January). Engineering design thinking, teaching, and learning. *Journal of Engineering Education, 94*(1), 103–120.

Elkington, J. (1998). Accounting for the triple bottom line. *Measuring Business Excellence, 2*(3), 18–22.

Ferlie, E., Ashburner, L., Fitzgerald, L., & Pettigrew, A. (1996). *The new public management in action.* Oxford: Oxford University Press.

Fledderus, J., Brandsen, T., & Honingh, M. E. (2014). Restoring trust through the co-production of public services: A theoretical elaboration. *Public Management Review, 16*(3), 424–443.

Gelderman, C. J., Semeijn, J., & Vluggen, R. (2017). Development of sustainability in public sector procurement. *Public Money & Management, 37*(6), 435–442.

Kożuch, B. (2004). *Public management in the theory and practice of polish organizations.* Warszawa: Wydawnictwo PLACET.

Kramer, R. M. (1999). Trust and distrust in organizations: Emerging perspectives, enduring questions. *Annual Review of Psychology, 50*, 569–598.

Kramer, R. M., & Cook, K. S. (2004). *Trust and distrust in organizations: Dilemmas and approaches* (pp. 1–18). New York: Russell Sage Foundation. isbn:9780871544858.

Lewicki, R. J., & Bunker, B. B. (1996). Developing and maintaining trust in work relationships. In R. M. Kramer & T. R. Tyler (Eds.), *Trust in organizations:*

Frontiers of theory and research (pp. 114–139). Thousand Oaks: Sage Publications.

Lindberg, T., Noweski, C., & Meinel, C. (2010). Evolving discourses on design thinking: How design cognition inspires meta-disciplinary creative collaboration. *Technoetic Arts: A Journal of Speculative Research, 8*(1), 31–37.

Margolin, V., & Buchanan, R. (1995). *The idea of design*. Cambridge: The MIT Press.

McKnight, D. H., Cummings, L. L., & Chervany, N. L. (1998). Initial trust formation in new organizational relationships. *Academy of Management Review, 23*, 473–490.

Offe, C. (1999). How can we trust our fellow citizens? In M. E. Warren (Ed.), *Democracy & trust* (pp. 42–87). Cambridge: Cambridge University Press.

Osborne, S. P., & Strokosch, K. (2013). It takes two to tango? Understanding the co-production of public services by integrating the services management and public administration perspectives. *British Journal of Management, 24*, S31–S47.

Ostrom, E. (1996). Crossing the great divide; co-production, synergy, and development. *World Development, 24*(6), 1073–1088.

Ostrom, E. (2000). Collective action and the evolution of social norms. *The Journal of Economic Perspectives, 14*(3), 137–158.

Park, S. M. (2009, October 1–3). *Toward the trusted public organization: Untangling the leadership, motivation, and trust relationship in U.S. federal agencies*. This paper will be presented at the 10th National Public Management Research Conference, Columbus, Ohio.

Pestoff, V. (2012). Co-production and third sector social services in Europe: Some concepts and evidence. *VOLUNTAS: International Journal of Voluntary and Nonprofit Organizations, 23*(4), 1102–1118.

Pestoff, V., Osborne, S. P., & Brandsen, T. (2006). Patterns of co-production in public services. *Public Management Review, 8*(4), 591–595.

Petukienė, E. (2010). Coproduction of public services: Individual versus collective customer participation. *Iešoji Politika Ir Administravimas Public Policy and Administration, 32*, 137–147.

Raport Bureau of European Policy Advisors. (2011). *Empowering people, driving change: Social innovation in the European Union* (pp. 36–38). Luxembourg: Publications Office of the European Union.

Roam, D. (2010). *Draw your thoughts*. Gliwice: Wydawnictwo Helion.

Rotter, J. B. (1966). Generalized expectancies for internal versus external control of reinforcement. *Psychological Monographs: General and Applied, 80*(1), 1–28.

Rudkin, I. B. (2015). *Design thinking for entrepreneurs and small businesses*. Gliwice: Helion.

Schaltegger, S., Bennett, M., & Burritt, R. (2006). Sustainability accounting and reporting: Development, linkages and reflection: An introduction. In

S. Schaltegger, M. Bennett, & R. Burritt (Eds.), *Sustainability accounting and reporting*. Dordrecht: Springer.

Schaltegger, S., & Burritt, R. (2000). *Contemporary environmental accounting*. Sheffield: Greenleaf.

Scott, A. (1999). Trust law, sustainability, and responsible action. *Ecological Economics, 31*, 139–154.

Seddon, J., & Brand, C. (2008). Debate: Systems thinking and public sector performance. *Public Money and Management, 28*(1), 7–9.

Sienkiewicz-Małyjurek, K. (2016). Production innovation in public management at local level, Zeszyty Naukowe Politechniki Śląskiej Seria. *Organizacja i Zarządzanie, 89*(1949), 421–435.

Six, F. (2007). Building interpersonal trust within organizations: A relational Signaling perspective. *Journal of Management of Governance, 11*(3), 285–309.

Sobota, D., Bojar, W., & Zajdel, M. (2014). Design thinking as a method of intensifying regional development. *Marketing i Rynek, XXI*(10), 183–189.

Sześciło, D. (2015). Co-management as a co-production of public services. *Zarządzanie Publiczne, 1*, 19–20.

Van de Walle, S. (2010). New public management: Restoring the public trust through creating distrust? In T. Christensen & P. Lægreid (Eds.), *The Ashgate research companion to new public management* (pp. 309–320). Aldershot: Ashgate.

Wawak, S. https://wawak.pl/pl/content/podejscie-procesowe.

The Dynamics of Public Trust in Organizational Cooperation

Mutual Trust: Joint Performance of an Operations Strategy Implementation— Securing the Value Chain by Preparedness

Vesa-Jukka Vornanen, Ari Sivula, Yang Liu,
and Josu Takala

11.1   INTRODUCTION

"The need for the daily construction of the public safety" was the topic of a New Year's speech by the President of the Republic of Finland in 2017, as well as the topic of this chapter. A common value chain was presented in this speech: "Finland acts in a way that takes into account individuals, who in return contribute to a common objective." The Supreme Commander of the Finnish Defense Forces also clarified the civil society's comprehensive security objectives with a quality expectation: "You feel good when no one feels sick; therefore, help what you can. Know reasonably your responsibility, even for yourself, therefore, do what you are able to" (see http://www.presidentti.fi/public/default.aspx?contentid=3563 40&nodeid=44810&contentlan=2&culture=en-US).

V.-J. Vornanen (✉) • A. Sivula • J. Takala
University of Vaasa, Vaasa, Finland

Y. Liu
Jinan University, Guangzhou, China

B. Kożuch et al. (eds.), *Managing Public Trust*,
https://doi.org/10.1007/978-3-319-70485-2_11

Customer expectations in the municipalities are persistent. Municipalities in Finland still face disturbances in their operational environments. Despite several governmental streamlining projects since 2005, development is intensifying and operational disturbances are increasing (Limnéll 2014). Hence, organizational cooperation will benefit all competitors in this race. The gap between quality expectations and the performance of different operators makes the implementation of equality challenging. The prolonged disturbances are particularly damaging to the most disadvantaged people. There is a need for a new approach to improve civil society's ability to fill the security gaps.

The displeasure springing from the inequality is shared by the people and feeds the growth of populism. Irresponsible behavior in social media is part of the hybrid threat. Furthermore, the functioning of social networks is disturbed by provocations, which weakens mutual trust. Faith in internal security is purposefully undermined through denial-of-service attacks, the trolls of the info-wars, hate speech and pictures, and even fake news. Through this, the threat map of society has been redrawn.

All individuals have experienced negative events. There, where human interest in a common goal has ceased to exist, the expected value chain is at its weakest. Because of these unfortunate events, the detection of weak signals should be included in the development of municipal critical support services. On this playing field, every player of the team is important and their home runs are valuable to society. The required change management should occur close to the customer interface. The prevention of social exclusion is supported by social capital, which bolsters confidence in the inclusion and expands efforts in the hybrid organization's operational level.

This was the introduction of the lead author's public defense on February 17, 2017 at the University of Vaasa: "The objective of transformational leadership is how the division of labor by enhancing the social capital will be strengthened, and improved confidence in the inclusion again. Social capital is a resource for crowdsourcing, which must be ensured." In the study, organizational cooperation and the division of labor were examined to develop the necessary quality level. A manager's transformational leadership plays a key role here. Quality management enables high-quality operations, resulting in high-quality service, which provides the expected outcomes and meets the objective of customer satisfaction. The customer needs to start a chain that ends in satisfying the customer's need. The value is generated between those endpoints. The value-creation chain can be presented in accordance with the continuous

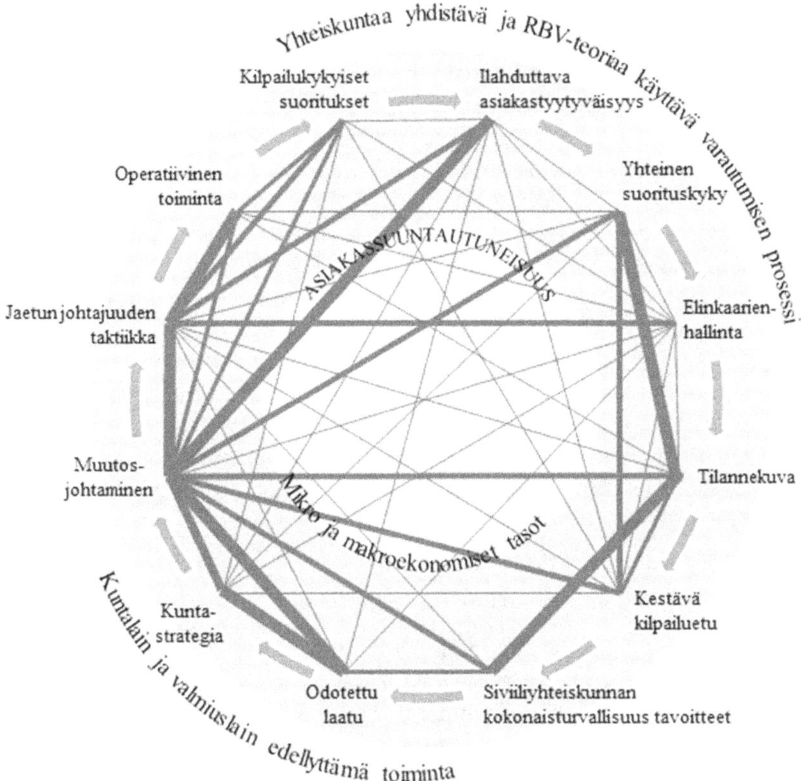

Fig 11.1 Abstraction of an innovative preparedness process (Vornanen 2017: 89; Vornanen et al. 2016)

development cycle as a process. Figure 11.1 presents the preparedness process, which was the key finding of the study in terms of managing internal security. The model of the preparedness process shows a pragmatic world. As an "internal roundabout," the model illustrates the action research that was executed between 2009 and 2015 in Western Finland (Vornanen 2017: 51–67).

Instead of a static presentation, the preparedness process model is continuous and dynamic. Simultaneous implementation of the security strategy for society and the municipal strategy (macrolevel policies) occurs by implementing the target unit's operations strategy (microlevel policy). The method of implementation opens interaction and action pathways to the wider inclusion, and thereby the safety of the individual, community, and societal levels. The model brings together large numbers of people. For each individual to be equally important, he or she is viewed as the customer. Thus, the preparedness process directs all actors toward the customer-oriented common objectives of internal security, and thus the joint performance (Vornanen 2017: 87–93, Vornanen et al. 2016).

In terms of the local baseball culture, the widest pathways in the preparedness process are found between the pair with the most home runs (Vornanen 2017: 89). The preparedness process is the response to the public sector's key challenge of finding new ways of operating, both vertically and between different levels of government. The preparedness process sheds light on the critical task chains of the networked value system (Vornanen 2017: 166; Vornanen et al. 2016). By mutual trust, the task forces function as a hybrid organization. By targeting critical operations in a customer-convincing way, a hybrid organization should aim toward positive qualities (Kano et al. 1984) as a focus of organizational cooperation (Vornanen 2017: 189–191).

11.2   Rebuilding Public Safety

The corresponding author's action research was a six-year project. The work was carried out in a municipal organization's middle management, which was a turbulent environment. Two municipal phenomena united there: statutory steering and the real-time economy (Vornanen and Takala 2014: 240). The facility services unit's activities were adjusted to be in the category of the 20 largest cities in Finland when the new City of Seinäjoki was established on 1 January 2009, after the merger of three municipalities. The municipal merger was neither an automatic guarantee of the success of the new municipality nor a normal situation in any municipality's continuum. However, the disturbance in the continuum was a good starting point for the research.

The municipal merger offered opportunities for the new municipality (Meklin and Paatelainen 2006). To make the necessary changes, municipality decision-making needed to be supported. Through the target unit, three research articles examined the implementation of the strategy before, during, and after the disturbance. As a situational factor, trust in joint solutions should lead the new municipality in the right direction. The new strategies needed to be implemented in such a way that confidence in the future would be strengthened. Therefore, all actors' competitiveness factors had to be measured to look at the direction of development. According to the ongoing situation and recovery from it, the indicators of the development direction could be verified through organizational cooperation (Vornanen 2017: 7–8).

A key problem was how the operations strategy could be carried out in such a way that the joint performance is realized. The research problem was solved in a way that responded to the following subquestions: How could it be ensured that the various teams operate under a common strategy? How could dynamic capabilities be built to maintain the critical public property? How can residents and support service roles in preparedness be identified and how can their common roles be developed? The theoretical framework of the study was a dynamic construction. It was refined a few times during the action research (Kasanen et al. 1991) and combined several theories with a resource-based view (Wernerfelt 1984; Kano et al. 1984; Carlzon 1987; Porter 1985; Williamson 1991; Rannisto 2005; Jalonen 2007; Ranta and Takala 2007; Slezak 2013). The study's methodology aimed to solve real-world problems and thus contribute to the discipline in which it is applied (Vornanen 2017: 26–35).

In action research (Lewin 1946), the researcher seeks to influence the research target. Therefore, the study included an interventionist work hypothesis: the old organizational cultures and actions must unite and change to a new one, because individuals must survive the disturbance and seek sustainable competitiveness (Vornanen 2017). In the study, validity and reliability have been improved with detailed material, use of a multiple-approach research method, and reflections on the generalization of the results. The work is based on the multiple strategies for realizing the city's values in accordance with the statutory guidance (Vornanen 2017). The research is related to the author's maintenance manager post, alongside his preparedness liaison officer duty. The official job position sets the actions and results in an evaluation of their effectiveness. Officials gave a mission to the maintenance manager: planned maintenance (Vornanen 2017) to create a systematic and unified code of conduct for the unit. The procedures were produced by teamwork and examined in relation to quality expectations. The author's manuals were used as tools for implementing the strategy, including a quality guidance handbook, risk management manual, and orientation manual for employees (Vornanen 2017). The implementation and updating of projects during the action research produced material for the published articles, and vice versa, thereby deepening the preparedness process.

11.2.1   Further Insights from Other Publications

The first research article on the topic focused on operations management (Vornanen et al. 2013). The study uses analytical models to clarify operational priorities (Takala et al. 2005, 2007). After the unit's respondents completed questionnaires, the answers were analyzed using an analytic hierarchy process software program. In implementing a sustainable competitive advantage for proactive operations (Liu 2013), the following indexes were calculated in the study: critical factor index, manufacturing strategy, leadership, outcome, total leadership, and overall competitiveness with technology levels. The results indicate how the unit's organizational levels work in parallel according to the unit's operations strategy before, during, and after a disturbance. For general operations, some critical factors with regard to resources are development, information technology, cooperation of processes, and customers. The system was developed with a Computerized Maintenance Management System (CMMS) provider, thus leading to a practical win-win-win solution. The obvious benefit of using the sustainable competitive advantage methodology was its ability to make the structures of the organizations and strategies transparent for developing action. The study results were used to develop the quality guidance handbook (Vornanen 2017).

The second research article aimed to present a path to joint performance—that is, how to build dynamic capabilities for public critical asset maintenance (Vornanen and Takala 2014). The study examined the Sand Cone-model and the Kano-model content linkages to the Council's Action Plans of the 20 largest municipalities in Finland. The publication is based on a case study, supplemented by content analysis and surveys from the first article. The case study explains the implementation of multi-focused strategies for the order fulfillment process in the common value chain. The dynamic capabilities were used for several strategic actions. The study utilized Balanced Critical Factor Index (BCFI) analysis to examine network partners. The most significant contributions of the paper were in the task of resource allocation to achieve multi-focused strategic goals (Vornanen 2017).

The third research article merged society actors in the development of a joint performance perspective (Vornanen et al. 2016). In the context of preparedness, joint performance is subject to securing the value chain. Customer orientation is a common factor in the public, private, and third sector organizations; their operations with households and individuals' everyday lives; and the overall logistic society. To promote a combination of these factors and their joint performance, there is a need for a hybrid management. The management implemented a preparedness analysis and classification system (PACS) for hybrid organizations, transformational leadership, and crowdsourcing. The PACS shed light on local hybrid and crowdsourcing usage in preparedness. Crowdsourcing provides knowledge and resources for private, public, and third sector organizations. Activities are supported by the real-time PACS system, which creates a common situational awareness of how to secure the value chain by implementing operations strategies (Vornanen 2017).

11.3   Preparedness in the Support Process Tasks

11.3.1   *How to Support a Hybrid Organization*

The Emergency Powers Act requires municipalities to prepare for disturbances in advance. The new municipality has more than 600 buildings and over 400,000 square meters of floor area, with the premises managed in a customer-oriented way. Public buildings are common to all and form a networked value system: from the children to grandparents, from military to other authorities, everyone has some kind of experience and/or expectation from public buildings. If the use of a public building is disturbed, the value chain for a building user does not function as expected. Therefore, there is a need for a planned maintenance that functions in a customer-oriented manner in all situations (Vornanen et al. 2013).

To fulfill the municipality's needs, the lead author interacted with the following partners: as a representative of the City of Seinäjoki at the Regional State Administrative Agency; as a doctoral researcher of the University of Vaasa; and as a research and development engineer for the unit's business partners (Vornanen et al. 2013). The actions supporting organizational cooperation (e.g., meetings, negotiations, exercises) were grouped according to four factors: government, civil society, research, and business using a sample from October 2014 to June 2015 (Vornanen 2017). The factors were further grouped into four categories: two management levels (hybrid management and hybrid organization's operations) and two action columns (process and information technology [IT]; data streams include social media for crowdsourcing purposes).

Six of 22 supportive actions focused on organizational cooperation with security partners. These were in the government category at the upper level of hybrid management, at the top of the process column: two meetings with the Pori brigade of Defense Forces, participation in the

Confederation of Finnish Construction Industries RT's exercise as a pool of the National Emergency Supply Organization, participation in the provincial situational picture exercise at the Police University College, and two joint security group meetings at the Regional State Administrative Agency. Four of 22 supportive actions focused on the development of information and communication technology. These were in the business category, at the level of the hybrid organization's operations, at the bottom of the IT column: negotiations with the access control system supplier, building information modeling companies, and military logistics.

Most of the supportive action focused on organizational cooperation with internal partners, such as school principals and the rescue department; these were in the civil society category at the level of the hybrid organization's operations, at the bottom of the process column. This is a category near the field where support operations take place. The study itself is in the research category at the upper level of hybrid management, at the top of the IT column. This is a category of attractive quality and is a place of findings. The results in this category create a path for a sustainable competitive advantage. Maintaining society's vital functions through cooperation between several actors is indispensable. The critical support services of the municipality cooperate with sectors such as food, health, finance, industry, and security. Local public services contain a variety of precautions against threats to society. On the other hand, the resources, operational capability, and operating cultures of different municipalities also vary (Vornanen 2017).

Preparedness is ensuring the disturbance-free performance of tasks. For this reason, municipal strategic plans and the municipal sector's annual plans are too broad and vague to be applied weekly, daily, or even hourly. There is a need to control and monitor the outputs. The realization of all 149 issues of the 2009–2013 municipal strategy with the hundreds of statutory duties required the cooperation of several actors. The strategies' processing was based on content analysis. In this method, the material is reduced to parts, which are conceptualized and finally organized into a new entity. This method connects the results to a wider context and other research results on the phenomenon (Vornanen 2017). Implementing the strategy required strategic choices from the target unit, such as the following: Is the performance of the support service activities directly or indirectly affecting the strategic plan? Because the environment is turbulent, should the resources be allocated to full-time critical issues? Are there enough resources to implement multitasking? The target unit's customer-oriented evaluation items from the municipal strategy were placed on a strategy map in a logical order. The acronym "SIPOC" (supplier-input-process-output-customer) clarified the order of the strategic entities (Kaplan and Norton 2004). A SIPOC-based strategy map of the unit also examined how the unit's operations strategy could be constructed (i.e., what to do and how) (Vornanen 2017).

At first, the logistics success factors (readiness, agility, and leanness) were combined with the unit's operations strategy (Takala and Rautiainen 2003). They affect the unit's competitive factors of time, cost, and quality (Vornanen 2017). Together, the maintenance manager and supervisor develop and implement work outlines so that employee job satisfaction affects customer satisfaction. In this way, the desired resource efficiency affects the flow efficiency. In other words, the support service performs its own core business while supporting the customer's operations and common goals (Vornanen 2017). Therefore, there is a need for a flexibility. If a sudden disturbance occurs, the order fulfillment process becomes more challenging. Some prolonged disturbances may turn into crises. Therefore, a holistic view of the consumption of resources and capabilities is also necessary and should occur early enough to sense and respond to changes.

The facility services unit had to build a sensing and responding system to achieve multi-strategic goals and ensure their achievement (Vornanen 2017). For example, the unit's customer has a need to use a building for safety. The customer's needs are served by a value chain, which is particularly important in major emergencies and disruptions. In addition to evacuation situations, the unit has to produce information on which buildings are more flexible for different uses. This helps customers to achieve cost-effective recovery from disruptions to the normal situation. To detect changes in the customer's operational environment, the unit constructed a centralized control room (CCR). The CCR collects data, then compares and verifies information about automation systems and processes. If there are any deviations in the measurement data from the control factors, the CCR sends an alert to the decision-maker at the relevant authority. In Finland, emergency management is based at the relevant authority, with other parties providing support. This is the key idea of the civil society's concept for comprehensive security. The mode of operation deepens mutual trust, which adds the necessary flexibility to the organizational culture. The CCR is a managerial implication to enhance operational effectiveness (Vornanen et al. 2013, 2016; Vornanen and Takala 2014). Figure 11.1 illustrates how the activities of the hybrid organization began by implementing the municipal strategy, along with the work to produce an innovative model of the preparedness process.

11.3.2   Quality: The Pacemaker of a Hybrid Organization

The challenge of preparedness can be characterized by the daily implementation of public safety. Without safety, there is no well-being. Safety is built up on a daily basis by security and supportive actors. This requires a set of organizations and their aligned actions. Responding to quality expectations mean that planned maintenance had to be redefined from the point of view of the municipality. According to the Local Government Act, the mayor/municipal manager is responsible for the implementation of precautionary actions. In action research, the preparedness process in the municipality was coordinated by the preparedness liaison officer. He reported directly to the mayor/municipal manager (Vornanen et al. 2013). As a sign of success, the collaborative procedure was confirmed as an official mode of action on June 2017.

A municipal building's life-cycle quality should be ensured by planned maintenance. During the action research, planned maintenance was condensed into four task chains: predictive maintenance services; corrective maintenance and repair services; reactive, technical surveillance and maintenance services; and employment and assistant maintenance services. Assistant maintenance services are particularly important as they can be used to help develop the division of labor and to ensure the duties of the service provider. Municipal buildings are in many ways part of the critical infrastructure and the internal security. From a broader perspective, assistant maintenance is an asset of the local government; it implements municipal employment obligations. Internal security is a vital basic function in society that needs to be ensured. Employment serves the people's inclusive experience and thus is an important role in connecting people in society. An innovative approach is to combine the simultaneous implementation of both (Vornanen 2017).

The strategic entities were presented using the SIPOC model. The unit's combined strategic objectives for service production were followed throughout the project. The establishment of the CCR responded to the strategies and quality expectations through four key policies of the unit's operation strategy: public asset criticality, customer focus, high-quality personnel, and trust.

11.3.3   Strategy for Public Asset Criticality

In the new municipality, all technical premises must be addressed only as real estate for technical use; all unofficial storage should be stopped to improve the efficient use of real estate. This operation led to the creation of the municipal organization's internal marketplace. To manage the internal market and create subsidized projects for assistant maintenance, the target organization implemented a centralized recycling center (CRC). The CRC's mission is to reduce the need to buy new furniture thus reduce the municipality's annual budget. The CRC enables accounting tasks to measure the speed of recycling fixtures. For example, when a table is no longer useful for customers, it can be modified, repaired, or disassembled for recycling.

The customer feedback was excellent because every unit has a limited budget for fixtures. When the budget is in use, the purchasing unit will determine individual needs for larger entities and implement acquisitions. This process takes a year according to the municipalities' financial guidelines. The CRC was able to meet customers' needs quicker than the budgeting/procurement process (Vornanen 2017).

11.3.4   The Customer-Focused Strategy

In all municipal functions, a common factor is operational floor space and fixtures. During a premise's maintenance activities, the fixtures need to be moved to a temporary location before maintenance begins then need to be restored after completion. The transfer operations are assistant actions for the target unit's task chains and an example of identifying the content of the work. The assistant team has made it possible to reallocate transfer-intensive tasks. The division of labor had a positive impact on the quality of core services. The arrangement underlined the importance of assistant logistics for the municipality residents (Vornanen 2017).

11.3.5   Strategy for High-Quality Personnel

One of the common entities among all municipal administrative sectors in Finland is an obligation for subsidized employment. This employment degree-based function maintains the public workforce in the municipalities. The support service unit formed a team to fulfill the needs of subsidized employment. As a member of the team, it is possible to also be a job applicant. Every trainee was treated like an internal customer, and the mission was the same for all situations. This is because the staff has a high average age in the task chain. According to the code of conduct, the retirement of employees has been taken into account in the unit's continuity management (Vornanen and Takala 2014).

11.3.6   Strategy of Trust

The basis of maintenance is to maintain the ability to function. To achieve objectives, the maintenance manager drives the internal control, which requires two important factors: personnel and the ability to produce value-added information. These factors make it possible to support implementation of multiple strategies through shared leadership and creation of the joint performance in the CCR. The CCR is the resource-based information-generating counterpart (Wernerfelt 1984; Vornanen 2017) for the command center of the municipality or the Civil Defense Districts. These districts are led from their own regional command centers, which operate under the main command center of the area. To form cross-border processes between these districts and to make them functional in all situations, it is essential to get things into the right hands at the right place and time. The use of resources for the common objectives of many actors requires a regional coordination point in addition to the lead contact. The unit's quality is implemented through the CCR, which is organized by a SIPOC assessment, customer satisfaction inquiries, and quality guidance (Vornanen 2017).

11.3.7   Summary

The study explained the customer's values for the unit's planned maintenance before, during, and after a disturbance. A municipality's critical support services are an inherent part of assistant logistics, which is based on the statutory tasks of the municipality. The logistical actors in public safety differ in their emphases on operations related to a crisis. All of the previously mentioned actors are united by a common goal, which can be presented on a common public sector's strategy map (Vornanen 2017).

11.4 MUTUAL TRUST: JOINT PERFORMANCE IN A HYBRID ORGANIZATION

Finally, we examine the challenge of meeting customer-driven quality expectations. The municipality's supported employment challenge lies in how the workplace relationship between long-term employees and short-term job-seeking customers is maintained. It is not easy.

The author received a letter from an unemployed person, 1 year after his subsidized employment ended and 2 days before the 2017 presidential New Year speech. The individual wrote that the target organization's working relationship had been perfect for him, but he could not understand why some other individuals had longer subsidized employment relationships than he did. However, The individual's next job period was in the target unit's service provider, whereas others had not received this placement.

The challenge of municipal subsidized employment lies in the division of labor choices and understanding of the objectives. In other words, will the unit provide on a short work training relationship for many jobseekers or a long work training relationship for only a limited number of job applicants? In 2016, the facility services unit provided work training for 68 jobseeker-customers through a division of labor—a high proportion for a 75-employee unit. The subsidized employment ratio was 91%. The unit's personal work design and couching were successful.

As mentioned previously, maintaining mutual trust is challenging. The value chain of subsidized employment can break if the next actor has a small number of contracts. A simple explanation could be that the local labor market does not work. Two operators may not be enough to secure this kind of value chain. However, these two operators can be the beginning of an entire value network. Security and humanitarian actors, as well as a chain of service and production companies, are partners in the society's security strategy implementation (Vornanen 2017).

The municipality's critical support services connect to the value chain of local subprocesses. A common goal and cooperation should define a positive identity experience for the actors. Tasks and events in the preparedness process should generate creativity. They provide possibilities for the municipality support service unit to secure its customers's value chain. Securing the common value chain occurs by implementing the unit's operations strategy. This is management through a customer-driven, networked value system. It tells what part of the whole we all want you to be, and we are together (Vornanen 2017). Three managers assessed the reliability and the results of the action research. The results were evaluated and confirmed by a weak market test (Vornanen 2017).

11.5   Chapter Summary

We are committed to common goals—not because they are easy, but because they are hard. Mutual trust, as a result of an organizational cooperation, is a set of performances in a networked value system. To succeed, the perceived quality should be continually attractive. The preparedness process gathers performances to achieve and secure a civil society's comprehensive security goals. Overall, the system promotes the well-being of residents and vitality of the municipalities. The unit's operations are controlled in such a way that the right hands are in the right place to make right things in the right amount at the right time (Vornanen 2017).

During a disturbance, municipal management follows a hybrid management approach, as follows. Data are collected and critical factors are evaluated in advance to determine the necessary cooperation. From this information, planned and practiced workflows are developed, with trust for the expertise of the actors before the disturbance and, especially, during the disturbance. Securing the value chain requires cooperation to maintain a reliable situation in all scenarios. Information is gathered to form a common situational awareness, with collaboration and shared knowledge required before any decision making. As a result, mutual trust and organizational cooperation occur (Vornanen 2017).

References

Carlzon, J. (1987). *The moment of truth*. Sydney: Harper & Row Pty Ltd.

Jalonen, H. (2007). *Kompleksisuusteoreettinen tulkinta hallinnollisen tehokkuuden ja luovuuden yhteensovittamisesta kunnallisen päätöksenteon valmistelutyössä. Akateeminen väitöskirja* [Complexity-based interpretation of integrating effectiveness and creativity in the preparation of municipal decision-making. Academic dissertation]. Tampere University of Technology. Publication 693.

Kano, N., Seraku, N., Takahashi, F., & Tsuji, S. (1984). Attractive quality and must-be quality. Hinhitsu. *The Journal of the Japanese Society for Quality Control, 14,* 39–48.

Kaplan, R. S., & Norton, D. P. (2004). *Strategy maps: Converting intangible assets into tangible outcomes*. Boston: Harvard Business School Press.

Kasanen, E., Lukka, K., & Siitonen, A. (1991). Konstruktiivinen tutkimusote liiketaloustieteessä. [A constructive research in business economics]. *Liiketaloudellinen aikakausikirja, 40*(3), 301–327.

Lewin, K. (1946). Action research and minority problems. *Journal of Social Issues, 2*(4), 34–46.

Limnéll, J. (2014). *Kyberaika muuttaa sotia ja konflikteja* [Cyber time transforms wars and conflicts]. Helsingin Sanomat. 1.1.2014. Online: http://www.hs.fi/kotimaa/a1405826705250

Liu, Y. (2013). Sustainable competitive advantage in turbulent business environments. *International Journal of Production Research, 51*(10), 2821–2841.

Meklin, P., & Paatelainen, S. (2006). *Seinäjoen, Nurmon ja Ylistaron voimavarojen kokoamista ja yhdistämistä koskeva selvitys* [Research on the pooling and consolidation of resources in Seinäjoki, Nurmo and Ylistaro municipalities]. Online: http://www.pronurmo.info/selvitys.pdf

Porter, M. E. (1985). *Competitive advantage: Creating and sustaining superior performance*. New York: Free Press.

Rannisto, P.-H. (2005). *Kunnan strateginen johtaminen. Tutkimus Seinänaapurikuntien strategiaprosessien ominaispiirteistä ja kunnanjohtajista strategisina johtajina*. Akateeminen väitöskirja. [Strategic management of the municipality. Research on the characteristics of the strategic processes of neighboring municipalities and municipal leaders as strategic leaders]. Acta Universitatis Tamperensis 1072. Tampere.

Ranta, J.-M., & Takala, J. (2007). A holistic method for finding out critical features of industry maintenance services. *International Journal of Services and Standards, 3*(3), 312–325. Vaasa: University of Vaasa, Department of Production.

Slezak, S. (2013). *Why corporate cultures needs to adopt risk management*. Global risk insights. Online: http://globalriskinsights.com/2013/11/why-risk-management-needs-to-be-integrated-in-corporate-culture/

Takala, J., & Rautiainen, M. (2003). *Measuring customer satisfaction and increasing It by choosing the right development subjects*. The 2nd International Conference of Logistics & Transport, LOADO 2003.

Takala, J., Hirvelä, J., Hiippala, P., & Nissinen, V. (2005). *Management and deep leadership sand cone model for human resource allocation*. 4th International DAAAM (Automation & Manufacturing) Conference, ATDC (Advanced Technologies for Developing Countries), Slavonski Brod, Croatia.

Takala, J., Hirvelä, J., Liu, Y., & Malindzag, D. (2007). Global manufacturing strategies require "dynamic engineers"? Case study in Finnish industries. *Industrial Management & Data Systems, 107*(3), 326–344.

Vornanen, V-J. (2017). *Joint performance – Preparedness in the municipal transformation 2009–2015: Securing the value chain by operations strategy implementation*. University of Vaasa, Acta Wasaensia 369, Finland, p. 243.

Vornanen, V.-J., & Takala, J. (2014). Towards joint performance: Building dynamic capabilities for public critical asset maintenance. *Management, 9*(3), 239–257.

Vornanen, V.-J., Liu, Y., & Takala, J. (2013). Implementing sustainable competitive advantage to the public sector's management system – By sense and respond methodology in facilities services unit's preparedness. *Management and Production Engineering Review, 4*(3), 76–86.

Vornanen, V.-J., Sivula, A., & Takala, J. (2016). Hybrid management in preparedness: Utilizing cooperation and crowdsourcing to create joint performance in the logistic society. *Management, 11*(2), 152–170.

Wernerfelt, B. (1984). A resource-based view of the firm. *Strategic Management Journal, 5*(2), 171–180.

Williamson, O. E. (1991). Strategizing, economizing, and economic organization. *Strategic Management Journal, 12*(S2), 75–94.

CHAPTER 12

Trust in Public Organizations: An Explanation for Noncooperative Behavior

István Takács and Katalin Takács-György

12.1   Introduction

Trust (or a lack of trust) is an indicator of the relationship between two parties. The concept presumes the existence of uncertainty or risk in the relationship (Rousseau et al. 1998). There is an information asymmetry between the two partners regarding the issues of the partnership—that is, they do not know the same things to the same depth and level of detail. Decisions may be made without full knowledge or without knowing the response of the partner (Lane and Bachmann 2000); thus, a lack of knowledge is replaced by trust. The actors in a trust relationship depend on each other: The actions of one party are determined by the expectations regarding the actions of the other party (Dasgupta 1988); therefore, expectations affect decisions. The trust relationship is started by one of the partners. The originator would expect that the vulnerability from accepting the risk will not be exploited by the other partner in the relationship (Lane and Bachman 2000)—in other words, the other partner will not show opportunistic behavior. The previous experiences of the partners and the common experiences inherited in the culture of the community

I. Takács (✉) • K. Takács-György
Óbuda University Budapest, Budapest, Hungary

© The Author(s) 2018
B. Kożuch et al. (eds.), *Managing Public Trust*,
https://doi.org/10.1007/978-3-319-70485-2_12

regarding the possible (or rather, expected) behavior of the other party determine the probability of establishing a trust relationship.

In his famous book *The End of History and the Last Man*, Francis Fukuyama (1992) discussed the battle between Hobbes and Hegel—that is, the liberal democracy versus *"thumos"* (the desire for recognition). He stated that the battle is over and humankind is heading toward a globalized liberal democracy based on mutual respect. It is obvious that the former situation requires a very strong public confidence within individual nations and among different nations. However, three decades after this book, the human race has strayed very far from the end of history because a long range of heightened conflicts, strengthening xenophobia, increasing fear from terrorism, and the deliberate reinforcement of this fear (by raising awareness of increasing risks, either presumed or real), which further amplify the distrust between different social groups. All of these examples also show that trust development depends on several different factors.

Many factors—from historical "imprinting" to selection mechanisms—have contributed to the development of trustful attitudes in a certain group of people. According to a paraphrase, which has been attributed to Darwin but was actually said by Meggingson (1963): "It is not the strongest of the species that survives, nor the most intelligent, but rather the one most adaptable to change." This suggests that selection mechanisms also contribute to the development of trust attitudes, which are characteristic in social groups. Gallo (2016) cited Hallowell and Raley's paper (1994), in which the authors stated that symptoms of attention deficit/hyperactivity disorder are typical for many inventors and innovators. That is how America had been established: the mass appearance of adventurers and people who were regarded as "deviant" in their own social environment determined the features of the white American population later. For African Americans, their settlement in America was not the result of a voluntary decision; thus, there had been no similar type of selection process in their case.

It has been conjectured that there are evolutionary reasons behind strong cooperation willingness and its preconditions. For example, consider the social trust of Viking-descendant Scandinavians and sea people in general: their cooperation willingness and social trust are often much higher than that of other people. The interdependency between others is huge during long sea journeys: the people with the greater chance of survival trusted each other and the captain of the ship, whereas those who did not cooperate were lost at sea (i.e., trust = survival and distrust = destruction). The situation was totally opposite in continental areas where different troops ravaged the communities; here, distrust was more reasonable in terms of survival (i.e., trust = destruction and distrust = survival). These were the "outcomes" of typical trust attitudes. In this context, trust is a product that is formed on the basis of experiences (reward and punishment; i.e., the yield), individual risk aversions, and interest relations. All interactions (and often, the lack of interaction) mean risk. It can be presumed that—either instinctively or deliberately—the individual or the organization aims to optimize this risk. In modern economies and societies, entering as the third actor, governments (the establishment) distort the information relationships among partners. They use different regulatory or economic means (e.g., the promise of social security, provision of earmarked subsidies) to temporarily or permanently divert expectations and, consequently, the actions of one or both parties. In this context, the topic can be discussed hereinafter as an economic issue.

By drawing on the experiences of other social sciences and utilizing the revealed connections and regularities, modern economics tries to describe and model social-economic processes with new economic theories. There have been two outstanding new theories in economics in recent decades: new institutional economics and game theory. Both theories also use the results of psychology and sociology sciences in the explanation of observed economic phenomena.

The subject of economic thinking is the human being and the performance resulting from the different interactions among people or their groups. New institutional economics, among other things, aims to explain the economic correlations of decisions with the help of transaction cost theory. Depending on whether human relations are examined on the basis of noncooperative or cooperative game theory, game theory explores the reasons why the "players of the game"—the actors of social relations and events—behave as they do. Through a discussion of these relationships, this chapter explores the economic reasons for noncooperative behavior.

12.2   Transaction Costs of Cooperative Behavior

New institutional economics focuses on the analysis of institutions (e.g., markets, organizations, legal norms), in the frames of which economic processes are occurring. Its aim is to explain the structure and efficiency of economic institutions as well as the economic behavior of people

(Schumacher 1973) based on the synthesis of neoclassic microeconomics, economics, and organizational theory (Kieser and Ebers 2014). This theory is searching for answers to the following questions:

1. Which organizational form and which types of coordination problems of economic processes have the relatively lowest cost and the highest efficiency?
2. What are the impacts of exchange problems, costs, and efficiency on the setup and transformation of institutions?

The theory sets up a four-factor model, the factors of which are the institution, the exchange transaction, cost, and efficiency. The theory (Kieser and Ebers 2014) consists of the following parts: agency theory, property rights theory, and transaction cost economics theory. The theories have more sensible presumptions about the actors of economy than the previous economic theory and explain the economic events through the behavior of individuals. They presume that there are information limits in human behavior, as well as fraud, self-interest, and limited rationality (Klein et al. 1978).

The agent theory—and especially its normative line, the principal-agent theory—focuses on asymmetric information during the cooperation of participants and the related opportunistic behavior. Asymmetric information can always be tracked down if there is cooperation between two or more parties. Due to information asymmetry, there can be a moral hazard and adverse selection among the cooperating partners. There is moral hazard if at least one factor cannot be observed in the course of cooperation and it cannot be laid down in the contract (Royer 1999). The limited observability may mean that the agent does not make appropriate, optimum efforts from the aspect of the principal.

Holmstrom (1982) introduced the concept of moral hazard. According to this, if the partners in a group are awarded on the basis of joint efforts and at least one input cannot be observed by the others, it will encourage the individual agents to withdraw themselves from the joint effort (free-rider behavior). Social norms, peer pressure (Kandel and Lazear 1992; Barron and Gjerde 1997) and dynamics (Radner 1986) contribute to reducing moral hazard. Peer pressure means that the members of the group are afraid of the consequences of breaching the written and unwritten rules laid down by the group as well as violating the social norms, which can be external (sin, guilt) or internal (shame) effects. The "chief" appointed within the group may be able to reduce moral hazard as dynamics is said to dissolve moral hazard (Barron and Gjerde 1997; Radner 1986). In case of repeated "games" over several periods of time (supergame), the group members are able to observe the efforts and actions made by fellow members in the previous period; thus, the information asymmetry may disappear. It should be clear, however, that it only works if real-time information is available. If this is not the case, none of the parties can synchronize their actions with the other party on the basis of information.

Asymmetric information may lead to adverse selection (Akerlof 1970) when one of the parties is unable to recognize an important characteristic of the other party (e.g., preparedness, true intention, honesty). Thus, the former party may fall victim to the misleading and deceptive behavior of the latter party. The issue of social trust can also be explained using the example of the development of autocratic systems. In most of these cases, the intentions of and the expectation connected with the leader—who was elected according to the group norms—are separated. This will destroy public confidence.

Transaction cost theory is important from the aspect of cooperation among economic actors because it is an explanatory model for the development of different structures. The first milestone of the theory is the work of Coase (1937) (The Nature of Firm). In terms of theory development, the work carried out by Coase (1960) and Williamson (1985) was outstanding. The theory examines the efficiency of transactions within a given institutional framework, how the scarce resources are used, how the assets and services are exchanged (production costs), and how the resources (transaction costs) are used for managing and organizing exchanges (Kieser and Ebers 2014). It is based on three behavioral presumptions:

1. *Limited rationality.* Although the transaction partners want to act rationally, they end up with partial success because they have limited information and information-processing ability.
2. *Opportunism.* The participants in the transaction follow their own interests in developing exchanges. They also take the chance that they use tricks, mislead, or withhold information, etc. The consequence of this is that the partners in the transaction face problems (imperfect information and/or opportunism) that reduce their net profit; therefore, they develop different institutional solutions and regulations with different efficiency in order to treat the problems.

3. The actors avoid risks.

Transaction costs occur in connection with market transactions and exchanges. These can be costs related to acquiring information or concluding and monitoring contracts. The size of costs involved in the organization and management of transactions (transaction costs) depend on transaction-specific investments, uncertainty, and frequency (Williamson 1985). Uncertainty may be regarding the outcome of a deal or behavioral uncertainty, which can lead back to opportunistic behavior. The consequence in both cases is that the transaction cost as well as uncertainty is increasing. The costs also depend on the frequency: the more frequent are the deals among partners, the lower are the transaction costs.

By examining the issue of public trust and cooperative behavior starting from the basics of the transaction cost theory, we can conclude that different actors of society try to optimize their own risks as a result of the information asymmetry existing within the society. The rational behavior of individuals is that they do not like to change. They will consider change if the transaction costs related to the maintenance of the current state (e.g., the losses due to the lack of changes) are higher than the costs occurring due to changes and the possible losses due to risks connected with changes—that is, whether the losses due to non-action are higher than the costs of action or not.

Cooperation also involves self-restraint, which means giving up possible benefits. This also belongs to the transaction costs of cooperation. The lack of social trust reduces cooperation willingness and, at the same, increases the social transaction costs. Corruption and tax evasion are typically such phenomena.

12.3   "TIT FOR TAT": STRATEGY REFLECTS EXPERIENCES

Observations made by ethologists regarding different animal groups can help one to understand human behavior and the operation of society, although we would like to believe that these are exclusive characteristics for human beings. Mérő (2017) used analogies to describe that the competitiveness of actors operating in an economic space distorted by influencers (e.g., government) will disappear in a competitive sphere out of this space. He mentioned as an example the experience of the Mowats while researching the behavior of wolves (Mowat 1963). While conducting field observations in the wolves' habitat, the researchers realized that if they urinated around their lodging (similarly to the wolves, who mark with urine the place they regard as their own), then the wolves would stop destroying their tent every night. The animals probably found it reasonable that there was a small area that belonged to the intruding couple, because after that point, the wolves left the researchers alone. The effort of the wolves (producing enough urine for marking the area and then actually marking it) is the price for regarding the area as their own. Evolution has confirmed that it was worth taking these markings seriously and observing them. Thus, private ownership has been developed among wolves.

The conditions, however, may lead to situations that contradict the general evolution experiences. This has been supported by the behavior of wolves living on Isle Royale in Lake Superior (Mech and Cronin 2010). These wolves do not waste their energy on marking their area because there is no need for marking on the island (an isolated environment). The large and less mobile moose have totally displaced the quick reindeers, which live in herds; thus, wolves can easily hunt down their prey. The area has no value for wolves and it is not worth making any effort to own it; however, it also means that wolves have become so lazy that they would not be competitive with other wolves under normal conditions in the struggle for food. Whether we want it or not, the story of wolves has many lessons for understanding the development of social trust. The game theory approach also helps us to understand the impacts of changing factors of the economic environment, explain correlations, and find in-depth arguments for them.

Game theory says that economic processes (and all social interactions) can be explained as a game of two or more players, who make decisions in the game (Kreps 2005). The usual starting point in the explanatory models is that the decision is rational (the player is homo economicus) and an identity can be expected in decisions due to the lack of changes in terms of the condition system. The economic decisions about cooperation are determined on one hand by information asymmetries and on the other hand through experiences. Regarding the latter, the "tit-for-tat" principle prevails (Axelrod 1984), which means that it is more difficult to obtain and retain trust than to lose it.

According to noncooperative game theory, the players make their decisions independently; thus, there is no self-restraint in decision-making and they aim to maximize payoffs. It is not irrelevant in decision-making whether the decision-maker knows the decision of the other player or not.

The so-called normal form, representing the possible alternatives of decisions made by participants, shows the parallel decisions (made without knowing the decision of the other player). The extensive form—as a decision tree—is the graphical depiction of decisions; here, the sequence of decisions can also be seen, which also introduces a cause-and-effect relationship. The normal form is the depiction of the payoff to players in a matrix (P), in the cells of which the due payoff of strategy pairs are listed (see Takács 2012). The rows show the strategies of one player (in our case, A), while the columns show the other player (in our case, B). The result of rational choice is that the player picks the option that offers a more favorable payoff (profit) for them. As a result, there are equilibrium decision pairs called Nash equilibriums. If each player has chosen a strategy and no player can benefit from changing strategies while the other players keep theirs unchanged, then the current set of strategy choices and the corresponding payoffs constitutes a Nash equilibrium. This also means that when one player changes strategy, the other player should review their strategy and modify accordingly. Thus, time has become an important factor (i.e., who goes first), which, in return, leads to decreasing trust.

The researchers of game theory have examined several cases for the development of "games," which may provide the basis for economic modelling. With regard to the topic of the present paper, we considered games for which the following conditions were met: (1) there are two players, (2) each player has two different possible strategies, (3) the players do not have perfect information, and (4) the game is not zero-sum. Several games met these conditions, including Battle of the Sexes, Hawk-Dove, Cul-de-Sac, Prisoner's Dilemma, Deer Hunting, and War of Resources. The trust in the other player determines the performance of individual players in all models, but to a different extent. The concepts of Prisoner's Dilemma and Deer Hunting were used for modelling. The normal form of depicting the two games is the same, but the content of the payoff matrix is significantly different.

The adaptation of game theory models helps to explain the economic brakes of trust development. The model divides the players of the social group into two units; thus, the case can be discussed as if only two players participate. It is obvious, however, that the advantages of one group, which are visible to the other group, encourage those with unfavorable conditions to modify their decisions. If a player moves from one group to the other, the power relations as well as the payoffs for players also change. A detailed description of the model is discussed in detail in Takács (2012).

The main outcomes are introduced by generalizing the model in relation to public trust.

The decision-making problem to be discussed is an actual problem in the rural communities of Central and Eastern European countries: how the state subsidies provided for agricultural enterprises (i.e., intervention by a third party) affect cooperation among business partners (farmers)— that is, how the subsidies may weaken the need for trust. The number of actual participants is significantly higher than two, but in most cases they can be divided into two groups: (1) those owning or investing in machinery and (2) those who have no machinery and do not want to invest in machinery. These groups can be replaced with two players. The payoff for individual players comes from the balance of possible revenues (production, providing services and possible subsidies for the producers) and costs (variable costs of production separating the variable costs of machine use, which is the subject of examination in terms of decision-making; costs of machinery services replacing own machinery; fixed costs of allocating assets [amortization] and opportunity cost of using resources). The different models analyze the impact of third-party interventions on the farmer's decision-making.

The payoffs should be interpreted at the individual player level because the participants make their decisions individually. It is also obvious, however, that if the number of elements of the two groups changes (due to the strategy shift of individuals), the local supply-demand relation is also adjusted. This influences the individual cost elements and the value of yield components of the participants—that is, the payoff of individual participants will be different. The sum of individual payoffs gives the cumulated payoff of the community. The individual aims to maximize his or her payoff (total yield), but it is obvious that the optimum of the community (maximum yield available by the community) is not necessarily at the maximum of the individuals. The possible strategies of players A and B are the following:

- First strategy of player A: Invest and offer services (A1)
- Second strategy of player A: No machinery, no investment, looking for services (A2)
- First strategy of player B: Invest and offer services (B1)
- Second strategy of player B: No machinery, no investment, looking for services (B2)

The payoffs of model variants are summarized in Fig. 12.1. The figure shows the payoffs of the two players for the upper right payoff pairs according to the normal form in relation to the machinery service fees (which are determined by local service market competition). It can be declared that there is no dominant strategy. For most of the games, however, the Nash equilibrium can be recognized (payoff pairs are shown in bold), which indicates cooperation willingness (i.e., the faith of one party that the other will provide services so that he or she does not have to purchase machinery, as well as the willingness of the other party to meet this need with his or her own available machinery). These payoff pairs are Pareto efficient but not fair. The fair strategies (ensuring the same payoff) are not Pareto efficient, except for those cases when the fee of services results in the same payoff for both parties in the given model variant. This can be regarded as the balance price of services because in different situations the participant receiving lower payoff will be urged to change his strategy to increase his income. (This decision-making situation is some-

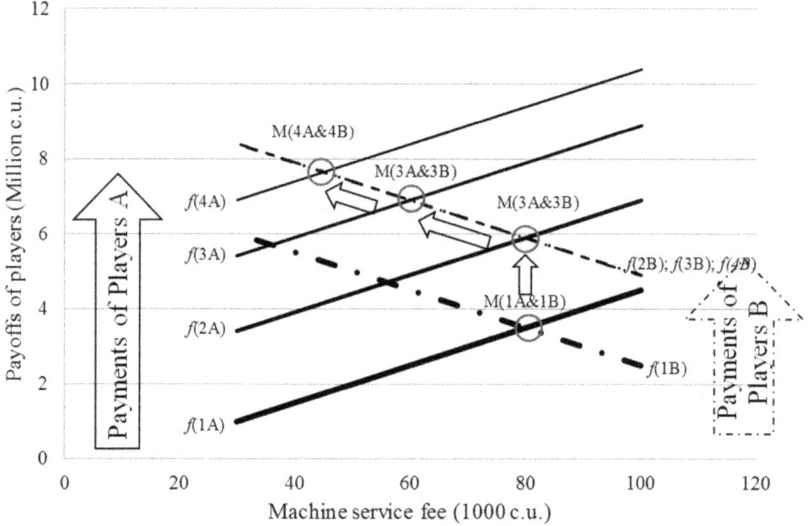

Fig. 12.1 Payoffs of players in relation to the machinery service fees by modelling the impact of subsidies. The strategies of players are as follows: A = invest and offer services; B = no machinery, no investment, needs services (wants to cooperate)

what similar to the problems in the Deer Hunting game.) If the fee of service is the same as its variable cost, it is not worthwhile for the service provider to provide services; however, the person utilizing the service can realize significant (unjustly higher) extra income.

The production and investment subsidies have a considerable impact on the actual payoff and the one perceived "in the heads" of farmers. These will result in lower equilibrium service charges and relatively high income differences next to the actual prices on the services market; therefore, they will encourage those without machinery to invest in it. Suppliers tend to count on used machines with considerable residual value (which, according to our experience, amounts to approximately 30% of the original purchase price); many farmers take this into account when they make investment decisions but do not calculate the time value of money. For this latter situation (decision-making practice), the payoff for those with no machinery can be increased if they invest, which will not encourage cooperation either. According to model calculations for 10-year maturity and based on the current value of payoffs, the above statements do not change significantly whether or not there are interim strategy shifts. The experiences have confirmed that the present value of the payoff pairs moves toward being equitable after the investment decision. However, the joint actual payoff of the two players would decrease compared to the theoretically achievable level.

In summary, the intervention of a third party should reduce the consideration of efficiency criteria (reducing risk awareness). The differences in payoff encourage strategy shifts until the payoffs are levelled. In addition to the relatively small deviation between the yields of the two strategies, the consideration of existing risks and individual benefits also encourage investment—that is, noncooperative behavior (see the dilemma of Deer Hunting, where the decision is a sure rabbit or an uncertain deer). Considering all of the above (supported also with rational arguments), the need for trust decreases due to the intervention of a third party. The producers lose the maximum payoff, which could be realized together with cooperation through more efficient, joint, and coordinated machinery investments and machinery use.

12.4   INFORMATION ASYMMETRIES: GAMES
FOR MAXIMIZING YIELDS

In the decision-making process, all participants make decisions on the basis of their own knowledge. However, risk aversion also affects an individual's decision-making, as well as the influence of the environment on the risk awareness of the individual (whether it weakens or strengthens risk awareness). It is obvious that the existing information asymmetry between individuals has a considerable impact on the strategy chosen. However, the fact that market regularities also prevail in this medium cannot be ignored.

To support these correlations, the model introduced in the previous section can be further developed. One of the key elements of the amended model is that the fee of machinery services—depending on supply and demand—will change according to a hyperbolic equation, which converges to the variable cost of services (a service provision cannot be expected below that level). The other essential criterion is that a player will only change strategy if the difference between payoffs before and after the strategy shift reaches or exceeds the transaction costs of strategy shift as well as the costs of risk connected with no strategy shift (an expected loss if the strategy is not changed).

Regarding cooperation, it is worth examining A1–B2 or A2–B1 strategy pairs, which are mirror images of each other. If all players choose Strategy 1 (i.e., everyone buys their own machinery), then there is no need for cooperation. If all players choose Strategy 2 (i.e., no one buys their own machinery), then there would be no chance to cooperate, even if everyone was willing. The payoffs of the A1–B2 strategy pair are summarized in Fig. 12.2, which shows the average individual payoffs (farm income) of two player groups. On the left side of the curves, when the total available capacity of player A does not cover the total capacity need of player B, then player B suffers losses. There is a substantial difference between the average individual income of player A and player B; the difference can even exceed the transaction costs of a strategy shift, thus encouraging player B to purchase his or her own machinery.

The optimum of the payoffs is at the maximum of the aggregated income of the community. In theory, before the optimum point, player B is in an advantageous position because the fee for using the services is lower than the operation cost of the player's own machinery. As demonstrated previously, the subsidies decrease the impact of market forces (S1,

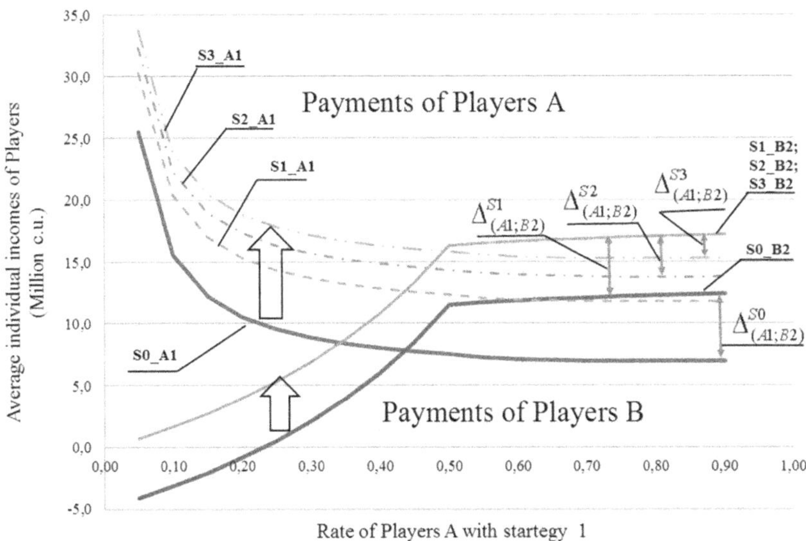

Fig. 12.2 Individual payoffs (income) of players in relation to hired machinery services by modelling the impact of subsidies. The strategies of players are as follows: A = invests and offers services; B = does not have own machinery, demands services (wants to cooperate); Sx = scenario x

S2, and S3 scenarios) because they reduce the average individual (operating) income difference between the alternatives below the transaction costs of a strategy shift. If an increasing number of farmers choose to purchase their own machinery, then the total income and machinery efficiency at the community level will decline; at the same time, it will unnecessarily increase the state support payments.

12.5   Winners and Losers in Noncooperative Behavior

Information asymmetry among economic actors leads to decision risks, which affect the results of the decision-maker. As demonstrated, there are winners and there are losers. The experiences of the individual are built on their behavior and their trust attitudes. The answer for the same question can be different when someone is asked generally versus when they are asked about a particular person. It is a frequent phenomenon that, for example, an individual prefers or rejects a social group but has a totally opposite opinion about a person belonging to that group. The outcomes of examinations regarding the cooperation willingness—which is closely related with trust issues—provide good insight to its operation at the community level.

The correlations between trust and cooperation willingness have been explored by Baranyai and Takács (2010) through personal interviews, questionnaire surveys, and in-depth interviews in South-East Hungary, Southern Great Plain region, Békés County. The research involved private farmers from three statistical micro regions. The sample was selected using the so-called snowball method. The interview subjects were selected randomly from farmers who indicated their willingness to participate. The questions of the in-depth interviews were linked to the questions in the questionnaire in order to control them or describe them in detail.

The data included 132 farms after data cleansing, with 23 in-depth interviews. The following presumptions and criteria were used for the development of the research model, in an analogy to the tank model used in engineering research:

- The selected regions (regarding the topic of examination) form a closed system.
- To examine trust, parties should know each other and the relationship network should be mappable.
- The examined settlements can be regarded as one system in terms of geographical, economic, cultural, and social criteria.

The possible number of elements in the sample is limited on the basis of conditions. Statistically, the sample is representative at the local level, but not at the country or county levels. Therefore, if the presumptions regarding closed systems are confirmed and supported by other research, the outcomes collected from the examined region can be generalized because the region does not show any essential economic-social differences from other key agricultural areas of the country. The data were evaluated using the Sholtes (1998) trust model, which places trust in the matrix of loyalty and capability. At high loyalty and high capability, there is the trust; in another cases, there are sympathy (at high loyalty and low capability), respect (at low loyalty and high capability), and mistrust (at low loyalty and low capability).

Examining trust in a general sense, the respondents had difficulties distinguishing between trust generally in other people and trust particularly in fellow farmers. This can also be explained by their lifestyle because social relations mostly coincide with business relations. Those respondents were typically the heads of smaller farms, where farming was part of their life to a lesser extent. They farmed only to supplement their income and they had full-time jobs in other enterprises, sometimes in other settlements; thus, they have wider social relations. These respondents gave more differentiated answers.

Evaluating the trust in fellow farmers on a scale of 1–7, the result was slightly above the median (3.77 [$s = 2.13$] on average). The responses moved on a wide scale. In all, 20% of respondents did not trust anyone, 20% trusted others at a very low level, 30% had an average trust level, and another 30% indicated a high trust level. Cross-tabulation analyses indicated that only age had a close association with the level of general trust, with younger farmers typically trusting their fellow farmers more than the older generation.

Measurements of trust in loyalty versus capability were also made on a scale of 1–7 by answering several questions (Baranyai 2010). With regard to trust in loyalty, it can be concluded that respondents trusted that their fellow farmers would keep their promises (average: 3.69) a bit more than they trusted that fellow farmers would not be opportunistic in the case of any (positive or negative) changes regarding the conditions of farming (average: 3.47). The difference was significant between the two averages according to paired t-test (or adequate on the basis of the Kolmogorov–Smirnov test).

There were no significant differences between the averages of responses regarding trust in capability. All of the possible responses measuring faith in capability received higher average marks than questions used for measuring loyalty. The level of trust in capability of fellow farmers was proven to be statistically higher in the sample than the trust in loyalty. Although responses given to general trust and loyalty trust were closely correlated, it is interesting that the value of correlation between trust in loyalty and general trust was rather low, which indicates that professional trust has a completely different dimension in the assessment of respondents.

Cross-tabulation analyses showed that the impact of age and income-dependency in relation to loyalty in trust can be regarded as statistically proven. On the basis of regression analysis, the impact of age was slightly stronger according to the beta coefficients. However, age and income dependency were inversely correlated; thus, older respondents were less trusting of the loyalty of fellow farmers and more skeptical regarding the fair behavior of fellow farmers. There was a similar negative tendency in the case of income dependency: farmers with greater income dependency on agricultural activities were more likely to avoid any "vulnerability" (risk) that would endanger their livelihood through trust. In terms of trust in the capability of fellow farmers, only the impact of age was proven to be significant: the higher was the age, the lower was the trust.

12.6   CHAPTER SUMMARY

This chapter discussed the economic aspects of noncooperative behavior of partners in terms of game theory. Trust is a fundamental requirement of collaboration and cooperation among partners. Modern economic theories (i.e., the new institutional theory) and game theory provide new approaches to this issue. In connection with the existing trust level among different partners, the chapter examined the economic and social benefits or losses of participants and which factors affect the individual utility functions, as determined by personal preferences, yields, and social transaction costs.

Because of information asymmetry between participants and a lack of confidence, individual and social expenditures are higher than economically reasonable instead of the optimum. From the aspect of game theory, economic processes can be regarded as a game of two or more players, who make decisions in the game. Explanatory models usually start from the point that the decision is rational (the player is homo economicus); identical decisions can be expected because the condition system remains unchanged. The decision of partners to cooperate is determined by the information asymmetry among them, as well as by the different experiences of the participants. With regard to the principle of the "tit-for-tat" effects acquiring as well as keeping the trust is more difficult as its loss.

The implementation of the normal form of noncooperative game theory was prioritized in the research. According to noncooperative game theory, the players make decisions independently. Thus, there is no self-restraint during decision-making, and everyone aims to maximize their own profits. However, this depends on whether the decision-maker knows the decision of the other player(s). The normal form of noncooperative game theory is appropriate for describing decisions made simultaneously (i.e., without knowing the other player's decision).

REFERENCES

Akerlof, G. (1970). The market for 'lemons': Quality uncertainty and the market mechanism. *Quarterly Journal of Economics, 84*(3), 488–500.

Axelrod, R. (1984). *The evolution of cooperation.* New York: Basic Books.

Baranyai, Z. (2010). *Az együttműködés elméleti és gyakorlati kérdései a magyar mezőgazdasági géphasználatban* (Theoretical and practical questions of cooperation in agricultural machine use in Hungary) (Ph.D. thesis). Gödöllő.

Baranyai, Z., & Takács, I. (2010). Willingness to cooperate among field crop farms: An illustration from Hungary. *Food Economics – Acta Agriculturae Scandinavica Section C Economy, 7*(1), 11–24.

Barron, J., & Gjerde, K. (1997). Peer pressure in an agency relationship. *Journal of Labour Economics, 15*(2), 234–254.

Coase, H. R. (1937). The nature of the firm. *Economica, 4*(16), 386–405.

Coase, H. R. (1960). The problem of social cost. *Journal of Law and Economics, 3*, 1–44.

Dasgupta, P. (1988). Trust as commodity. In D. Gambetta (Ed.), *Trust. Making and breaking cooperative relations* (pp. 49–72). New York: Basil Blackwell.

Fukuyama, F. (1992). *The end of history and the last man.* London: Penguin Books.

Gallo, C. (2016). *The storyteller's secret: From TED-speakers to business legends, why some ideas catch on and others don't.* New York: St. Martin's Press, LLC.

Hallowell, E., & Raley, J. (1994). Driven to distribution: Recognizing and coping with attention deficit disorder from childhood through adulthood (p. 45), New York: Anchor Books, 400 p. In C. Gallo (2016), *The storyteller's secret: From TED-speakers to business legends, why some ideas catch on and others don't.* New York: St. Martin's Press, LLC.

Holmstrom, B. (1982). Moral hazard in teams. *Bell Journal of Economics, 13*(2), 324–340.

Kandel, E., & Lazear, E. P. (1992). Peer pressure and partnerships. *Journal of Political Economy, 100*(41), 801–817.

Kieser, A., & Ebers, M. (2014). *Organisationstheorien* [Organization Theories] (7th Auflage, p. 524). Stuttgart: Kohlhammer.

Klein, B., Crawford, R., & Alchian, A. (1978). Vertical integration, appropriable rents, and the competitive contracting process. *Journal of Law and Economics, 21*(2), 297–326.

Kreps, D. M. (2005). *Game theory and economic modelling (Clarendon Lectures in Economics).* Oxford: Oxford University Press.

Lane, C., & Bachmann, R. (2000). *Trust within and between organizations.* New York: Oxford University Press.

Mech, D., & Cronin, M. A. (2010). Isle Royal study affirms ability of wolves to persist. Letter to the Editor. *Biological Conservation, 143*, 535–536.

Megginson, L. C. (1963). Lessons from Europe for American business. *Southwestern Social Science Quarterly, 44*(1), 3–13.

Mérő, L. (2017). *Aminek nincs ára* [Of which has not price]. *HVG.* 16.04.2017.

Mowat, F. (1963). *Never cry wolf.* Toronto: McClelland and Stewart.

Radner, R. (1986). Repeated partnership games with imperfect monitoring and no discounting. *The Review of Economic Studies, 60,* 599–611.

Rousseau, D. M., Sitkin, R. S., Burt, C. B., & Camerar, C. (1998). Not so different after all: A cross-discipline view of trust. *Academy of Management Review, 23*(3), 393–404.

Royer, S. J. (1999). Cooperative organizational strategies: A neo-institutional digest. *Journal of Cooperatives, 14,* 44–67.

Schumacher, E. F. (1973). *Small is beautiful – Economics as if people mattered.* London: Blond & Briggs.

Sholtes, P. R. (1998). *The leader's handbook: Making things happen – Getting things done.* New York: McGraw-Hill.

Takács, I. (2012). Games of farmers – To cooperate or not? *Annals of the Polish Association of Agricultural and Agribusiness Economists, 14*(6), 260–266.

Williamson, O. E. (1985). *The economic institutions of capitalism.* New York: The Free Press.

CHAPTER 13

Trust in an Integrated Territorial Investment

Agnieszka Chrisidu-Budnik

13.1 Introduction

Other than satisfying the collective needs of citizens by providing them with various public goods, the objective of territorial self-government is to strengthen the potential of a specific social system by creating social capital—the core component of which is trust (Coffé and Geys 2005; Warner 2001; Wallis and Dollery 2002; Morphet 2008). The contemporary concept of trust, just like the Weber model of management, is an implication of the industrial revolution. Until the end of the 1990s, trust was seen as the basis of interorganizational cooperation and a source of eliminating conflicts in the course of any cooperation between specific entities.[1] However, no detailed analyses of the category of trust itself, its nature, or its basis have been conducted.

As late as 1979, Niklas Luhmann, a German legal sociologist and pioneer of research on the significance of trust, wrote that there was a relatively small number of scientific publications that considered trust as their main topic (Luhmann 1979: 8). Paradoxically, the process of globalization, which helped to intensify the relations between different types of organizations and their mutual interdependence—as well as the digital revolution, which furthered these relations and interdependencies—led to the temporary

A. Chrisidu-Budnik (✉)
University of Wroclaw, Wroclaw, Poland

B. Kożuch et al. (eds.), *Managing Public Trust*,
https://doi.org/10.1007/978-3-319-70485-2_13

marginalization of the significance of trust; it was acknowledged that technology is able to replace trust. However, when the processes of globalization and digitization started to become superimposed on each other, with specific political processes leading to the diffusion of public authority and consequently the crystallization of the perspective of a network state, trust was again considered to be an important mechanism of collaboration. This is because technology is not a sufficient substitute for trust, which is necessary for building effective mechanisms of shared management. The processes of searching for a dynamic balance between centralization and decentralization, which can be interpreted as a move away from government toward shared management or governance, have now started to be noticed in the literature (Marinetto 2003).

13.2   CONTRACTUALISM: THE HEART OF THE NETWORK STATE

The paradox of simultaneous centralization and decentralization has become a catalyst of the constitution of interorganizational connections, which increasingly frequently constitute an instrument for implementing political decisions and a mechanism for fulfilling public tasks. Networks have been defined as "fixed models of social relations between interrelated actors, formed around political issues and programmes" (Kickert et al. 1999). A network state is therefore created by relatively stable nonhierarchical relationships connecting entities/actors of different origins that have common objectives; to achieve these objectives, they activate the transfer of multiple resources between themselves.

The outlook for a network state as a formal determination of thinking includes the notion of governance, which reflects the mechanisms making public decisions that take into account the complexity, diversity, and internal conflict propensity of the social world, the interdependence of public and non-public entities appearing in it (which are involved in a variety of network systems), and the need to coordinate a higher level (metagovernance) that requires not a monocentric center of authority and hierarchy but a heterarchy. A network state is made up of relatively autonomous pluralist social systems, the existence of which is a consequence of the said process of diffusion of authority. Authority has been concentrated to date in hierarchical structures spread out in four independent directions, toward supranational organizations, territorial self-governments, independent transnational structures, and a self-organizing local community.

The diffusion of authority has resulted in the redefinition of bases of thought about the organizational structure. In addition to the hierarchical structure, which is typical of the industrial epoch (the exemplification of which was the Weber model of bureaucracy as a model of development), one can observe adaptation and performance in the postindustrial age, the tendency to form horizontal structures based on collaboration, joint decision making, and joint creation. Contemporary global civilization challenges the interdependence of phenomena, the rate of change, uncertainty, and risk, which generate comprehensive and excessively complicated challenges for exclusively hierarchical structures to satisfy. The imperative of responding to these challenges through the creation of specific solutions requires the acceptance of new forms of coordination of collective efforts, which adopt the form of networks that I shall hereinafter refer to as *collaborative systems*.

The joint appearance of a hierarchy (vertical structure: the form of a pyramid) and heterarchy (a horizontal structure: the form of a matrix) is visible within the organizational structure.[2] The heterarchy undermines the dichotomous breakdown into autonomous agendas of reality: the public sector (the state) and the private sector (the market) (Di Maggio 2001: 75; Jessop 2002). In this sense, the heterarchical structure, as an endemic feature of the digital revolution, is an alternative to the Weber model of perfect bureaucracy assuming that public and private interests are completely separate. The consequences of this are important.

At the theoretical level, there cannot be talk of the existence of an autonomous hierarchical structure (e.g., organizing the performance of public services directly), which constitutes a foundation and the definitive source of legitimacy of actions. In a heterarchical structure, public services are provided in cooperation with independent institutions, fully market entities, municipal companies, public-benefit organizations, nongovernmental organizations, and specialized public institutions. At the same time, the dynamics of a state are determined within the heterarchy by a never-ending social process of coordination between various entities. Therefore, the social order from the point of view of a network state consists of the sum of the relationships. Coordination is not based on hierarchical links but on horizontal links, the foundation of which is the interdependence of the interests and objectives of entities constituting the network structures.[3]

A network state is based on contractualization processes that reflect the demonopolization of public institutions and the transfer of some of their tasks to nongovernmental organizations or private entities, with which contracts are signed for the performance of specific tasks. The range of areas in which the administration works with entities, thereby holding the role of a partner, is increasing. The phenomenon of the involvement of the administration in contractual relations means a significant increase in the application of the contract as a tool of operation of public administration; this is called *contractualism*. Contractual forms of fulfilment of public tasks include both civil law contracts and public law contracts, primarily administrative contracts.

Apart from the matter of what trust is, it should be emphasized at this point that the functions of trust in a network state appear in terms of the coordinates of a catalyst and stabilizer of the collaboration. The function of the catalyst referred to here arises from the following two facts: (1) the presence of the relationship of trust between the parties to the cooperation facilitate its activation, which applies to *ex ante* trust; and (2) the development of a relationship of trust between the parties to the cooperation over its duration increases the effectiveness of its operations, which applies to *in tractu* trust. The function of the stabilizer determines the consistency and durability of the cooperation. In hierarchical structures, a stabilizer of cooperation understood in this way is located at the peak of the pyramid; in heterarchical structures, it does not have a specific location but remains "fuzzy." Trust as a stabilizer of cooperation blocks its participants so that, even if specific centrifugal trends appear, the cooperation is not subject to the process of destruction.

13.3   Nature of Trust

Contemporary trust is a subject of interest to many scientific disciplines: sociology, economics, psychology, and management sciences, to name just a few. The interdisciplinarity of the category of "trust" enhances its structure, but makes consensus to find its essence and nature difficult (Rousseau et al. 1995). Therefore, a summary definition of the relationship of trust is extremely difficult because of the ambiguity of the term itself and the variety of methods used in contemporary science to study its mechanisms. This interdisciplinarity of the category of "trust" means that it is an area of reality of interest fulfilled by various disciplines of science, which study the various aspects of the same phenomenon. Of course, this interest, despite being common, is of a different nature in the case of the science of administration and different in the case of, for instance, psychology and sociology. The science of administration itself does not study the process of trust, but is interested in the results of studies on it obtained by psychology and sociology.

It would be difficult to discuss the current status of research on trust in the individual scientific disciplines in one chapter; thus, relying on a review of the literature, I am limiting myself to the observation that there is no single commonly accepted definition of trust. There is a narrower or wider description of this phenomenon, but it can be separated into two elements constituting a *sine qua non* condition for the emergence of a relationship of trust.

The first element is the risk constituting the probability of a loss perceived and estimated by the decision-maker, which may (but does not need to) become reality (Chiles and McMackin 1996; MacCrimmon and Wehrung 1986). Risk is often described with the use of the term "probability"—namely, such a threat that the probability of its appearance is greater than zero and less than one.

The significance of risk in a relationship of trust was especially highlighted by the Nobel Prize winner in economics, Olivier Williamson. Williamson claimed that a relationship of trust is based on a calculation; therefore, the relationship based on the calculation should be described in the language of the calculation for which the term *risk* is most appropriate (Williamson 1996). There is feedback between risk and trust; risk creates opportunities for demonstrating trust, which could lead to decision-making that is subject to a specified degree of risk. At the same time, it should be noted that risk can strengthen confidence when the behavior expected of the partner becomes reality.

Risk, as an element of trust, is present in Bachmann and Inkpen's definitions, which state that trust is a decision-making process—that is, the decision of one party to rely on another party under conditions of risk. The trustor permits his or her fate to be determined by the trustee and risks that he or she will experience negative outcomes if the trustee proves untrustworthy (2011). Currall and Judge interpreted trust as the behavioral reliance on another person under a condition of risk (Currall and Judge 1995). Coleman identified trust with the situation in which the risk one takes depends on the performance by another actor (Coleman 1990).

The second element is interdependence. The participants of specific structures are mutually dependent on each other through common objectives. Interdependence exists if specified structures have to affect each other so that the change in the condition of one structure implies a change in the condition of another structure. In 1949, in his theory of social interdependence, the U.S. social psychologist Morton Deutsch isolated two types of interdependence: (1) positive interdependence, the manifestation of which is cooperation and collaboration; and (2) negative interdependence, the manifestation of which is rivalry and competition (Deutsch 1949). A third type of interdependence is noticed today, which is characterized by the simultaneous appearance of cooperation and competition between the same entities. This type of interdependence is called coopetition.

It appears that, in the political science created by Russell Hardin, the concept of encapsulated interest is close to Morton Deutsch's theory of interdependence. According to Hardin, trust is a manifestation of encapsulated interest and is based on the fact that the addressee of the trust has an interest in maintaining positive relations with the entity offering the trust; this interest is an incentive for the person to be a trustworthy entity to be accepted and to satisfy the expectations of the trusting entity (Hardin 2002). The degree of interdependence of the parties to the cooperation forces them to "manifest" attitudes of trust.

A review of literature enables the isolation of concepts highlighting the element of interdependence, other than Hardin's. According to Hosmer, trust is the expectation by one (entity) of ethically justifiable behavior (i.e., morally correct decisions and actions based on ethical principles of analysis) on the part of another (entity) in a joint endeavor or economic exchange (Hosmer 1995). According to Zaheer, trust is the expectation that an actor (1) can be relied on to fulfill obligations, (2) will behave in a predictable manner, and (3) will act and negotiate fairly when the possibility for opportunism is present (Zaheer et al. 1998). Klijn defined trust as a stable positive expectation by A of B's intentions and the motive for refraining from opportunistic behavior, even if the opportunity arises. Trust is based on the expectation that A will take B's interests into account (Klijn et al. 2010).

13.4   Relational Contracts in Public Administration

In the context of heterarchy, the issue of coordination is important—namely its ability to exercise control over the course of events, the synchronization of actions of entities involved in the processes of fulfilling public tasks. The logic of the functioning of hierarchical structures primarily rests with formal governance. In heterarchical structures, coordination is based to a greater extent on relational governance. The basis for developing relational governance was the theory of the American lawyer Ian Macneil, with regard to relational contracts. Relational contracts are defined as relations based on personal trust, namely those in which the choice of the partner to the cooperation takes place as a result of the individual relationship of trust that is binding on him, or when this relationship arose during the lasting contractual relationship.

The theory of relational contracts started to be used in the 1990s in administrative sciences to explain the mechanisms of contracting for the performance of public tasks. Initially, it was positioned at the opposite end to the formalized and detailed contracts, which are typical of new public management. There is currently a move away from the dichotomous division, positioning the above two coordination mechanisms at two basic interrelated levels: institutional and behavioral. The former refers to the specificities of the provision of specific public services, whereas the latter focuses on the nature of the interactions with other entities. The acceptance of the coexistence of two levels—institutional and behavioral—has become an analytical framework through which hybrid governance is identified.

13.5   Integrated Territorial Investment

The structure of the network state described above, as well as the relational contracts, appears in the so-called Implementation Act on the principles of implementing financial cohesion policy programs in the 2014–2020 financial perspective.[4] Article 30, para. 1 of the Act applying Regulation (EU) No. 1303/2013 of the European Parliament and of the Council of 17 December 2013 (Article 36) has introduced integrated territorial investments, which constitute a new instrument of territorial development. In turn, the National Spatial Management Concept 2030,[5] as a political act of a forward-looking nature rationalizing the intentions of the lawmakers,[6] has established a so-called functional area—an encapsulated spatial system consisting of functionally-related lands with common and uniform development objectives.

Integrated territorial investments are both a qualitatively new instrument and a model of cooperation between territorial self-government entities. The use of the term "instrument" is related to the creation of joint integrated projects for comprehensively solving the problems of specific city and territorial self-governments that are affected by it—namely the said functional areas. The use of the notion of a "model" highlights the need for cooperation of self-governments which, together with the voivodship authorities, identify the objectives to be achieved and designate the investments, the fulfillment of which enables the achievement of the previously identified needs.

The issue of integrated territorial investments is already relatively well described in the literature on the subject. Thus, in this paper, I am limiting myself to just the context of trust, which I believe enables the identification of those observations that enhance the characteristics of such a network partnership. Integrated territorial investments force the self-government authorities to change their existing views on development management. This model of cooperation prevents the enclosure of individual self-government units within their structures; quite the opposite, it not only motivates but obligates them to cooperate.[7] To benefit from this instrument, the self-government authorities are forced to relate to the socioeconomic reality (functional area) *in toto* and not through structures exposing their particular interests and often ambitions. At the same time, in promoting the development of joint territorial projects that are to receive co-funding from the EU budget for 2014–2020, this model counters their fragmentation and dispersion—that is, the multidimensional process of breaking down investments into a number of autonomous sections within individual self-government structures.

Therefore, in the process of implementing integrated territorial investments, hybrid coordination mechanisms are of fundamental significance. They contain the said two functions of trust: a catalyst and a cooperation stabilizer. An important context of trust is the need to institutionalize partnerships—that is, to formalize the cooperation of territorial self-government bodies used to implement joint actions within integrated territorial investments. There are two aspects to the institutionalization of cooperation. The first is related to the need to establish an institutionalized form of partnership—a so-called union of integrated territorial investments. The second, which is related to the first and constitutes its derivative, is the institutionalized obligation to generate a coordinated strategy to obtain greater overall benefits and reduce overall losses. The institutionalization of these two aspects constitutes an incentive for self-governments to jointly identify and analyze needs and investments, which will imply greater effects than the sum of the individual actions within specific territorial self-government units. The foundations of the coordination in the integrated territorial investments are not hierarchical ties; rather, the structural framework of the model of cooperation forms horizontal ties.

The functions of trust in integrated territorial investments must be seen in the context of commitment. Commitment is a positive attitude to collaboration, as well as the readiness to make efforts to achieve the objectives of a collaboration with partners (Numemela 2003). Commitment reduces the said risk and is reflected in the quality of communication between the partners, which is directly related to sharing information and ideas. This translates into the efficiency of the cooperation—effectiveness, benefit, and economy. The literature mentions various bases of commitment that are also described as sources of trust. Four bases of commitment are of fundamental importance in integrated territorial investments:

1. Contractual commitment: The basis is a contract, which is treated as a social institution under which the parties undertake to be truthful and kind and to comply with obligations.
2. Identification: The basis is shared values, objectives, tasks, and conditions of cooperation.
3. Relational: The basis is the quality of previous relationships between territorial self-government units, enabling conclusions to be drawn about the future conduct of the other party to the collaboration.
4. Institutional: The bases are the legal regulations and institutions serving to protect trust.

In Poland, the observation of the practices of institutionalizing partnerships for implementing integrated territorial investments justifies the observation that that it has not progressed without problems. The barriers to formalizing cooperation primarily appeared in polycentric functional areas dominated by at least two large cities that aspire to perform the functions of the leader in integrated territorial investments. The excessively highly intensive competition between them means that, acting independently, they often duplicate the functions and investments, while being unable to develop a coordinated strategy within the framework of the coopetition. Difficulties in institutionalizing the partnership and, therefore, a lack of strategy synchronizing the priorities of the partners in time and space are the results of a deficit of commitment in specific territorial self-government units. In the polycentric functional areas, the barrier to the establishment of a partnership was primarily the lack of commitment based on identification.

The element encouraging the institutionalization of the cooperation is the interdependence between the partners to the cooperation. According to Deutsch, interdependence is the central component of cooperation; it makes the results or the extent to which the objectives of one party to the cooperation are achieved dependent on the other. In this sense, interdependence leads to the elimination of risk and the intensification of the positive perception of the common interest and/or benefits of the given relationship (Gulati 1995).

13.6   Chapter Summary

Public administration was never an autarchic structure; it was forced to collaborate with various entities to efficiently achieve its objectives. Cooperation is currently largely based on relational contracts. Cooperation is implemented by both public international entities, as well as central and territorial self-government administrations. Integrated self-government investments are an example of horizontal cooperation between territorial self-government units. Cooperation relationships are a much broader category than relationships based on trust. Trust is one of the foundations for taking up cooperation.

In integrated territorial investments, trust makes the establishment of cooperation easier and reduces transaction costs accompanying the conclusion of every agreement (trust as a catalyst of the cooperation). The party to the cooperation that trusts believes that the partner in the cooperation will not behave opportunistically; therefore, acting on the basis of trust, it can reduce transaction costs, even though trust does not eliminate the risk associated with the cooperation.

However, it is important to emphasize that, when the degree of trust between the participants is low or there is no trust between them, the cooperation operates as a result of the legal regulations, the institutions that they serve to protect, and the enforcement of the law (institutional commitment). In integrated territorial investments, trust has a role that is similar to the law because it satisfies the need for certainty, predictability, and order. Trust and the legal system can therefore be seen as two mechanisms encouraging cooperation.

The function of trust as a stabilizer of the cooperation should be viewed in two contexts: resource and social. The resource context of trust applies to tangible and intangible resources (trust), which economically and organizationally bond integrated territorial investments. It is worth mentioning that the structural context of trust is an important component of a network state and the hybrid mechanisms of coordination because it is related to the elimination of barriers to cooperation, the effective performance of contracts, and the exchange of an economic and extra-economic nature with the partners to the cooperation. The social context of trust is applied to the positioning of social relationships that take place in the integrated territorial investments—that is, reliance on interpersonal bonds. The effectiveness of the collaboration within integrated territorial investments is determined not only by interdependence, but also by the social structure of earlier interpersonal relations, from which territorial self-government units obtain information about the predictability of their partners.

Notes

1. Attention should be drawn to two complementary lines of research that shaped the modern paradigm of trust in the phase of the industrial revolution. The first became pronounced in the area of economic sciences, which Olivier Williamson called transaction cost theory (Williamson 1991). The second line, which arose in the area of legal science, is S. Macaulay's and I. Macneil's relational contract theory (Macaulay 1985; Macneil 1978).
2. The term "heterarchy" was introduced into science in the mid-1940s by the American cyberneticist and neuropsychologist, W. S. McCulloch (McCulloch 1945). The exemplification of a heterarchy—elements of an equivalent position in and, similarly, the potential of the impact that can constitute a component part of a hierarchical system or form a separate structure—in the 1950s became an array structure, which broke away from the Fayol principles of unity of management and unity of giving orders. However, by the 1980s, this term had been forgotten and rediscovered by management science and political science. J. Ogilvy referred to heterarchies as noncentralized and distributed centers of authority (Ogilvy 1977; Ogilvy 2002).
3. I am deliberately not discussing the imperfections of a heterarchy here. However, it should be noted that "network structures are—in fact—flexible, but may be too comprehensive to respond quickly to new challenges. Furthermore, responsibility is inevitably "diluted" in such structures. New bodies of authority can also develop in them with insufficient legitimacy" (W. Hoffmann-Riem 1999: 379).
4. The Act on rules the principles of implementing programmes regarding the financial cohesion policy in the 2014–2020 financial perspective (Journal of Laws of 2014, item 1146).
5. Resolution No. 239 of the Council of Ministers of 13 December 2011 on the adoption of the National Spatial Management Concept 2013 (M.P. 2012 item 252).

6. Article 47, para. 3 of the Act on spatial planning and development of 27 March 2003 (Journal of Laws of 2003, item 778).
7. Therefore, cooperation of territorial self-government bodies is *a sine qua non* condition for gaining access to hybrid financing, both from the European Regional Development Fund and European Social Fund. In Poland, the integrated territorial investments instrument is necessarily implemented in voivodship cities and areas that are functionally related to them (it may optionally be implemented in other towns and cities and areas functionally related to them). Funds for integrated territorial investments are available under the regional operational programs and the so-called program reserve and can, for example, be used to develop sustainable transport connecting the city with its functional area, promote energy efficiency, revitalize functional areas of cities, strengthen innovation and technological development, and/or improve nature and/or the environment of the functional area.

REFERENCES

Bachmann, R., & Inkpen, A. (2011). Understanding institutional – Based trust bilding process in interorganizational relationships. *Organization Studies, 32*(2), 281–301.

Chiles, T. H., & McMackin, J. F. (1996). Integrating variable risk preferences, trust, and transaction cost economics. *Academy of Management Review, 21*(1), 73–99.

Coffé, B., & Geys, B. (2005). Performance and social capital: An application to the local government level. *Journal of Urban Affairs, 27*(5), 485–501.

Coleman, J. (1990). *Foundations of social theory*. Cambridge: Harvard University Press.

Currall, S. C., & Judge, T. A. (1995). Measuring trust between organizational boundary role persons. *Organizational Behavior and Human Decision Processes, 64*(2), 151–170.

Deutsch, M. (1949). A theory of cooperation and competition. *Human Relations, 2*(2), 129–152.

Di Maggio, E. (2001). Conclusion: The futures of business organization and Paradoxes of change. In E. Di Maggio (Ed.), *The twenty-first-century firm: Changing economic organization in international perspective* (pp. 210–244). Princeton/Oxford: Princeton University Press.

Gulati, R. (1995). Social structure and alliance formation patterns: A longitudinal analysis. *Administrative Science Quarterly, 40*(4), 619–652.

Hardin, R. (2002). *Trust and trustworthiness*. New York: Russell Sage Foundations.

Hoffmann-Riem, W. (1999). *Strukturen des Europäischen Verwaltungsrechts – Perspektiven der Systembildung* [Structures of european administrative law – Perspectives of systemic formation]. In E. Schmidt-Assmann &

W. Hoffmann-Riem (Eds.), *Strukturen des Europàischen Verwaltungsrechts*. Baden-Baden: Nomos.

Hosmer, L. T. (1995). Thrust: The connecting link between organizational theory and philosophical ethics. *Academy of Management Review, 20*(2), 379–403.

Jessop, B. (2002). *The future of the capitalist state*. Cambridge: Polity Press.

Kickert, W. J., Klijn, E. H., & Koppenjan, J. F. M. (1999). *Managing complex networks. Strategies for the public sector*. London: Sage Publications.

Klijn, E. H., Edelenbos, J., & Steijn, B. (2010). Trust in governance networks: Its impacts on outcomes. *Administration and Society, 42*(2), 193–221.

Luhmann, N. (1979). *Trust and power*. Chichester: Wiley.

Macauly, S. (1985). *An empirical view of contract. Wisconsin Law Review, 465,* 465–482.

MacCrimmon, K. R., & Wehrung, D. A. (1986). *Taking risks: The management of uncertainty*. New York: Free Press.

Macneil, I. R. (1978). Contracts: Adjustment of long-term economic relations under classical, neoclassical, and relational contract law. *Northwestern University Law Review, 72*(6), 854–905.

Marinetto, M. (2003). Governing beyond the centre: A critique of the anglo-governance school. *Political Studies, 51*(3), 592–608.

McCulloch, W. S. (1945). A heterarchy of values determined by the typology of nervous nets. *The Bulletin of Mathematical Biophysics, 7*(2), 89–93.

Morphet, J. (2008). *Modern local government*. London: Sage Publication.

Nummela, N. (2003). Looking through a prism-multiple perspectives to commitment to international R&D collaboration. *The Journal of High Technology Management Research, 14*(1), 137–138.

Ogilvy, J. (1977). *Many dimensional man: Decentralizing self, society, and the sacred*. New York: Oxford University Press.

Ogilvy, J. (2002). *Creating better futures: Scenario planning as a tool for a better tomorrow*. New York: Oxford University Press.

Rousseau, D. M., Sitkin, S. B., Burt, R. S., & Camerer, C. (1995). Not so different after all: A cross-discipline view of trust. *Academy of Management Review, 23*(3), 393–404.

Wallis, J., & Dollery, B. (2002). Social capital and local government capacity. *Australian Journal of Public Administration, 61*(3), 76–85.

Warner, M. (2001). Building social capital: The role of government. *The Journal of Socio-Economics, 30,* 187–192.

Williamson, O. E. (1991). Comparative economic organization: The analysis of discrete structural alternatives. *Administrative Science Quarterly, 36*(2), 269–296.

Williamson, O. E. (1996). *The mechanism of governance*. New York/Oxford: Oxford University Press.

Zaheer, A., McEvily, B., & Peronne, V. (1998). Does trust matter? Exploring the effects of interorganizational and interpersonal trust on performance. *Organization Science, 9*(2), 141–159.

PART V

Public Trust in Different Countries

CHAPTER 14

Managing Public Trust in Turkey

Fatih Çetin and Özge Demiral

14.1   Introduction

Global trust literature suggests that trust is closely associated with national cultures and work values. Also, antecedents and consequences of trust vary across cultures. Trust studies on Turkey link trust and trustworthiness to the Turkish culture by integrating cultural values into work values in organizational relationships. Beginning with these premises, we discuss trust, trust-culture linkages, and trust management in Turkey by focusing on Turkish public and business organizations.

The next Sect. 14.2 explains the meaning(s) of trust in Turkish culture from a multidimensional approach. Section 14.3 presents the literature review on trust and trust management scholarship at both the organizational and multinational level. Section 14.4 demonstrates public trust in institutions, business, chief executive officers (CEOs), system, national governments and public services provided by governmental institutions comparing Turkey to other cultures. Section 14.5 discusses the key characteristics of trustworthiness behaviors in Turkey. Lastly, this chapter finishes with concluding remarks in Sect. 14.6.

F. Çetin (✉) • Ö. Demiral
Niğde Ömer Halisdemir University, Niğde, Turkey

   225
B. Kożuch et al. (eds.), *Managing Public Trust*,
https://doi.org/10.1007/978-3-319-70485-2_14

14.2   The Meanings of Trust in Turkish Culture

Culture consists of the reciprocal interactions orchestrated by societal rules. It is a kind of collective mind programming that distinguishes members of one group from another (Hofstede et al. 2010). A variety of dynamic factors, including culture, affect trust. The Organization for Economic Cooperation and Development (OECD 2016) defines a cohesive society as one where citizens mutually trust each other and public institutions. In this definition, trust is a key indicator of social cohesion. Based on the question "Generally speaking, would you say that most people can be trusted or that you need to be very careful in dealing with people?" Figure 14.1 shows that 36% of all interviewees thought most people can be trusted. In Nordic countries, over 60% of interviewees trust each other while only 13% trust each other in Chile, Mexico, and Turkey. Among the non-OECD countries, levels of trust were usually lower than OECD countries, with Colombia having the lowest share of trusting citizens. In Turkey, the share of total people reporting trust in others was less than 13%, a third of the average in OECD countries. Young people between 15 and 29 years old were roughly 15% in Turkey, and 35% for the OECD.

Multinational differences in interpersonal trust have spurred researchers to study trust as a multidimensional and multi-disciplinary phenomenon. Determining how countries differ culturally and how these differences impact business relationships takes prominent interest in international business and management literature

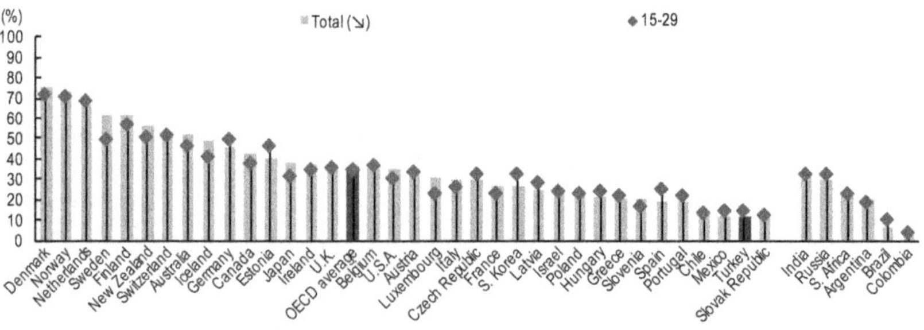

Fig. 14.1 Percentage of people reporting trust in others, 2014 (Source: OECD's (2016) presentations on the World Value Surveys and European Values Survey)

Concerning cross-cultural differences, Hofstede's (1980, 2001) leading works on culture classify cultural dimensions as "power distance", "individualism", "masculinity", "femininity", and "uncertainty avoidance". Power distance is the degree to which less powerful members of a society assume that power is not equally dispersed in society. Individualism is a preference for a loose bond with society in which members are expected to take care of themselves. Collectivism is the opposite of the individualism, in that it is the preference for a tight bond with society in which individuals take care of other members of society in exchange for unquestioning loyalty. Masculinity implies a preference for achievement, assertiveness, and material rewards for success. Femininity, however, values cooperation, caring for the weak, and quality of life. Uncertainty avoidance is the degree to which members of a society feel discomfort with indefinite situations. In Hofstede's (1980, 2001) studies on the values of people in 50 countries, Turkish culture was high in power distance, collectivism, femininity, and uncertainty avoidance.

From the values perspective, some studies showed how cultural values shape trust relationships. A study indicated that trustworthiness in Turkish culture depends on the quality of the relationship between individuals and the feeling of being valued by others (Wasti and Tan 2010). A cross-cultural study proposed the significance of benevolence in Turkish trust-building (Mayer et al. 1995). The antecedents of benevolence are intimacy, unselfish behavior, personalized generosity, and protection in supervisor, peer, and subordinate relationships. Intimacy involves displaying affectionate closeness in a relationship. Unselfish behavior means showing more concern for others than for oneself, even at the expense of one's own needs or wishes. Personalized generosity is the quality of being kind to others, or a willingness to give valuable things to others. Lastly, protection involves protecting the interests of others. The results showed the influence of collectivistic values on trust relationships in Turkish culture.

Paternalism as a kind of leadership style also explains the meaning of interpersonal trust in Turkish culture (Aycan et al. 2000). Paternalism is a supervisor-subordinate relationship where supervisors play the role of a father to provide support and protection for those under their responsibility (Aycan and Kanungo 1998). Paternal supervisors are concerned with the private problems of subordinates, make initiative-based decisions for subordinates if necessary, and create a family-like climate. In conjunction with the paternalistic role of supervisors, subordinates show deep loyalty, trust, and respect to them in return for their care and protection. Interpersonal trust between supervisors and subordinates develops similarly to father-child relationships in Turkish culture.

14.3   Studies on Trust and Trust Management in Turkey

Trust studies on Turkish culture address trust and trust management at the organizational and national levels. At the organizational level, the studies focused on interpersonal trust with using samples of leaders, negotiators, coworkers, doctors, teachers, students, employees, employers or entrepreneurs. National level the studies were relatively limited, and dealt with cultural differences in trust between societies.

14.3.1   Organizational-Level Studies

Organizational trust literature on Turkey confirms that trust is a multidisciplinary and multidimensional subject. Almost every study used a survey methodology with a cross-sectional design. The most influential studies explored the relationships between organizational trust and psychological empowerment (Ergeneli et al. 2007; Ertürk 2009), organizational deviance (Demir 2011), organizational commitment (Tezergil et al. 2014; Akgündüz and Güzel 2014; Top et al. 2015), organizational citizenship behaviors (Yıldız 2015), organizational identification (Ertürk 2009), organizational silence (Okur 2016), perceived organizational support (Ertürk 2009; Sezgin 2015), job satisfaction (Tezergil et al. 2014; Top et al. 2015), entrepreneurial behaviors (Sezgin 2015), mobbing (Baş 2011; Ertürk 2016), and organizational performance (Erdem 2003). The results showed that most of these relationships were mutual with a two-way causality. These complex relationships led some researchers to examine possible mediating effects of organizational trust (Akgündüz and Güzel 2014; Yıldız 2015; Sezgin 2015; Karapınar et al. 2016).

Beyond intra-organizational relationships, some studies highlighted the importance of inter-organizational trust when businesses from different industries are linked through buyer-supplier relationships (Oba and Semerciöz 2005; Eser 2012). In those circumstances, informal institutional arrangements, cooperation and satisfaction, and the duration of the relationship were the main factors for building trust in Turkish culture.

14.3.2   Cross-Cultural Approach: Country-Level and Regional Studies

A limited number of qualitative and quantitative studies adopted a cross-cultural approach to examine trust in Turkey. Some of the results indicated the antecedents of trust and the attitudes and perceptions of trust were culturally different (Wasti et al. 2011; Semercioz et al. 2011; Kale 2013; Chien et al. 2016), and go beyond the business relationship domain (Wasti et al. 2011).

Integrating cultural dimensions into inter-organizational buyer-supplier relationships, Wasti and Wasti (2009) proposed a detailed trust model to identify the antecedents of trust in Turkish culture. They found it was not the duration of relationship, but consistent, positive behaviors between suppliers and buyers that affected inter-organizational trust. They also found the greater the support from a powerful party (the buyer), particularly in the early stages of the relationship, the higher the trust developed in the relationship. The continuity of the relationship had a stronger positive effect on inter-organizational trust. Communication content that allows partners to know each other promotes inter-organizational trust. Lastly, reciprocal stock ownership was not associated with interorganizational trust in the Turkish culture. Consequently, they suggested that at the organizational level, dependency on manufacturer purchases, the degree of dependence on the buyer's technological or financial support, the existence of foreign partnerships, and the duration of supplier operation matter in supplier-buyer relationships in Turkey.

Other cross-cultural studies focused on the cultural differences in adaptation of trust scales. Wasti et al. (2007) proposed that respondents from collectivist and high power distance cultures can misinterpret some items of the trust scales which are originally developed individualistic and low power distance cultures. This ambiguity emphasizes possible biases while adopting trust scales from dissimilar cultures. However, several institutions provide interculturally harmonized and comparable data, which the next section uses to compare Turkey's public trust indicators with those of other countries.

14.4   Public Trust in Turkey: Multinational Comparisons

Given the rapid increase in political, social, and economic globalization, worldwide trust trends will doubtlessly affect local tendencies. Based on its recent global surveys, the Edelman Trust Barometer (2017) reveals that trust is in crisis around the world that people's trust in businesses, government institutions, non-governmental organizations, and media has declined significantly. As general trust indices of the Edelman Group illustrate (Fig. 14.2), the percentage share of the total population declaring trust in their institutions (government, business, media and non-governmental organizations) is higher than 50% in only 8 of 28 countries. This indicates that on average, people distrust their institutions in 20 countries, including Poland, Brazil, and Turkey.

The important aspect of trust is people's confidence in their national governments, which is essential for a cohesive society in countries with state-owned institutions. Figure 14.3 depicts the confidence citizens have in governmental institutions across countries, and in many countries, trust in the government was either low, declining, or both. Compared to the OECD average (about 42%), people in Nordic countries expressed higher levels of confidence in their governments, while rates were lower in Slovenia, Portugal, Poland, and Spain. Among non-OECD countries, confidence in national governments was highest in India and Indonesia, and lowest in Colombia. For Turkey, people trust in governmental institutions more than they do in other people.

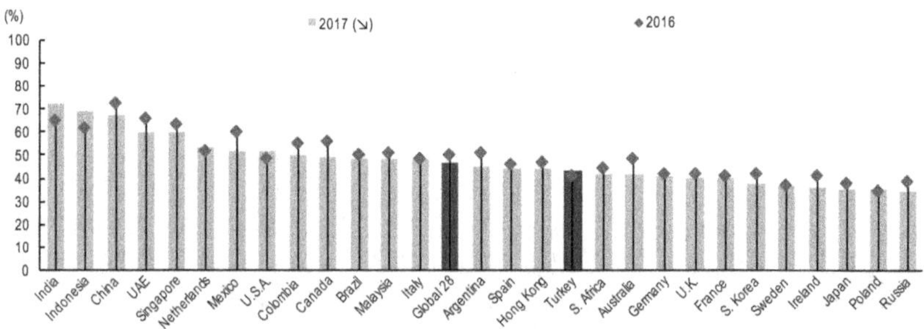

Fig. 14.2 Average trust of the general population in institutions: 2016 vs. 2017 (Source: Authors' compilation from Edelman Trust Barometer (2016, 2017))

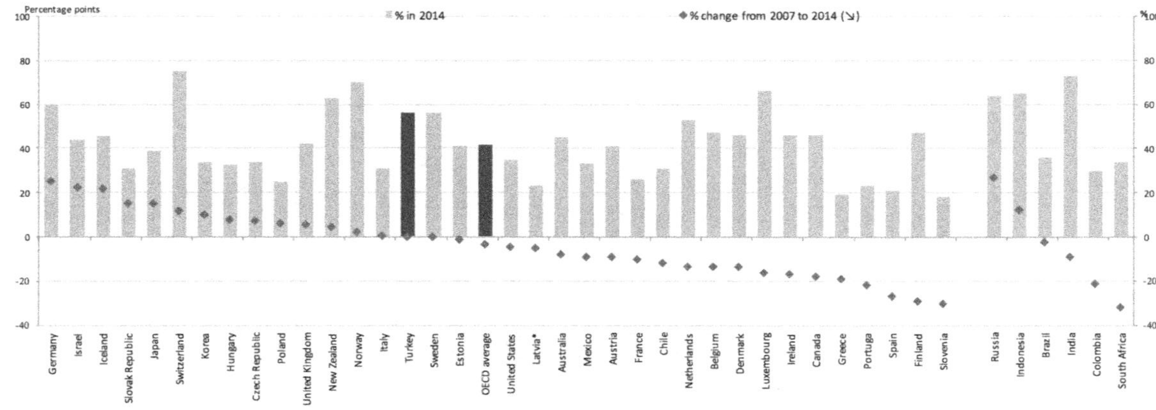

Fig. 14.3 Percentage of people reporting trust/confidence in their national government, 2014 and change since 2007 (*Latvia joined the OECD in July 2016. Data refer to the percentage who answered "yes" to the question: *Do you have confidence in national government?* Source: OECD's (2015) presentation from Gallup World Poll)

Public trust in government institutions is vital for the success of public policies that depend on behavioral responses of the public. Since governments influence public trust, OECD (2017) listed areas for governments to strengthen trust, such as reliability, responsiveness, openness, better regulation, integrity/fairness, and inclusive policy-making. For reliability and responsiveness, governments have an obligation to minimize uncertainty in the economic, social, and political environment and improve the quality of public services, respectively. Openness shows the transparency of government policy-making. Proper regulation as an important factor for justice, fairness, the rule of law, and public services reflects to implementing good regulatory practices for everyone in society. Integrity/fairness as crucial determinants of trust indicates transparency, credibility and impartiality of governance. Finally understanding and participating in public policies can strengthen public institutions. Empirical research confirms that when these characteristics are present in governments, they promote trust between public institutions and citizens regarding public transportation, the judicial system, local police, education, and healthcare. The opposite is also true when public institutions fail in these obligations, leading people to mistrust in not only governmental institutions, but also each other, since people learn to distrust (OECD 2017).

14.5   Trustworthy Managerial Behaviors in Turkey

The Great Place to Work Institute (2017) emphasized the importance of trustbased work cultures in business organizations and defined a great workplace as one where employees trust the people they work for, have pride in what they do, and enjoy the people they work with. In the Trust Index Employee Survey (Great Place to Work Institute 2017), trustworthiness of organizational management is modelled by credibility (open communication, and competent and honest management), respect (incentive and appreciation, cooperation with employees, caring), fairness (objectiveness, equal payment and treatment), pride (proud of the job, teamwork, and business success), and camaraderie (sincerity and trust, friendly environment, working for a common goal). The Trust Index Employee Survey results showed that the features of great workplaces in Turkey were also highly consistent with those of global principles, and most of the highest scored businesses in Turkey are run by multinationals.

Trustworthiness occurs in dyadic relationships construct trust on cognition-based trust and affect-based trust. Cognition-based trust originates from the trustor's rational and systematic assessment of the trustworthiness of a trustee based on individual beliefs about peer reliability and dependability. Affect-based trust depends on a trustor's feelings toward a trustee beyond rational assessments. Affect-based trust is possibly affected by reciprocated interpersonal care and concern (McAllister 1995). Additionally, people can perceive others as having trustworthy personalities (Lewicki et al. 2006), which includes disposition-based trust, and is closely linked with affect-based trust. Dispositionbased trust refers to the personality trait for a general propensity to trust in others, although is expected to be affected by past experiences. Erdil's (2011) research concluded that this conceptualization of trust and trustworthiness was true in Turkey's case.

Several conclusions were drawn about Turkey from the study by İslamoğlu et al. (2012). Trustworthiness of managers depended on the support for subordinates, honesty, and fairness, being a team leader, providing a positive work environment, self-confident, not creating tension, sharing information, inspiring confidence, competency, delegation, and concern for employees. Trust in colleagues required a willingness to succeed in one's own effort and competence, self-development, honesty and openness, affection, a non-exploitive attitude, tolerance, responsibility, not behaving politically, and agreeableness. The key contributors to the trustworthiness of subordinates were being a good person, working effectively and efficiently, valuing one's job, having discipline and work ethic, competent, hardworking, and sharing information. Trustworthiness of organizations is formed by honest and fair business attitudes, positive images, peaceful and just atmospheres, creating a sense of commitment, company profits, considering employees' needs, objective performance appraisals, concern and respect for employees, providing long-term employment opportunities, and providing training programs. Each of these traits is either cognition-based, affect-based trust, or both, and are closely linked to disposition-based trust.

14.6   Chapter Summary

Trust, as a key phenomenon of social cohesion, has attracted interest in the social sciences, both globally and in Turkish studies. A wide range of dynamic factors, including the culture, affects trust structures. From the cultural perspective, the main characteristics of Turkish culture are high in power distance, collectivism, femininity, and uncertainty avoidance. For those with collectivistic values, interpersonal trust relationships rest on benevolence, which is a result of intimacy, unselfish behavior, personalized generosity, and protection. Paternalism, a kind of supervisor-subordinate relationship, is another construct related to power distance in Turkish culture. With the influence of paternalistic values, interpersonal trust between supervisor and subordinate develops similarly to the father-child relationship in Turkish culture.

Turkish trust studies have explored the dynamics of inter-personal trust, intra-organizational trust, inter-organizational trust, and cross-cultural differences of trust. From the organizational level, research interests revolved around mutual interactions between trust and individual perceptions, attitudes, and behaviors. Despite the importance of trust across multiple levels in organizations, the literature focused on trust at the individual level in Turkey. This tendency seems to stem from the approach that individual features of trust also determine trust at the organizational level. Those studies concluded that intra-organization and inter-organization trust contribute to organizational goals. From the cross-cultural approach, studies focused on cultural differences in the antecedents, the attitudes, and perceptions of trust.

We discussed the origins of public trust and trustworthiness in both individuals and organizations, comparing Turkey to other countries. Trusting institutions (government, business, media, and non-governmental organizations) was relatively low for Turkey. Moreover, people generally trust national government more than other people.

Regarding workplace properties of credibility, respect, fairness, pride, and camaraderie, Turkish multinational organizations follow global principles of trustworthy management in Turkey. The antecedents of interpersonal trustworthy behaviors consist of cognitive, affective, and dispositional properties with a rational and systematic assessment, an interpersonal care and concern, and the personality traits, respectively. In Turkey, higher trust levels of individuals encourage constructive human affairs, well-functioning organizations, and healthy economic activities at the individual, organizational, and national level.

References

Akgündüz, Y., & Güzel, T. (2014). The effect of organizational trust as a mediator role on the relationship between organizational justice with organizational commitment. *Anadolu University Journal of Social Sciences, 14*(3), 1–18.

Aycan, Z., & Kanungo, R. N. (1998). *Paternalism: Towards conceptual refinement and operationalization.* Paper presented at 14th International Congress of Cross-Cultural Psychology, Bellingham.

Aycan, Z., Kanungo, R. N., Mendonca, M., Yu, K., Deller, J., Stahl, G., & Kurshid, A. (2000). Impact of culture on human resource management practices: A ten-country comparison. *Applied Psychology: An International Review, 49*(1), 192–221.

Baş, S. (2011). *Workplace mobbing and its relationship between job satisfaction and organizational trust: A study on Turkish academicians* (Unpublished master's dissertation). İstanbul: Yeditepe University.

Chien, S. Y., Sycara, K., Liu, J. S., & Kumru, A. (2016, October 9–12). *Influence of cultural factors in dynamic trust in automation.* Paper presented at the IEEE International Conference on Systems, Man, and Cybernetics' SMC 2016, Budapest, Hungary.

Demir, M. (2011). Effects of organizational justice, trust, and commitment on employees' deviant behavior. *Anatolia, 22*(2), 204–221.

Edelman Trust Barometer. (2016). Retrieved from: http://www.edelman.com/insights/intellectual-property/2016-edelman-trust-barometer/

Edelman Trust Barometer. (2017). Retrieved from: http://www.edelman.com/trust2017/

Erdem, F. (2003). Optimal trust and teamwork: From groupthink to team think. *Work Study, 52*(5), 229–233.

Erdil, S. (2011). *A model of dyadic trust: Turkish case* (Unpublished doctorate dissertation). İstanbul: Sabancı University.

Ergeneli, A., Arı, G. S., & Metin, S. (2007). Psychological empowerment and its relationship to trust in immediate managers. *Journal of Business Research, 60*(1), 41–49.

Ertürk, A. (2009). Exploring predictors of organizational identification: The moderating role of trust on the associations between empowerment, organizational support, and identification. *European Journal of Work and Organizational Psychology, 19*(4), 409–441.

Ertürk, A. (2016). Organizational trust of mobbing victims: A study of Turkish teachers. *Journal of Education and Training Studies, 4*(11), 49–57.

Eser, Z. (2012). Inter-organizational trust in franchise relationships and the performance outcomes: The case of fast-food restaurants in Turkey. *International Journal of Contemporary Hospitality Management, 24*(5), 774–790.

Great Place to Work Institute. (2017). Retrieved from: http://www.greatplacetowork.net/index.php

Hofstede, G. (1980). *Culture's consequences: International differences in work-related values.* Beverly Hills: Sage.

Hofstede, G. (2001). *Culture's consequences: Comparing values, behaviors, institutions, and organizations across Nations* (2nd ed.). Thousand Oaks: Sage.

Hofstede, G., Hofstede, G. J., & Minkov, M. (2010). *Cultures and organizations: Software of the mind* (3rd ed.). New York: McGraw-Hill.

İslamoğlu, G., Birsel, M., & Boru, D. (2012, June). *Trust scale development in Turkey.* Paper presented at the CASA E-Leader Conferences (June 4–6), Berlin.

Kale, M. (2013). Perceptions of college of education students in Turkey towards organizational justice trust in administrators, and instructors. *Higher Education, 66*(5), 521–533.

Karapınar, P. B., Camgöz, S. M., & Ekmekçi, Ö. T. (2016). The mediating effect of organizational trust on the link between the areas of work life and emotional exhaustion. *Educational Sciences: Theory & Practice, 16*(6), 1947–1980.

Lewicki, R. J., Tomlinson, E. C., & Gillespie, N. (2006). Models of interpersonal trust development: Theoretical approaches, empirical evidence, and future directions. *Journal of Management, 32*(6), 991–1022.

Mayer, R. C., Davis, J. H., & Schoorman, F. D. (1995). An integrative model of organizational trust. *The Academy of Management Review, 20*(3), 709–734.

McAllister, D. (1995). Affect – And cognition-based trust as foundations for interpersonal cooperation in organizations. *The Academy of Management Journal, 38*(1), 24–59.

Oba, B., & Semercioz, F. (2005). Antecedents of trust in industrial districts: An empirical analysis of inter-firm relations in a Turkish industrial district. *Entrepreneurship and Regional Development, 17*(3), 163–182.

OECD. (2015). *Government at a glance 2015.* Paris: OECD Publishing.

OECD. (2016). *Society at a glance 2016: OECD Social indicators.* Paris: OECD Publishing. https://doi.org/10.1787/9789264261488-en

OECD. (2017). *Trust and public policy: How better governance can help rebuild public trust* (OECD Public Governance Reviews). Paris: OECD Publishing.

Okur, F. (2016). *Investigation the relationship between organization silence and organizational trust* (Unpublished master's dissertation). İstanbul: Beykent University.

Semercioz, F., Hassan, M., & Aldemir, Z. (2011). An empirical study on the role of interpersonal and institutional trust in organizational innovativeness. *International Business Research, 4*(2), 125–136.

Sezgin, O. B. (2015). *The role of organizational trust in the relationship between perceived organizational support and intrapreneur behavior* (Unpublished doctoral dissertation). İzmir: Dokuz Eylül University.

Tezergil, S. A., Köse, A., & Karabay, M. E. (2014). Investigating the effect of trust, work-involvement, motivation and demographic variables on organizational commitment: Evidence from IT industry. *International Journal of Business and Management, 9*(12), 111–122.

Top, M., Akdere, M., & Tarcan, M. (2015). Examining transformational leadership, job satisfaction, organizational commitment and organizational trust in Turkish hospitals: Public servants versus private sector employees. *The International Journal of Human Resource Management, 26*(9), 1259–1282.

Wasti, S. A., & Tan, H. H. (2010). Antecedents of supervisor trust in collectivist cultures: Evidence from Turkey and China. In M. N. K. Saunders, D. Skinner, N. Gillespie, G. Dietz, & R. J. Lewicki (Eds.), *Organizational trust: A cultural perspective* (pp. 311–335). Cambridge: Cambridge University Press.

Wasti, S. N., & Wasti, S. A. (2009). Antecedents of trust in buyer-supplier relations in developing countries: The case of the Turkish automotive industry. *TODAİE's Review of Public Administration, 3*(1), 157–180.

Wasti, S. A., Tan, H. H., Brower, H. H., & Önder, Ç. (2007). Cross-cultural measurement of supervisor trustworthiness: An assessment of measurement invariance across three cultures. *The Leadership Quarterly, 18*(5), 477–489.

Wasti, S., Tan, H., & Erdil, S. (2011). Antecedents of trust across Foci: A comparative study of Turkey and China. *Management and Organization Review, 7*(2), 279–302.

Yıldız, H. (2015). *The relationship between positive psychological capital, organizational trust and organizational citizenship behavior: A case study* (Unpublished doctoral dissertation). Balıkesir: Balıkesir University.

CHAPTER 15

Managing Public Trust: Cases from Taiwan

Lee, Tzong-Ru (Jiun-Shen) and Chun-Yu Chien

15.1 INTRODUCTION

Trust "plays an important and integral role in achieving and sustaining organizational effectiveness" (Clubert and McDonough 1986). An individual who trusts will act capably and loyally when the actions they take involve risk (Lewis and Weigert 1985). Public trust is defined as individuals' trust in an organization or a unit. Public trust in Taiwan can be divided into at least two parts: trust in government and trust in business.

There are many ways to build public trust, but they all boil down to doing more, thinking more, caring more, and being more accurate than the public's expectations. For example, information communicated to the public should always be accurate and the details of each transaction should exceed the public's expectations. In this way, people will have confidence in their governments and entrepreneurs who are working to produce these outcomes. If individuals have this confidence, they will no longer question the details of a transaction and are likely comply with the leadership with less resistance. It is more difficult for government officials or entrepreneurs

Lee, Tzong-Ru (Jiun-Shen) (✉)
National Chung Hsing University, Taichung, Taiwan

C.-Y. Chien (✉)
Asia University, Taichung, Taiwan

B. Kożuch et al. (eds.), *Managing Public Trust*,
https://doi.org/10.1007/978-3-319-70485-2_15

to successfully promote their policies and strategies to people who are less trusting of them.

Trust in government not only has implications in the compliance of citizens, but it also has political consequences (Chanley et al. 2000). The issues of crime, welfare, and the environment are of serious concern to citizens. In addition to government, trust is also a critical success factor in modern businesses: "There are many factors that lead to success…. However, nothing is more important than trust" (Porat 2017). Customers buy products and services from local companies as well as businesses in distant locations. Therefore, it is not always possible to address a customer's problem by meeting in person. The services provided and the problems that customers have are impersonal and becoming more complex (Porat 2017).

In this chapter, we present four representative cases of public trust. For each case, we discuss the roles played by the characteristics of relevance, psychology, risk, goodwill, and decision-making in the establishment of public trust, as follows:

1. *Relevance* refers to "an individual characteristic, as a characteristic of interpersonal relations, and/or as an institutional attribute" (Rosenbloom and Haefne 2009).
2. *Psychology* is "a generalized expectancy held by an individual or group that a word, promise, verbal, or written statement of another individual or group can be relied on. (Rotter 1967)". It is also believing. People will do what they have expected because of trust, and trust may have positive influence on behaviors (Psychology Wiki 2017).
3. *Risk* refers to the unwanted events that may or may not occur (Hansson 2004, p. 10; Eiser and White 2005).
4. *Goodwill* "is neither necessary or sufficient for trustworthiness" (Stanford Encyclopedia of Philosophy 2015).
5. *Decision-making* is the thought process of selecting from available options. A person weighs the positive or negative options and makes an effective decision (Business Dictionary 2017)

The four cases in this chapter are related to these characteristics of public trust with regard to the use of computer software, mechanisms of implementation, and behavior. We further examine the systems, mechanisms, and behaviors in these cases to demonstrate public trust in

Table 15.1 Characteristics of public trust in the four examined cases

	Case 1: Government	Case 2: Sinon Corporation	Case 3: Hot-pot restaurant	Case 4: Real estate developer
Relevance	X	X	X	
Psychology	X		X	
Risk	X			X
Goodwill	X	X		X
Decision-making	X	X		X

government or organizations. Table 15.1 lists the characteristics of public trust in the four case studies.

Each case in this chapter is divided into three parts: (1) identification of the problem, (2) description of ways to solve the problem, and (3) discussion of the related characteristics of public trust.

15.2   Case 1: A Government Rebuilds Public Trust

Problem: Food Safety Crisis

The Republic of China (Taiwan) attracts both domestic and foreign tourists because of its year-round warm weather, beautiful scenery, history, and cuisine (Tourism Bureau, Republic of China [Taiwan] 2016). Taiwanese cuisine, snacks, and beverages are even promoted by the government to attract tourists. For example, many foreigners want to try pearl milk tea and crushed ice with toppings of mangoes, strawberries, or other seasonal fruits when they visit Taiwan. The proportion of people in Taiwan who eat outside the home is more than 70%. More than 3.3 million people eat out every day, with approximately 1.7 million people eating out every meal (Global Views Monthly 2007).

The general public has limited exposure to the food manufacturing process. Approximately 85% of mothers in Taiwan reported wondering if their food is safe. They are worried about food security policies and food safety in Taiwan (Yang 2015). Melamine-poisoned milk was imported from Mainland China to Taiwan in 2008; plasticizer was added to drinks in 2010; ractopamine-tainted beef was sold in 2012; low-quality rice was found to be mixed with Taiwanese rice, a number of cooking oils were mislabeled and contained an inferior oil instead (Bo 2013), and undisclosed additives were added in beverages and breads in 2013; antibiotics were found in eggs and excessive pesticides in bubble tea in 2014; and undisclosed preservatives were added to dried tofu and excessive pesticides to bubble tea in 2015. Food safety and poor quality raw materials are problems not only in Taiwan: Europe and the United States also experienced a series of food safety problems. For example, in 2013, beef was mixed with horse meat in Europe; furthermore, tainted eggs, spinach, and peanut butter caused damage to customers' health in the United States. Because of these food scandals, consumers have been losing trust in enterprises and government. Food safety thus has been a primary concern in Taiwan.

Solution: Rebuilding Public Trust Through Food Safety Policies and Practices
To avoid another food crisis in Taiwan, Former Taiwanese President Ma Ying-Jeou announced efforts "to create a food safety agency within [my] government in an effort to combat problems with tainted food and other food safety concerns" (News Desk 2014). After the food safety incidents, more authorities were set up to monitor and ensure the product quality. Food traceability and Good Agriculture Practices (GAPs) were implemented in Taiwan to decrease the risks of food safety and sustainable agricultural environment.

Food labels allow consumers to know what ingredients are in their food and beverages. However, some manufacturers use low-quality ingredients and unclear labeling to deceive customers. Thus, the government inspects food products regularly to see if the food has been mislabeled or unsafe ingredients were added.

A. *Food safety policies*

After the food safety incidents, the government of Taiwan established policies to make people feel at ease and save the country's reputation as "The Kingdom of Food." The policies (Tsai 2015) are as follows:

1. Implement source control and set up a poison management agency: To avoid downstream contamination in food products, upstream source management is critical. Tracing harmful substances and banning the use of chemical fertilizers, harmful chemicals, and harmful additives are necessary to prevent food risk.

2. Rebuilding the production management system: The traditional food hygiene management system required end products to be clean, safe, and free of pesticides. However, food and agricultural products should be controlled from the source, with production processes that follow international standards (e.g., Hazard Analysis and Critical Control Points, Taiwan Good Agricultural Product, ISO22000, risk assessment mechanisms). A traceable production database and a system for recording raw materials, additives source, production processes, product distribution channels, and sales targets should be established. All documentation should be retained for 5 years.
3. Comprehensive inspections for imported products and self-produced products: In Taiwan, 70% of food sources are imported from other countries. These products should be checked rigidly and importers should provide the proper certifications. For the domestic production, the government should manage the chemical pesticides and fertilizers used in agriculture. Environmentally-friendly farming methods will protect water and soil.
4. Increasing the number of imported agricultural products.
5. Modifying the food security laws: Individuals should also independently supervise food safety. To curb illegal food production and manufacturing, the government will provide the rewards to the whistleblowers.

B. *Food traceability*

The development of a safe agricultural system has been a goal of the Council of Agriculture (COA) in Taiwan. The COA has established traceability and certification systems for agricultural products, developed organic agriculture, and strengthened animal and plant health inspections and quarantines (Council of Agriculture 2017). The traceability and certification systems aim to standardize the quality of agricultural products and processed agri-products. The traceability and related certification regulations have been promulgated; nine certification institutes were accredited in 2007. In addition, in the same year, protocols were established on good agricultural practices for 140 agri-products. The COA set up a website called the Taiwan Agriculture and Food Traceability system. Seventeen regional certification institutes make up a nationwide service network established by the COA. Furthermore, 100 terminals were installed in various supermarkets to trace the sales of agri-products.

Food traceability is used to identify the origin of food, feed ingredients, and food sources. In this way, consumers can be protected when products are found to be faulty (International Union of Food Science and Technology 2012). Food traceability is used by manufacturers and farmers. Unique codes are stored, presented, and transmitted in variety ways, such as ear tags for livestock, barcodes, electronically via radio frequency identification tags, and readable printed data. Hardware and software are used to store and retrieve data. If the consumers want to know what sources or ingredients are in the products, they can check the records on traceability.

Customers can purchase clearly labeled agricultural products at the market, which contain tracking and traceability information. To learn more about the production and agricultural information, consumers in Taiwan can check the COA website at http://taft.coa.gov.tw. Here, consumers can access product records as recorded by the farmers and trace the products after they leave the farms.

C. *Good Agriculture Practices*

With the improvement of living standards, people are paying more attention to food safety. Pesticide residues in agricultural products are a very important issue. However, people cannot visually identify the presence of pesticide residues. Therefore, the Agriculture and Food Agency of the Council of Agriculture created a Good Agriculture Practice label to indicate the safety of fruits and vegetables (Council of Agriculture, Executive Yuan 2017).

The GAP label encourages farmers to use pesticides correctly, take responsibility for their products, and provide high-quality fruits and vegetables to customers. There are two characteristics of the GAP label: (1) the producers need to follow the regulation of pesticide usage; and (2) the label must be traceable. The two leaves on the label represent agriculture, whereas the three red circles indicate that the farmers should follow reasonable pest control, use recommended agents, and comply with the safe harvest period. In addition, the red circles also indicate that products have been through counseling, examination, and control. The numbers on the bottom of the label are a identification code by which customers can trace the producer's information.

Characteristics of Public Trust

Taiwan earned a worldwide reputation as a reliable food maker for over 50 years. Residents of Taiwan and tourists have enjoyed various delicacies in

Taiwan and trusted the food and drink that stores offered. However, after the food safety crisis in May 2011, at least 47 Taiwanese food and beverage manufacturers recalled more than 9000 products because of toxic chemical or artificial additives (Sun 2011). Trust in food producers was subsequently damaged.

To repair this trust, the Former President Ma Ying-Jeou made a public statement that lax inspections by local governments led to the crisis. He asked local municipalities to take these inspections of facilities and companies seriously. In addition, various government agencies have conducted regular inspections for food products that contain toxic chemicals or artificial additives in order to remove them from the market.

Furthermore, an agricultural product control system, food safety policies, traceability, and GAPs were implemented to make people feel safe and repair the reputation of "The Kingdom of Food." Traceability reduces risks in the production process and products, including food safety, sustainable agricultural, and employees' health. GAPs provide clear responsibility for all participants in food production. If a food safety incident occurs, the liability can be eliminated and the unsafe products can be removed from the market right away. Thus, producers can reduce the impact from affected consumers.

The best way to control and reduce risks is to use a combination of GAP and a traceability system. With this approach, every group of products can be examined strictly. The faulty products can be disposed of immediately, fraudulent data will be effectively reduced, and production processes can be controlled to minimize harm to the environment and humans. In addition, the government of Taiwan should control the source of raw materials and products, rebuild production management, and inspect imported products and self-produced products comprehensively. Citizens should monitor and report any illegal food production or manufacturing to prevent the sale of harmful products in the market.

15.3   CASE 2: SINON CORPORATION SOLVES THE ISSUE OF FOOD SECURITY AND HELPS SMALL FARMERS THROUGH TRANSPARENCY

In Taiwan Fresh Supermarket, a television screen is playing an advertisement that shows how farmers grow their vegetables and fruits. They are proud of what they have planted, and these crops are now sold in Taiwan

Fresh Supermarket. Sinon Corporation's Taiwan Fresh Supermarket provides fresh fruits, vegetables, fish and meat products, high-quality dry goods, and dairy products through 41 stores in the Central Taiwan region. Since Sinon Corporation has run supermarkets, health and organic foods have been sold there. The company only contracts with farmers who use limited pesticides.

Sinon Corporation was founded in 1955 and built on a basic foundation of honesty. It provides a safe and rewarding working environment for the employees and offers high-quality products and services to the customers. Simon Chemical Group provides formulated and technical products, raw materials, intermediates, and finished goods to customers in more than 60 countries. The products that Sinon Corporation sells are fertilizers, plant hormones, seed treatments, synthetic fertilizers, organomineral fertilizers, organic fertilizers, organic seed treatments, inoculants, and natural plant hormones.

Sinon Corporation is a leading distributor of agrochemicals, fertilizers, agricultural equipment, and seeds in Asia. While other companies have strived for discovering the new molecules, Sinon Corporation has devoted resources to make the environment safer and cost-effective. With high standards (ISO 9001, ISO 17025, OHSAS 18001 certified), Sinon Corporation's state-of-the-art quality assurance program exceeds the standards required by FAO and OECD (Sinon Corporation 2016).

Problem: Information Is Not Transparent
Many dishonest businesses use chemical materials in products to reduce production costs or increase the flavor of products. Advances in technology and science contribute to overuse of products that increase risk in food safety in recent years.

Solution: Enhance the Value of Small Farmers and Provide Fresh and Nontoxic Produce
Even though Sinon Corporation sells fertilizers, plant hormones, and pesticides to farmers, it is an advocate for food and environmental safety. Sinon Corporation sells products to farmers, then keeps records on who has purchased fertilizers, plant hormones, and pesticides. Thus, Sinon Corporation knows which farmers use less pesticides on their farms. The operators of Taiwan Fresh Supermarket then sign contracts with these farmers, as they insist on selling natural, healthy, fresh, high-quality, safe produce.

Videos are shown in Taiwan Fresh Supermarkets to inform customers about the farmers who produced the nontoxic fruits and vegetables. The fruits and vegetables are inspected before delivery to Taiwan Fresh Supermarkets. The website of Taiwan Fresh Supermarket provides "Fresh Food News" to inform the consumers about the qualifications of the vegetables, meat, fruits, fish, bread, and dry goods.

To ensure the food safety, Taiwan Fresh Supermarket provides a freshness and safety guarantee, including contract farming and traceability. The steps in the contract farming to traceability process are as follows:

1. Approximately 300 supply centers are used as resources to select farmers for the contact farming.
2. The use of pesticides and fertilizers is monitored to ensure quality.
3. Field testing ensures the correct use of pesticides and the soil safety.
4. Traceability is used for vegetables.
5. The food can be traced from the place of origin to the consumers' dining tables, which ensures that the resources are safe and secure (Taiwan Fresh Supermarket 2017).

Sinon Corporation aims to support local agriculture, small farmers, and small factories to provide the highest quality products to their customers. To this end, the following freshness and safety guarantees are made:

1. Freshness guarantee: Taiwan Fresh Supermarket guarantees the freshest products for consumers. For example, eggs, milk, and beer are only sold for 4 days. Peanuts are inspected for aflatoxin and are only sold for a month. Each egg is labeled with its production date.
2. Strengthening food safety: Taiwan Fresh Supermarket has been recognized by the Taiwan Agricultural Research Institute Council of Agriculture for 11 years. More than 30,000 pesticide residue tests have been performed—the most in the circulation industry. Taiwan Fresh Supermarket spends more than NT$ 10 million per year on food safety inspections.
3. Security guarantee: The products that Taiwan Fresh Supermarket sells do not have artificial additives, pigments, preservatives, or flavoring.
4. Natural and healthy food claims: The market does not sell genetically modified soy sauce and soybean products, and does not sell mixed rice.

5. Freshness and safety claims: Taiwan Fresh Supermarket promises consumers that fruits are fresh. Moreover, meat is inspected for antibiotics and sulfonamide. Vegetables are checked for agricultural residues by biochemical sifting.

Sinon Corporation contracts with small farmers and small factories because they are willing to disclose their manufacturing processes and adjust their production methods.

Characteristics of Public Trust

Although the government of Taiwan has made great efforts to improve food safety, the lack of manpower and resource management have been challenges. Establishing food safety by traceability, network monitoring, food inspections, and reporting are important. In this way, Taiwan Fresh Supermarkets guarantees the quality and safety of their products; furthermore, they provide customers with healthy foods and improved quality of life, increase farmers' incomes, and help to protect the environment. Customers therefore trust the products that are provided by Taiwan Fresh Supermarkets.

15.4   CASE 3: HARM FROM NEGATIVE WORD-OF-MOUTH

Problem: Negative Word-of-Mouth

Many consumers in Taiwan enjoy hot pots at restaurants. Recently, Hot Pot Restaurant A faced an allegation that they lost customers' reservations. Hot Pot Restaurant A has operated for almost 15 years and had a good reputation in the city. The Hot Pot Restaurant A operator is devoted to providing the best food and service to customers. The fruits, vegetables, and ingredients that Hot Pot Restaurant A uses are fresh; the operator goes to the markets to buy the materials personally. Before new employees are allowed to serve customers, they need to complete a full training program, which includes lessons on being patient and friendly with customers. The employees are required stand up straight and wear clean and neat uniforms, in addition to providing prompt service.

Recently, a customer, Ms. K, complained that Hot Pot Restaurant A provided terrible service on a community website. Ms. K went to Hot Pot Restaurant A last Saturday night. She made a reservation for 5 people 3 days prior. However, after the party arrived at the restaurant, the host informed them that he did not have a reservation. If they wanted to eat, the group needed to wait in line for at least 30 minutes. Ms. K argued with the host, but he did not apologize for the mistake. Instead, he impatiently asked Ms. K if she and her family wanted to wait in line. Because there were many guests waiting for the nearby restaurants and her family members were too hungry to find another restaurant, she and her family waited in line for 40 minutes to have dinner.

After Ms. K posted her complaint to the community website, many customers wrote responses about similar experiences. The operator of Hot Pot Restaurant A was informed of the complaints from his close friends, and he checked the posts on the community website right away.

Solution: Behavior Changes to Rebuild the Reputation
After the operator of Hot Pot Restaurant A was informed of the complaints, he decided to take the following actions to solve the problem:

1. Locate the complaining customers and apologize to them: To recover Hot Pot Restaurant A's good reputation as providing the best service in the city, the operator apologized to the customers through the community website.
2. The operator provided coupons for these to dine for free.
3. The operator investigated which employees received the reservation phone calls and did not take responsibility for the mistake.
4. He also decided to retrain all of his employees.

After the operator of Hot Pot Restaurant A apologized to the customers and retrained his employees, no more complaints were posted on the community website. Rather, customers and blogger began posting praise profusely. The operator did not ignore the complaints but dealt with them right away.

Characteristics of Public Trust
The effects of consumers' negative word-of-mouth could scare other customers away and cost a business large amounts of money. A company should directly face the negative word-of-mouth, apologize to the customers immediately, determine the problem, and correct the mistakes as quickly as possible.

15.5   CASE 4: BENEFITS FROM POSITIVE WORD-OF-MOUTH

Problem: Sales Rate Is Low
When Home Builder B was a child, he lived in a house that had a serious problem with the roof leaking. Thus, he did not like rainy days. In his mind, he told himself that once he became a businessman, he would build high-quality houses. He also believed that word-of-mouth would be the only way to help him sell more houses.

Home Builder B did not spend too much time to make his dream come true. He is different from other businessmen who build houses rapidly. He takes his time and builds the houses carefully, insisting on building high-quality houses. However, when the houses do not sell quickly, he does not hire a marketing team to help. He believes that word-of-mouth will increase his reputation, and people will be willing to buy the houses because of their loyalty. Even though only 40% of the houses sold in the beginning, he still believed the rest of the houses would be sold based on his good reputation. After residents have lived the houses for a few years, they realize that the quality of the houses really is better than the other houses on the market and recommend them to others.

Solution: Behavior Earns Consumers' Trust and Builds a Reputation
Positive word-of-mouth established a good reputation for the builder and resulted in more customers buying houses. When Home Builder B plans to build more houses, customers purchase pre-sale houses without the need for any advertisements.

Characteristics of Public Trust
A quickly built fancy house might attract buyers to purchase it quickly. However, eventually the consumers would recognize the low quality of their home and be angry about what they have bought. When consumers do not trust their home builder, they will not tell others to buy the houses. Home Builder B put the consumers as the first priority, building the best quality houses for them. Thus, consumers trust Home Builder B and recommend that others purchase his homes.

15.6   CHAPTER SUMMARY

The four cases presented in this chapter demonstrated the characteristics of relevance, psychology, risk, goodwill, and decision-making as they are related to public trust. Public trust in the Taiwan government was related to the characteristics of relevance, psychology, risk, goodwill, and decision-making. Public trust was built in this case using computer software. The second case of Sinon Corporation was related to the characteristics of relevance, goodwill, and decision-making as related to public trust. Public trust was built in this case by implementing various mechanisms. The third case of a hot-pot restaurant is related to the characteristics of relevance and psychology by behavior. Public trust was built in this case by behavior. The last case of the home builder was related to the characteristics of risk, goodwill, and decision-making. Public trust was built in this case is behaviors.

Consumers shopped at Taiwan Fresh Supermarket because they trusted the safety and reliability of the foods and product. Home Builder B insisted on not hiring a marketing team to sell his houses, believing that word-of-mouth will increase his reputation and bring more customers to purchase his homes. Because Taiwan Fresh Supermarket and Home Builder B have excellent relationships between the operators/companies and the customers, the operators/companies get benefits from the customers by selling the products or houses. Customers get benefits from the operators/companies selling the inspected and verified products. The operators put the consumers' interests and goodwill first; in turn, the consumers trust the products provided by operators/companies. When operators/companies consistently provide customers with excellent products, they will not be hurt by negative word-of-mouth. However, if customers have a terrible experience with a company, the operators should apologize and address the problems right away.

A series of food-related scandals increased public concern about the reliability and safety of the food supply (Ferry 2015). The challenge of food safety is enormous, and people are concerned with toxic chemicals and artificial additives in their food products. To solve the food crisis, the government established rules and policies to enhance transparency and traceability in the food chain. Data about food is recorded and uploaded to the so-called food cloud—that is, "a joint project among the TFDA, COA, EPA to give all regulators ready access to data on food processors and their supply chains, as well as any ingredients that might impact the food market" (Ferry 2015). Because the ingredients of foods are recorded in the food cloud, people are able to trace what they eat.

Word-of-mouth and reputation are two major issues for enterprises. With positive word-of-mouth, more products will be sold. Positive word-of-mouth has positive impacts on the consumers' buying process and adoption of new products. In addition, positive word-of-mouth can reduce consumers' awareness of the product cost, change their attitudes, and enhance consumers' decision-making and purchase accuracy. In addition, word-of-mouth occurs not only in the neighborhood but also on the Internet. Some consumers also view the product information and recommendations on the Internet. A word-of-mouth marketing strategy can impact customer decisions, but negative word-of-mouth causes companies to lose business. To avoid negative word-of-mouth, the company should react to complaints right away.

The government, organizations, and businesses should use their expertise to produce products well and provide excellent service. If they exceed the public's expectations, then they will gain the public's trust. If doing so, the government, businesses, and organizations will be able to operate in a sustainable manner.

References

Bo, Y. L. (2013). Food safety in Taiwan is an important issue to address. *The China Post*, December 1 2013. Retrieved from: http://www.chinapost.com.tw/commentary/letters/2013/12/01/394921/Food-safety.htm. Accessed 26 Dec 2016.

Business Dictionary. (2017). *Decision making*. Retrieved from: http://www.businessdictionary.com/definition/decision-making.html. Accessed 10 July 2017.

Chanley, V. A., Rudolph, T. J., & Rahn, W. M. (2000). The origins and consequences of public trust in government: A time series analysis. *Oxford Journals, 64*(3), 239–256.

Council of Agriculture, Executive Yuan. (2017). *Good Agriculture Practice (GAP) Label*. Retrieved from: http://gap.afa.gov.tw/faq/. Accessed 10 Mar 2017.

Culbert, S. A., & McDonough, J. J. (1986). The politics of trust and organization empowerment. *Public Administration Quarterly, 10*(2), 171–188.

Eiser, R. & White, M. (2005). *A psychological Approach to understanding how trust is built and lost in the context of risk*. SCARR Conference on Trust, LES, 12th December 2005.

Ferry, T. (2015). How safe is Taiwan's Food? *Taiwan Business Topics*, 6 February 2015. Retrieved from: http://topics.amcham.com.tw/2015/02/taiwan-food-safety/. Accessed 26 Dec 2016.

Global Views Monthly. (2007). 外食人口大調查 全台330萬天天外食族逼近北縣總人口, 252期,6月號. Retrieved from: https://www.gvm.com.tw/Boardcontent_13117.html. Accessed 10 July 2017.

Hansson, S. (2004). Philosophical perspectives on risk. *Techne, 8*(1), 10–35.

International Union of Food science and Technology. (2012). *Food Traceability.* Retrieved from http://iufost.org/iufostftp/IUF.SIB.Food%20Traceability.pdf. Accessed 26 Dec 2016.

Lewis, J. D., & Weigert, A. (1985). Trust as a social reality. *Social Forces, 63*(4), 967–985.

News Desk. (2014). Taiwanese Government to Establish Food Safety Agency. http://www.foodsafetynews.com/2014/10/taiwanese-government-to-establish-food-safety-agency/#.WlXnaiWY2y. Accessed 10 Jan 2018.

Porat, S. (2017). Why trust is a critical success factor for businesses today. *Entrepreneurs.* Retrieved from: https://www.forbes.com/sites/vanguard/2017/07/05/how-to-save-for-retirement-do-these-3-things/#a7532c14dc38. Accessed 10 July 2017.

Psychology Wiki. (2017). *Trust (Social behavior).* Psychology Wiki. Accessed 13 July 2017.

Rosenbloom, A., & Haefne, J. E. (2009). Country-of-origin effects and global brand trust: A first look. *Journal of Global Marketing, 4,* 267–278.

Rotter, J. B. (1967). A new scale for the measurement of interpersonal trust. *Journal of Personality, 35,* 651–665.

Sinon Corporation. (2016). *Food Distribution.* Retrieved from http://www.sinon.com/food-distribution.htm. Accessed 12 Apr 2017.

Standford Encyclopedia of Philosophy. (2015). *Trust.* Retrieved from: https://plato.stanford.edu/entries/trust/. Accessed 12 July 2017.

Sun, C. (2011). Food safety crisis in Taiwan. *Sun Chlorella*, July, 5, 2011. Retrieved from: http://www.sunchlorella.com/whats-new/health-news/437.html. Accessed 26 Dec 2016.

Taiwan Fresh Supermarket. (2016/2017). *Food Safety.* Retrieved from: https://www.supermarket.com.tw/News_List.html. Accessed 12 Apr 2017.

Tourism Bureau, Republic of China (Taiwan). (2016). Taiwan. Retrieved from: http://www.taiwan.net.tw/m1.aspx?sNo=0001004. Accessed 10 Mar 2017

Tsai, Y. W.(2015). 食安五環改革方案, Retrieved from: http://iing.tw/policies/food_safety. Accessed 10 July 2017

Yang, C. Y. (2015). 民進黨母親節民調　8成媽媽不滿食安政策!ETNEWS. Retrieved from: http://health.ettoday.net/news/504350. Accessed 10 July 2017.

CHAPTER 16

The Role of Trust in Spatial Planning Processes: The Case of Poland

Agnieszka Chrisidu-Budnik and Jerzy Korczak

16.1   Introduction

The objective of any public authority is to achieve coherence between the existing legal order, the views on justice, and the legitimacy of the orderliness forming under its influence. In the case of administrative authorities, the mechanism of this coherence is based on different assumptions from (1) the area of civil law, where the principles of social coexistence are the reference area and to which the formation of civil law relations arising under the provisions of civil law should be adapted; or (2) the area of criminal law, where the feeling of justice and legitimacy of the provisions of substantive and procedural law arise with respect to the assessment of the harmfulness of the offence and its penalization. The principles of social trust and justified expectations developed in the legal doctrine during the search for the mechanism of coherence, which is specific to public administration.

A twentieth-century English philosopher, Martin Hollis, claimed that trust is an obvious fact of life, albeit an "exasperating one… [like] the flight of the bumblebee or a cure for hiccoughs: it works in practice but not in theory" (1998: 1). Here, Hollis described the characteristic element

A. Chrisidu-Budnik (✉) • J. Korczak
University of Wroclaw, Wrocław, Poland

© The Author(s) 2018
B. Kożuch et al. (eds.), *Managing Public Trust*,
https://doi.org/10.1007/978-3-319-70485-2_16

of the phenomenon of trust—its multifaceted nature and illusiveness. When trust is analyzed rationally, it appears to be possible to present it as a closed and coherent set of well-known mechanisms and processes. However, when this is done, the impression is that the most significant aspect of trust has not been included in the analysis.

Trust is a conceptual category that is present in various contexts of social sciences, especially in psychology—an area in which an individual's attitude is referred to the reality around him or her, based on a conviction about a positive or negative relationship of the interest between the internal (subjective) and external systems of values, objectives, and interests. This relationship is based on the knowledge acquired from common sense and faith, which arises from the conviction of the veracity of certain assertions, particularly when there is a lack of knowledge in their area. Trust based respectively on knowledge or faith induces individuals to expect a certain desired situation in the future compared with the current situation. This expectation of the future desired situation is reflected in those definitions of trust in which the attitude of waiting is highlighted (Klijn et al. 2010; Lewicki et al. 1998; Möllering 2006; Hosmer 1995). Meanwhile, trust based on knowledge is of an extrapolative nature. We form a vision of the future through our knowledge of the course of events to date, whereas trust based on belief is closer to hope. However, trust is fundamentally irrelevant for hope—we hope even if we do not trust a given relationship with reality.

The essence of trust is highly complex—not only by both of its sources, which are so different, but also because of the diversity of the objects of trust. In this chapter, trust is referred to people, society, and the institutions functioning in it.[1] In this light, we are aware that trust in public authorities is built on trust in their representatives (protectors of monocratic bodies and members of collegial bodies). However, objectively speaking, we should trust authorities regardless of the protector. In democratic systems of authority, an authority performs his or her function over a period of time (e.g., during a term of office, until dismissal, or until a change in personnel).

The mechanism by which trust in institutions and the people representing them overlaps was a subject of Anthony Giddens' analyses of trust in an abstract system. According to this British sociologist, the nature of modern institutions is strongly related to mechanisms of trust in abstract systems and especially trust in expert systems. In certain situations, trust in the abstract systems (bodies of public authorities) does not require any direct meetings with citizens. However, in the decided majority of cases, trust in the bodies of public authorities is being built through the so-called access points, namely areas where citizens meet with the protectors of the bodies of public authorities (Giddens 1990). Although trust is placed in a specific body of public authority and not in the protectors that represent it in the given context, the citizen and the protector of the body of public authority come into direct contact in the area described by Giddens as access points. The quality of these contacts creates trustworthiness of the specific abstract system—in this case, the specific body of public administration.

The need to distinguish trust and trustworthiness was noticed, among others, by the American political analyst Russell Hardin. Some researchers have applied the notion of trust and trustworthiness interchangeably as synonyms (Cummings and Bromiley 1996; Krot and Lewicka 2012; McKnight et al. 1998). However, the identification of these concepts appears to be erroneous, which is why they need to be clearly separated from each other (Caldwell and Clapham 2003; Ingenhoff and Sommer 2010; McKnight and Chervany 2002). Trustworthiness refers to the perceptions of another person, whereas trust is an activity related to the positive perception of credibility (Blois 1999; Chen et al. 2011; Mayer and Davis 1999).

According to Hardin, an important issue currently faced by societies is not a reduction in trust but a decline in trustworthiness, particularly over raising trustworthiness and the ability to cooperate in various spheres of social life (Hardin 2002, 2006). The distinction made by Hardin is extremely useful for analyzing trust in bodies of public authorities and the trustworthiness of these bodies. Trust is an attitude; the action that citizens can show to a specific impersonal body of public authority is its emanation. The concept of trust as an "encapsulated interest" was created by Hardin based on the assumption that the body representing the citizens in their activities will take into account their interests. An attitude of the citizen's trust to an authority appears when the citizen has grounds for accepting the assumption that it is in the interest of the body to behave in a manner that is trustworthy at a given time and in given terms.[2] In turn, trustworthiness is a resource that strengthens and consolidates trust.

Trustworthiness in the processes of spatial planning is built on two mechanisms: behavioral and institutional. The behavioral mechanism can potentially be activated in the said access points during the citizen's direct contact with the protector of the body of public authority. The consequence of the assessment by the citizen of expert knowledge (cognitive aspect) and the sense of duty to act (emotional aspect) of the protector of public authority is precisely the ability to build this trustworthiness. The institutional mechanism creates the quality of the legal regulations. The wording of specific legal acts can potentially sustain confidence in the bodies of public authority, such as by taking into account the public personal rights of an ownership nature in the spatial planning processes. However, building trustworthiness solely on the basis of the institutional mechanism is impossible; the question of "Do you trust the law?" is ridiculous and pointless. The question always needs to be clarified because it is only about trusting or not trusting specific people—the protectors of the bodies of public authority, who apply the law in practice.

The concept of trust as an encapsulated interest. The entity endowed with trust considers the interests of the trusting entity to be its own only because his or her interests are encapsulated in the interests of the trusting entity. In principle, there is no room in the relationship between the citizen (the unit) and the bodies of public authority. However, this does not mean that the concept of trust as an encapsulated interest in the spatial planning processes is not reflected in individual cases; we shall return to this issue later in the chapter.

In the spatial planning process, in principle, trust is of a one-sided nature because it is a specific unit endowed with a given object of trust. In the case of trust in a person, the person who is endowed with trust does not need to return the same trust in the person trusting him or her. Therefore, in the literature on the subject, attention is drawn to the element of goodwill of the addressee of the trust, which may be referred to as favorable intentions or confidence that the results of the other party's activities will be appropriate from the point of view of the trusting person (Dunn 1988; Misztal 1996).

The failure to reciprocate the trust does not mean there is a complete lack of feedback between the parties in a specific relationship, or even an intentional impact on cultivating an attitude of trust on the part of the entity interested in obtaining the trust. For this reason, the manipulation of public trust—which involves obtaining the trust of people by institutions or individual people, such as candidates standing for elections to various posts—is distinguished in social psychology as a subject of its studies. Therefore, in this chapter, attention will be focused on the factors by which the bodies of public authority gain the trust of the participants of spatial planning in the spatial planning process.

The participants in spatial development are the addressees of the planning instructions as investors or owners of properties located within the area of the individual land use plans. The condition of a conflict of interest may be said to permanently constitute a part of the spatial planning and development process. At the same time, the reasonable expectations of these participants in the spatial planning process with respect to the bodies of public authority, which determine the extent and method of this development in their planning, must be taken into account.

The system of dependencies described above between the bodies of public authority and the participants of the spatial planning process can be used to transfer arrangements, which are characteristic of the management of business institutions, to the area of the activity of public administration. The literature on the subject in the area of public management, as well as the management of business organizations, draws attention to the significance of interorganization collaboration. The effectiveness of inter-organization collaboration depends, among other things, on the creation of effective communications between the participants in the collaboration, their mutual commitment, and their acceptance of responsibility for its results, which expresses a certain level of trust between the participants of this process of collaboration (Chrisidu-Budnik and Korczak 2012; Korczak 2015).

16.2 Conflicts of Interests and Stakeholders in Spatial Planning

An important feature of space—understood empirically as the surface of Earth[3] (namely, its finite and simultaneously limited nature)—appears in all considerations of the issues of spatial planning. Just like time, space is a good that an individual receives in a specified quantity and cannot increase. Even though modern technologies enable humans to explore both the interior of the globe and the area around it, the scale of this exploration does not yet play an important role in solving the problem of the limitation of the surface of Earth (for this reason, artificial islands and polders are not particularly significant).

In past stages of the development of human civilization, humans improved parts of Earth's surface by populating them (e.g., by chopping down forests) and developing them (e.g., through developments for residential and commercial purposes). Humans brought about the situation in which space became a threatened good, which arose from the excessive concentration of business activity in certain areas, with the simultaneous irreversibility of these processes. The parts of Earth's surface that remain undeveloped today can only be found on the parts of the globe that are adverse to human existence (e.g., desert climates, polar areas, mountainous regions above a certain elevation). Thus, further development is taking place on land that has already been developed.

The limited nature of space gives rise to competition between entities interested in its development and, consequently, creates a conflict between them, as well as a conflict between their objectives, the interests of the existing users of these areas, and the neighboring land. Competition is a natural phenomenon of a market economy. If space is treated as an item that is subject to business processes, starting from trading of real property to investing on real property in order to conduct business on it, competition between potential purchasers and investors is justified and natural. However, the conflict between users of space does not always lead to its better use and decidedly involves many entities, from the participants of the conflict themselves to the bodies of public authority that are responsible for spatial planning.

These conflicts appeared in Poland with particular strength in the period of systemic and economic transformations, which began in 1990. At that time, there was a confrontation of the optimal use of space with the aim to rapidly increase business activity related to the liberation of individual entrepreneurship. The Polish legal doctrine draws attention to the negative role of legislation in shaping conflicts, indicating numerous examples of inconsistencies, gaps, and conflicts in the provisions of the law. Even the Concept of the Country's Spatial Development[4] emphasizes the following:

> "The current legal regulations do not resolve the fundamental problems of spatial management. [...] they reinforce the adverse phenomena, blocking development opportunities in all urbanized areas, support the dissipation of developments and the extensive use of space, [...] create a barrier to public and private investments, making it difficult to modernize cities and shape public spaces, as well as conducting large scale urban planning operations".

In accordance with the Act on spatial planning and development of 2003,[5] the formation of the spatial policy by the bodies of public administration and the principles of determining development and construction on sites are based on two rules applied in parallel: spatial order and sustainable development. In accordance with Article 2, Item 1 of the Act, spatial order is understood to mean shaping space and creating a harmonious whole. It takes into account in the structured relations all the considerations and functional, socioeconomic, environmental, cultural, and composition/aesthetic requirements. Meanwhile, sustainable development, as defined in Article 3, Item 50 of the Environmental Protection Law,[6] is socioeconomic development in which political, economic, and social activities are integrated, with the observance of a natural balance and the durability of the fundamental processes of nature. This integration has the purpose of ensuring that both current and future generations are able to satisfy their basic needs.

Spatial planning emerged as a result of human activities that were aimed at creating living conditions for man in settlements by skillfully combining the method of planning the habitat with the existing system of nature and the infrastructure that is created—namely, the urban and rural direction. In particular, almost from the very beginning, urbanism was an area of constant friction between the economic perspective, where the priority is the economic use of the commercial attributes of space and its transformation towards the economization of its use from the architectural point of view, emphasizing not only the functionality itself of the structures that are built but also its aesthetic attribute. Therefore, the urbanistic perspective of spatial planning permanently contains a conflict between three values: *utlitas* (usefulness), *firmitas* (durability), and *venustas* (beauty).[7] So-called city charters, such as the Card, the Leipzig Charter on Sustainable European Cities 2007), the Green Paper on territorial cohesion of 2008, and the EC Communication "Action Plan on Urban Mobility" of 2009, refer to these values in the formation of spatial order and sustainable development. This is because they all believed that the borders of city developments are largely exhausted and only a reasonable urban policy can remedy this problem. However, the purely economic expectations of investors, primarily property developers, largely do not take into account beauty and usefulness; however, durability is generally questionable, despite the applicable technological and material standards. Spatial planning is effective if the economic and architectural outlook, as well as the ecological outlook today, do not reduce the environmental capital; in addition, the balance between them must be maintained for a long time, while respecting the interests of future generations.

Since at least the mid-nineteenth century, a modern distinction between private space and public space has developed. Private space is designed by one entity, which is usually its user. In the spatial planning process, public space is designed by the competent bodies of public administration, which is used by multiple users who frequently represent divergent interests. In most European countries, other than developing planning legislation, the nineteenth century was also a period of the emergence of modern territorial self-government. The units and, most frequently, the municipalities were equipped, almost from the beginning, with rights that have been named as planning authority in the legal doctrine,[8] whereby this is the sphere of land use plans with a high degree of detail. In Poland, the spatial planning process applies to private land as well as public spaces constituting the property of municipalities, counties, and voivodship self-governments or the State Treasury in the development of these spaces. Spatial planning applies to the interests of various categories of entities (users of public space) wishing to have the right to jointly decide on the ways and directions of their development. Spatial planning should also take into account the public subjective rights of a freedom nature.

Users of public space are essentially stakeholders of the spatial planning processes. The term "stakeholder" in the context of spatial planning means various users of public space who have their individual expectations, needs, and interests regarding space. Each of the stakeholders has trust expressed with the help of epistemic formulations ("is convinced that," "expects that," "believes that"), which reflect his or specific, individual interests regarding the shape, organization and method of developing space. The following categories of users of public space can be distinguished:

1. Owners of land driven by economic motives are stakeholders who wish to sell it at a profit, convert it according to their needs, or use it without making changes.
2. Possessors of land and structures and lessees.
3. Investors (individual and institutional investors) looking for appropriate sites, including property developers.
4. Nongovernmental organizations that pursue noneconomic motives, such as ecological, aesthetic, or axiological motives.
5. Users of facilities or devices located in public space. This especially applies to the municipality's inhabitants, who appear in various roles as users of specific public goods and services.
6. The bodies of public authority, which are responsible for the functioning of a particular space, its development, and search for and maintenance of a balance between values constituting the Vitruvian triad.

The position of the bodies of public authority in the spatial planning processes is unique because they represent one of the categories of stakeholders and, simultaneously, constitute an entity that is supposed to reduce and resolve conflicts and tension arising between stakeholders. It should simultaneously be noted that the greatest intensity of conflicts and tensions related to space and the methods of its management in the spatial planning system are concentrated in the municipality.[9] This is because this unit of territorial self-government is equipped with numerous authoritative powers and constitutes a fundamental element of the system of planning authorities. In the light of the provisions of the aforementioned Act on spatial planning and development, the formation and pursuit of a spatial policy within a municipality, including the adoption of a structure plan for the municipality and its land use plans, is one of the municipality's own tasks. Decisions of the municipality's competent authorities have the greatest impact on the legal and actual situation of the stakeholders interested in the planning arrangements.

The involvement of the stakeholders in the planning process applies to two documents that are the most important for municipality's spatial policy: the structure plan and the land use plan. The interest of users of public space in being involved in the procedure of preparing and adopting the structure plan arises from the fact that the land use plan must be consistent with this document, which indirectly affects the legal situation of property owners. Therefore, if a specific area is assigned in the structure plan for the development of blocks of flats, this decision is binding on the land use plan. Consequently, the lack of involvement of a stakeholder in the procedure of preparing and adopting the structure plan means a lack of his or her influence on the structure plan and, as a result, the ineffectiveness of involvement in the processes of preparing the land use plan. The stakeholder would be able to bear an influence on the detailed assumptions of the plan, whereas his or her influence on the assignment of the land would no longer be possible. The land use plan, as an act of local law, is a fundamental source of information about the purpose and principles of development of the site and directly affects the legal realm of the stakeholder in the planning process. The universally applicable power of this Act is binding on the majority of the categories of users of public space mentioned above, who may clarify the realm of their rights and duties with respect to using space.

The spatial planning processes, in particular at the level of the municipality, are among the most sensitive and result in the most conflicts (Zdyb

1991). Space and its components, such as water, forests, agricultural and forest land, urban and rural areas, and cultural monuments are common goods. Users of public space expect the public authority to organize space in such a way that the values, which lay at the heart of the contemporary system of spatial planning, are respected both in the course of work on the land use plan and in the administrative decisions, on the basis of which the development conditions are specified to the investor in the absence of a land use plan.[10] Users of public spaces seen *en bloc* can therefore be convinced that the bodies of public administration take into account the universal system of values in the spatial planning processes and in the processes of issuing administrative decisions. This is an example of trust as a unilateral relationship, which is expressed by the previously mentioned epistemic formulations. These expressions can be found in the definitions of trust that refer to positive expectations regarding the other in a risky situation (Gambetta 1988; Das and Teng 2001; Faems et al. 2008), belief that the results of another person's intended action will be appropriate from one's own point of view (Misztal 1996: 9), and faith in people's motivations and capacities (Carnevale and Wechsler 1992).

Every conflict about the assignment of public space usually has two dimensions: the axiological and substantive dimensions. The axiological dimension manifests itself in the differences in the positions as to what needs to be protected. The substantive dimension applies to verifiable and observable economic, natural, and social phenomena. Two sources of conflicts can be specified in the spatial planning perspective and other planning documents: (1) the right of ownership and other substantive rights of citizens and (2) benefits from the goods of nature and the natural environment.

16.3   Types of Conflicts in the Area of Spatial Planning

The types of conflicts in the area of spatial planning are identified differently, depending on the criterion accepted as the basis for making the distinction. In this chapter, we are limiting ourselves to just two types of conflicts. In Poland, as has already been mentioned, there has been a distinction of public interest versus private (individual) interest since 1990, when the systemic and economic transformation began. The primacy of public interest applied to the planning process from the end of World War II until 1990, which was an inherent feature of the systemic conditions of that time. The transformation process brought a balanced treatment of these two categories—public and private interest—by law.

Spatial planning, which is one of the responsibilities of competent municipal authorities, results in them being in the middle of somewhat contradictory expectations. On the one hand, in accordance with the Act on spatial planning and development, the public interest is an important value that should be taken into account in the spatial planning process; this value should be reflected in the content of land use plans that are developed, both when its provisions apply to all stakeholders and when they apply to a particular citizen's legal sphere. On the other hand, it is precisely the competent municipal authorities that are required to make the decision on which of the interests—public or private—in a particular situation and in a given context should have primacy. Similarly, the competent municipal authorities need to assess the specific situation (private interest) in the given context (the municipality as the advocate of the public interest). Therefore, the objective is for the public authorities to settle which interest in the specific situation and in the particular context should be assigned the greater weight and value.

Using the level of identity of the private and public interest as the criterion for separation, three situations can be distinguished, which are also interesting from the point of view of the matter of trust in the spatial planning processes (Zdyb 1991: 222). The first is the situation of full identity, in which the public and private interests fully overlap. In this situation, there is no difference in the axiological and substantive layers. There is no conflict and no attitude of trust is needed. This is because the attitude of trust is needed when there is no knowledge (uncertainty) as to the behavior of the addressee of the trust and risk (Chrisidu-Budnik 2016). Trust is the readiness to take a risk on the basis of a positive expectation as to the behavior of the person endowed with the trust, regardless of the ability to control it (Mayer et al. 1995).

The second situation is partial identity of public and private interests. This is a situation in which the implementation of interest X hampers the implementation of interest Y. In a case with partial identity of interests, an element of uncertainty and risk appears and is reflected in the concept of trust as an encapsulated interest. In a situation of disharmony of interests, trust is a four-component relationship: the unit or group trusts the competent municipal authorities to take account of their interests in the land use plan. A trusts B that he or she will make decision x (i.e., A trusts B in terms of x) in the context of y (planning authority). The specific user of public space trusts the competent municipal authorities, if he or she has certain grounds for accepting that it is in the interests of those bodies to behave in a trustworthy manner in a specific situation and in the particular context. However, the trust of the user of public space is not targeted at the interest of the competent municipal authorities as such, but at whether the user's interest is encapsulated in the interest of the competent municipal authorities (i.e., these authorities acknowledge the interest of the user of the public space as partly their own).

The concept of encapsulating the interest of the user(s) of public space in the interest of the respective public authorities is a valid (extra-legal) mechanism of planning authority. The mechanism of trust of an encapsulated interest only has a chance of being activated if the stakeholders play an active role in the spatial planning process, at the stage of drafting and adopting the structure plan and the land use plans. This is because it is a stage of the planning processes in which there is a confrontation of interests, the setting of priorities, and the agreement of the possibility of encapsulating interests.

The third situation is a lack of identity. In this situation, the interests of users of public space and the interests of the competent public authorities are completely exclusive. In this situation, the antinomy of trust—namely distrust—appears. This exclusion of interest is particularly visible in the area of conflicts between the ecological perspective regarding nature protection and the concepts adopted by various bodies of public authority regarding their development and use.[11] These are the conflicts in the context of the development of urban public space, which is not the property of specific users but public property.

The conclusion to which we are heading is as follows. If we design a continuum of "conflict propensity"—with one end having situations in which there is full identity of interests and the other having situations of a lack of identity of interests—then trust and its role in the spatial planning process can only be identified within the interval between the extremities of the continuum defined in this way (Fig. 16.1).

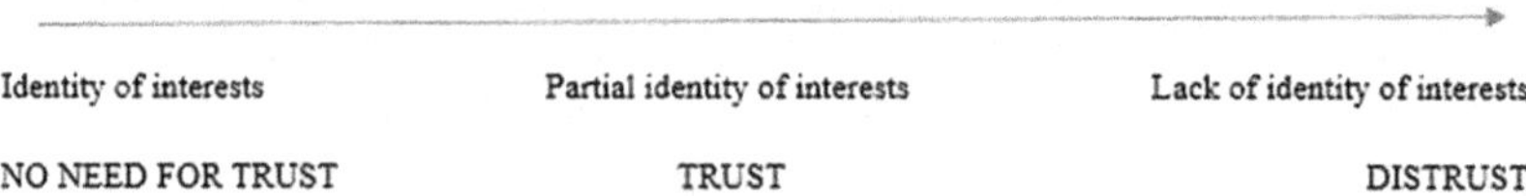

Fig. 16.1   Continuum of conflict propensity in the spatial planning processes

16.4   Trust and the Law in the Context of Spatial Planning

The spatial processes and contexts described in this chapter do not have simple solutions through the mere application of the provisions of the law. Social awareness must be built, in which space is a common good; therefore, everyone should feel obliged to protect it and take care to use it properly.[12] At the same time, it is interesting to outline the relationship between the law and trust. The review of the literature on the subject justifies making a distinction between two positions.

According to the first position, the law is a functional alternative to trust (Luhmann 1980; Barber 1983). The law and trust are two different social mechanisms; no fundamental convergence takes place between them in the complex, contemporary social order. According to this position, the legal regulations related to spatial planning are sufficiently autonomous that the claim is justified that trust has played any role as the actual grounds for coordinating specific problems regarding the shape, organization, and development of space.

According to the second position, trust and the law are complementary mechanisms. Legal regulations are seen as a source of so-called institutional trust (McKnight et al. 1998). The provisions of the law create a feeling of security and predictability in the given situation, determining the content of the decisions and behavior of the stakeholders of spatial planning. At the same time, the legal regulations are seen as the basis of credibility; this especially applies to the institutional mechanism mentioned previously.

The law is a method of obtaining the trust of the stakeholders of spatial planning. The following are three selected examples of obtaining the trust of spatial planning stakeholders through legal regulations:

1. *The ability to submit motions to the draft structure plan or land use plan:* When the announcement is made that work is starting on the adoption of the structure plan, the mayor announces the form that motions should take, as well as the time and place for submitting motions. Motions may contain postulates to introduce specific arrangements into the draft. They do not fundamentally involve contesting the wording of the resolution on starting to prepare the structure plan or the land use plan, as this act does not contain any substantive decisions.

2. *The public discussion that applies to the solutions adopted in the draft structure plan and the draft land use plan:* At the stage of preparing the structure plan, participation in the public debate means that the spatial planning processes in the municipality can gain greater acceptance and support. Therefore, potential conflicts can be eliminated in the phase of its implementation. At the stage of drafting the land use plan, it enhances the diversity of instruments of participatory democracy.

3. *Comments, the legal structure of which is included in the procedure of adopting the municipality's structure plan and land use plan:* In the comments, as opposed to the motions referred to above, it is possible to express a critical attitude to the substantive findings contained in the draft plan. It is therefore possible, for instance, to contest the course of a public road contained in the draft plan or demand a change of assignment of the land.

16.5   CHAPTER SUMMARY

Trust has many dimensions and can be included in various ontological categories. We have accepted that trust is a relationship and is able to assume the form of an encapsulated interest. Trust, as a unilateral relationship, is always addressed to bodies of public authority which, within the framework of planning authority, make decisions and create risks for individual stakeholders of spatial planning.

At least two types of risk should be distinguished in the spatial planning processes: (1) the risk of a possible breach of a broadly understood private interest; and (2) a risk appearing in the context of the development of public space, which is not owned by a specific category of users of public space (stakeholders). Foundations of trust based on axiology and subject matter can be found, especially in the latter case, in the perspective of the designed continuum of conflict propensity in the spatial planning processes—namely, expectations that the bodies of public authority will make responsible, fair, and professional decisions. The existence of a mechanism of trust in the planning sphere, as an encapsulated interest, is a derivative of the wish of stakeholders to participate and be involved in the procedures of preparing and adopting two fundamental documents: the structure plan and the land use plan.

Conflicts are an inherent part of the spatial planning process. Their solution, as well as the search for areas of encapsulating interests, is desirable in order to protect both the public interest and private interests. The rules for resolving conflicts regarding space are of a twofold nature: either clear and formal or indirect and informal. In the former case, the law organizes the relationships between the stakeholders on three levels of spatial planning and similarly creates conditions of stability, relative predictability, and rationality in the planning processes. In the latter case, trust becomes a convention between stakeholders directly in the planning process.

The law and trust can be perceived to be intangible resources. Law must be used, whereas trust may be used within the framework of the planning authority, namely in shaping the concept, directions of development, and the intended purpose of the space. The relationships between the law and trust are complementary: (1) the law can be a source of gaining trust; (2) the law may serve to safeguard trust; (3) trust can make the processes of resolving conflicts in spatial planning "more flexible."

Spatial planning is not only a sphere of public discourse but also a sphere of reconciliation and negotiation of interests. The quality of participation in the public discourse is a consequence of the degree of commitment of the stakeholders in the planning processes, the understanding of the planning procedures, the institution of motions and comments, and the functions that the public discourse is to fulfill in the spatial planning processes. This primarily applies to breaking the antinomy of public interest and private interests.

NOTES

1. Trust in pets, farmed and commercial animals etc., items (e.g., certain brands), substances (e.g., pharmaceuticals), and objects of religious cults is outside the scope of the considerations.
2. The concept of trust as an encapsulated interest in the public sphere was, in fact, already known in the Greek *poleis*. Citizens of these *poleis* who decided to enter into a defence relationship with Athens trusted, because—as Tukidydes emphasized—they saw Athens as being trustworthy, because it is guided not only by its own interest but also by the need to support others, which is included within this benefit. This motivation was just as important as the conviction that the so-called Delian League will be based on the principles of democracy, autonomy, participation, and freedom. The League lost its nature when it ceased to be voluntary, while the source of this process was the relativization of these principles and simultaneously the loss of the "power of trust." It was replaced by the conviction that any covenants are based on a balance between military and economic strength.

3. Of all the meanings, the term "space" in spatial planning refers to its physical aspect, which is the subject of physical geography, geometry, and their derivatives—namely cartography and surveying. Therefore, these are parts of Earth's surface inhabited by humans, who improved that space when settling and is developing it for his needs in life.
4. The National Spatial Development Concept, which was adopted on 13 December 2011, is currently being implemented in Poland.
5. The Act on Spatial Planning and Development of 27 March 2003 (Journal of Laws of 2016, item 778).
6. The Environmental Protection Law of 27 April 2001 (Journal of Laws of 2017, item 519, as amended).
7. The values, which were formulated for the first time by Marcus Vitruvius Pollio (hereinafter Vitruvius) in his work *De Architectura libri X*, constitute the so-called Vitruvian triad.
8. From the German "Planungshoheit." See more on this subject N-Ch. Kim, *Gemeindliche Planungshoheit und überörtliche Planungen. Ein Beitrag zur gemeindlichen Planungshoheit nach dem deutschen und koreanischen Recht*, Frankfurt 1998; U. Battis, *Öffentliches Baurecht und Raumordnungsrecht*, Stuttgart 2006.
9. The system of spatial planning adopted in Poland primarily arises from the Act of 2003 and, as is the case in other European countries, is based on three levels: the national, regional, and local levels.
10. In Poland, other than the statutory duties, the adoption of the land use plan is optional.
11. Conflicts have appeared recently in several places in Poland in recent years in the ecological perspective. The most publicized of these conflicts—in addition to the road crossing of the Rospuda River Valley by the Augustów ring road—was the conflict related to the Bialowieża Forest.
12. To justify such views, W. Jakimowicz even referred to John Paul II's encyclical *Centesimus Annus*, in which the Pope indicated encumbering a property owner with a "social mortgage" based on and, in principle, justified by the universal assignment of goods (Jakimowicz 2016).

References

Barber, B. (1983). *The logic and limits of trust*. New Brunswick: Rutgers University Press.

Blois, K. J. (1999). Trust in business to business relationships: An evaluation of its status. *Journal of Management Studies, 36*(2), 197–216.

Caldwell, C., & Clapham, S. E. (2003). Organizational trustworthiness: An international perspective. *Journal of Business Ethics, 47*(4), 349–358.

Carnevale, D. G., & Wechsler, B. (1992). Trust in the public sector: Individual and organizational determinants. *Administration and Society, 23*(4), 471–494.

Chen, C. C., Saparito, P., & Belkin, L. (2011). Responding to trust breaches: The domain specificity of trust and the role of affect. *Journal of Trust Research, 1*(1), 85–106.

Chrisidu-Budnik, A. (2016). Dimensions of trust in inter-organisational networks. *International Journal of Contemporary Management, 15*(1), 67–85.

Chrisidu-Budnik, A., & Korczak, J. (2012). Związek jednostek samorządu terytorialnego jako struktura sieciowa [Territorial self-government as a network structure]. *Samorząd Terytorialny, 2*, 86–103.

Cummings, L. L., & Bromiley, P. (1996). The Organizational Trust Inventory (OTI): Development and validation. In R. M. Kramer & T. R. Tyler (Eds.), *Trust in organizations: Frontiers of theory and research* (pp. 302–330). Thousand Oaks: Sage.

Das, T. K., & Teng, B. S. (2001). *Trust, control and risk in strategic alliances: An integrated framework. Organization Studies, 22*(2), 251–283.

Dunn, J. R. (1988). *Trust and Political Agency.* In D. Gambetta (Ed.), *Trust – Making and breaking cooperative relations* (pp. 73–93). New York: Basil Blackwell Inc.

Faems, D., Faems, D., Janssens, M., Madhok, A., & Van Looy, B. (2008). Toward an integrative perspective on alliance governance: Connecting contract design, trust dynamics, and contract application. *The Academy of Management Journal, 51*(6), 1053–1078.

Gambetta, D. (Ed.). (1988). *Trust: Making and breaking cooperative relations.* Oxford: Basil Blackwell.

Giddens, A. (1990). *The consequences of modernity.* Stanford: Stanford University Press.

Hardin, R. (2002). *Trust and trustworthiness.* New York: Russell Sage Foundation.

Hardin, R. (2006). *Trust.* Cambridge: Polity Press.

Hollis, M. (1998). *Trust within reason.* Cambridge: Cambridge University Press.

Hosmer, L. T. (1995). Trust: The connecting link between organizational theory and ethics. *Academy of Management Review, 20*, 379–400.

Ingenhoff, D., & Sommer, K. (2010). Trust in companies and in CEOs: A comparative study of the main influences. *Journal of Business Ethics, 95*(3), 339–355.

Jakimowicz, W. (2016). Jeszcze raz o wolności zabudowy [Freedom of construction once again]. In T. Bąkowski (Ed.), *Wolność zabudowy. Mity a normatywna rzeczywistość [Freedom of construction. Myths and normative reality]* (pp. 13–40). Gdańsk: Wydawnictwo Uniwersytetu Gdańskiego.

Klijn, E. H., Edelenbos, J., & Steijn, B. (2010). Trust in governance networks: Its impacts on outcomes. *Administration and Society, 42*(2), 193–221.

Korczak, J. (2015). Pozyskiwanie i umacnianie zaufania do władz publicznych przez współadministrowanie [Obtainment and trust consolidation in public authorities by coadministration]. In M. Stahl, M. Kasiński, & K. Wlaźlak (Eds.), *Sprawiedliwość i zaufanie do władz publicznych w prawie administracyjnym [Justice and trust in public authorities in administrative law]* (pp. 98–115). Warszawa: Wolters Kluwer.

Krot, K., & Lewicka, D. (2012). The importance of trust in manager – Employee relationships. *International Journal of Electronic Business Management, 10*(3), 224–233.

Lewicki, R., McAllister, D. J., & Bies, R. J. (1998). Trust and distrust : New relationships and realities. *Academy of Management Review, 23*(3), 438–458.

Luhmann, N. (1980). Trust. *A mechanism for the reduction of social complexity.* In *Trust and power. To works by Niklas Luhmann.* New York: Wiley.

Mayer, R. C., & Davis, J. H. (1999). The effect of the performance appraisal system on trust for management: A field quasi-experiment. *Journal of Applied Psychology, 84,* 123–136.

Mayer, R., Davis, J., & Schoorman, F. (1995). An integrative model of organizational trust. *The Academy of Management Review, 20*(3), 709–734.

McKnight, D. H., & Chervany, N. L. (2002). What trust means in e-commerce customer relationships: An interdisciplinary conceptual typology. *International Journal of Electronic Commerce, 6*(2), 35–53.

McKnight, D. H., Cummings, D. L., & Chervany, N. L. (1998). Initial trust formation in new organizational relationships. *Academy of Management Review, 23,* 473–490.

Misztal, B. (1996). *Trust in modern societies: The search for the bases of social order.* Cambridge, UK: Polity Press.

Möllering, G. (2006). *Trust: Reason, routine, reflexivity.* Amsterdam: Elsevier.

Zdyb, M. (1991). *Prawny interes jednostki w sferze materialnego prawa administracyjneg. Studium teoretyczno-prawne [Individual legal interest in administrative law. Theoretical and law study].* Lublin: Wydawnictwo Uniwersytetu Marii Curie-Skłodowskiej.

CHAPTER 17

Intellectual Capital Management and Trust in Public Administration in European Countries

Florinda Matos, Valter Vairinhos, and Ana Josefa Matos

17.1   Introduction

Global development presents significant challenges for public administrations that provide services to citizens. More transparent, innovative, effective, and efficient public administrations are needed. These administrations should be capable of managing scarce resources in complex political, economic, and social contexts. Starting with the growth of the economic crisis around 2008, the concept of trust has gained greater visibility, especially because more than 50 percent of all Europeans believe that success in businesses, in their country, depends on exploiting political connections. However, the countries where citizens perceive higher integrity and better governance are those that have managed to preserve higher levels of trust despite the economic crisis (European Research Centre for Anti-Corruption and State-Building [ERCAS] 2015). Trust in public administration is seen as a strategic factor for any country that wants to build a good reputation with its citizens and in the global market. This trust

F. Matos (✉) • V. Vairinhos • A. J. Matos
ICLab – ICAA – Intellectual Capital Accreditation Association,
Santarém, Portugal

© The Author(s) 2018   273
B. Kożuch et al. (eds.), *Managing Public Trust*,
https://doi.org/10.1007/978-3-319-70485-2_17

attracts investors and creates economic sustainability and social development. Likewise, trust guides ethical conduct and good governance, where public services are at the service of citizens' well-being.

In recent years, the interest of public managers in the practices of intangible management—namely knowledge and intellectual capital (IC) management—has increased. However, the effects of current management practices are not visible. In analyzing the current European public administration, some evidence indicates that the management of intangibles, namely intellectual capital, is inconsistent and formalized. Many practices of intangible management, implemented by agencies and public entities, are not aligned with the strategic guidance of the organizations (vision, mission, strategic objectives, strategies, and targets). Also, public organizations do not ensure the use of knowledge management and intellectual capital management to improve processes, products, and services, placing themselves at the service of the citizen (their client).

However, there is evidence of a possible cause-and-effect relationship between intellectual capital management and trust. Trust only exists if there is a transparent governance where knowledge is shared in decision-making processes and where citizens have access to knowledge. In countries where knowledge sharing is scarcer (e.g., dictatorships), trust in governments is lower. On the other hand, collaborative governance must necessarily include citizens in this process of sharing and creating knowledge. Frequently, formal processes of knowledge management are not very explicit. Often, we can only identify nonformal processes, which are very important to facilitate social control and the development of shared governance. These elements interact to increase trust.

This chapter presents an exploratory empirical study relating European countries' intellectual capital indicators to trust indicators. The source for the data on National Intellectual Capital used in this study is Lin and Edvinsson (2011, 2013). The Trust data are from Public Integrity and Trust in Europe, prepared by ERCAS (2015).

17.2   Literature Overview on Trust and Intellectual Capital

There are several definitions of trust in the literature; most of them are associated with behavior. To Mayer et al. (1995, 712), trust "is the willingness of a party to be vulnerable to the actions of another party based on the expectation that the other will perform a particular action important to the trustor, irrespective of the ability to monitor or control that other party." In the same line of thought, Rousseau et al. (1998, 395) defined trust as "a psychological state comprising the intention to accept vulnerability based upon positive expectations of the intentions or behavior of another." These definitions, as well as most of those identified in the literature, are based on the emotional aspects of individuals and are presented for studies carried out in an organizational context.

More recently, the concept of trust in public administration in European countries has also gained expression and is usually associated with the concepts of governance and corruption. For the World Bank (2017, 55), trust "is the probability that an actor assigns to other actors of delivering on their commitment, conditional on their past behavior. In the game theory literature, this is known as reputation" and "institutional trust refers to society's trust in organizations, rules, and the mechanisms to enforce them." Therefore, to the World Bank, trust is a fundamental aspect of governance and development, because trust is related with economic growth, as well as government performance.

The European Commission (2016) considered that societal changes will result in changes in public government, so trust in public services and public administration will increase. The Organisation for Economic Co-operation and Development (OECD 2015), for instance, stated that trust is usually a subjective phenomenon characterized by the belief and confidence that someone's actions will be right and fair. For Rose (1994, 18), "trust is a necessary condition for both civil society and democracy". For Hamm (2016), on the other hand, trust can be defined as the "willingness to accept vulnerability"—that is, the bigger the acceptance of vulnerabilities, the easier is the relationship between the trustor and the target of his or her trust.

However, several of the most cited articles related to trust take a more political and economic perspective, focusing on e-government and its connection with public trust. According to Kim (2005), a government in which people can trust requires accountability and a flexible administration—goals that can only be reached through trust because it can act as a catalyst for citizens' trustworthiness in the government.

For Bannister and Connolly (2011), however, the perception that citizen's trust in the government is decreasing is not universal; technology and e-governments might help to reverse this trend. Nevertheless, they support the view that more research is needed and state that, even though technology might change this trend, it cannot do it on its own. Van de

Walle et al. (2008) also mentioned this decrease in trust, suggesting that the research on trust should focus on why the issue of public trust is seen as a key element of the political and social agenda in certain moments and is completely absent in others.

Wang and Wan Wart (2007) presented a different perspective. They analyzed the perspectives of administrative experts about whether public participation could lead to an increase in public trust. Their results suggest that ethical behavior on the part of their superiors and a high-quality outcome can definitely enhance public trust and, posteriorly, may improve public services; however, more research is needed because their sample was limited. Furthermore, the OECD (2015) also presented the perspective that citizens' approval of their country's leadership and low perceived levels of corruption highly influence their trust in the government. In addition, Tolbert and Mossberger (2006) presented evidence suggesting that e-governments can enhance citizens' trust through the improvement of responsiveness and interactions with citizens. Thus, as Welch et al. (2005) stated, citizens' satisfaction with e-government is positively connected with trust.

The relationship between government transparency and public trust is also a subject mentioned in several articles. For example, the findings of Grimmelikhuijsen et al. (2013) suggest that the influence of transparency in citizen's trust in government can vary according to the countries' cultural context. Furthermore, Kim and Lee (2012) found a positive association between an e-government and the citizen's assessment of the services provided by an e-participation program.

A study conducted in the United States by Morgeson et al. (2011), however, adds a new outlook to this discussion. Their findings suggest that even though citizens' trust in a certain government agency might increase due to e-government, it cannot be generalized; in addition, it does not yet correlate with greater satisfaction and confidence in other government agencies or in the government itself. Moreover, Bouckaert and Van de Walle (2003) showed that the current measures of trust and satisfaction might be misleading in terms of good governance; as stated before, trust is very hard to measure and is not the only factor that influences citizens' confidence and views on good governance.

Therefore, there is not a consensus on the views relating e-government and public trust. Although more research on this topic is needed, some authors, such as Guiso et al. (2006) and Jordahl (2007), also presented interesting theories about trust. The former stated that trust might be lower in more heterogeneous communities, whereas the second presented economic inequality as a strong influencer in citizens' trust. Nevertheless, trust is considered to be a core element of social capital (Ortiz-Ospina and Roser 2016, Nahapiet and Ghoshal 1998, Inkinen et al. 2017, World Bank 2017), even though the literature that connects the concept of trust with intellectual capital is scarce. Bontis (1999), however, considered trust and culture to be intellectual capital drivers. To him, trust forms a link toward both inter- and intra-organizational cooperation. Leana and van Buren (1999) argued that the high social capital of universities results in a culture that promotes trust and cooperation.

The *Sixth Report on Economic, Social and Territorial Cohesion: Investment for Jobs and Growth* stated that "good governance is the support for institutional capacity of building, trust and social capital" (European Union 2014, 247). Similarly, the *JRC Science and Policy Report* (European Commission 2015) stated that trust helps to form the senses of community and belonging and to build social capital, namely in economic areas because it creates confidence in the regulatory capacity of public institutions.

Asiaei and Jusoh (2015) concluded that trust is imperative in the promotion and creation of IC, due to the fact that the act of sharing tacit knowledge is critical in the development of IC and trust is a major determinant of all IC components—namely human, structural, relational, and social capital. The authors, examining Iranian public companies, also concluded that investments in human, structural, and relational capital could improve the organizational performance of these companies.

Analyzing the worldwide venture capital investment flows from 2000 to 2012 and considering the effects of geographical, cultural, and institutional proximity as well as institutional and relational trust, Hain et al. (2016) concluded that trust can mitigate the negative effects of geographical and cultural distance. Furthermore, institutional trust is more relevant for investments in emerging economies and relational trust is more relevant for investments in developed economies. The authors considered the case of China to be a relevant demonstration of this situation. The case of China was also studied by Cumming et al. (2016), who concluded that there is greater insight into the determinants of fraud and increasing importance in the consequences of fraud and trust on business in China and beyond, namely because China ranks 83rd in *Transparency International*'s 2015 corruption perceptions index.

Inkinen et al. (2017) analyzed trust capital in Finland and considered expansions to the classic intellectual capital categorization, including renewal, entrepreneurial, and trust capital. Following other researchers, these authors considered that trust is a strategic factor in determining the sustainable competitive advantage. However, trust is not transferable between organizations because it depends on historical developments and is difficult to imitate. However, they considered that trust capital should be seen as an independent and distinct dimension of IC.

Thus, the problem of the evaluation of trust, as associated with the intellectual capital of countries, seems to lie in the fact that this factor is embedded into other IC dimensions (Inkinen et al. 2017). Even though there is much research that studies intellectual capital in the public sector, the approach to the issue of trust is very limited. To Kim (2005) and Asiaei and Jusoh (2015), the justification lies in the difficulty of accessing data on the management of intellectual capital in public services. Trust is an asset that is extremely hard to measure. Furthermore, it is usually measured in qualitative terms, is quite subjective, and is dependent on external and emotional factors. Despite the interest in the topic of trust in public administration, the difficulty in defining and measuring the concept has limited the research.

17.3   Data, Materials and Methods

Here it is presented a descriptive, multivariate study that aimed to highlight relationships in trust perception (TP) between European countries and National Intellectual Capital (NIC), as defined in Lin and Edvinsson (2011) and Lin and Edvinsson (2013). The data sources used in this work for NIC data were Lin and Edvinsson (2011) and Lin and Edvinsson (2013). As far as is known, this is the only published data about NIC. For TP, the dataset was assembled from several tables published in ERCAS (2015), which will be referred to here as ERCAS15. The data about NIC and its components' scores, which are from the period of 2005 to 2008 and cover only data from 27 of 42 European countries, was published in Lin and Edvinsson (2013) and updated in Lin and Edvinsson (2011) to include data covering the economic crisis.

To study the relationship between NIC scores from European countries and TP, a specific data set with 17 rows (the number of European countries for which there data for both NIC and TP) and 28 variables was built. The sources mentioned previously presented fully documented, high-quality univariate and bivariate analysis (scatter plots and correlations) of the involved variables. This work used biplots methodology

(Gabriel 1971 and Galindo 1986) to detect possible associations among the whole set of variables (four components of NIC) and 23 variables related to attitudes on TP and to thus obtain a holistic picture of the relationship between NIC and TP. The biplots were elaborated using the software Biplots PMD (Vairinhos and Galindo 2004).

17.4   DATA ANALYSIS

In this study, biplots were used to construct a global synthesis of the data available, aiming to identify and characterize the concepts subjacent to TP for distinct European countries and relate those perceptions with the level of NIC and its components. When interpreting biplots in the figures, the following conventions should be noted:

- Variables are represented by vectors (red), whose angles represent the correlations between them.
- Countries are represented by points (blue points), whose mutual distances represent the dissimilarity.
- Angles between countries and variables indicate the relevance of a variable to explain what happened in a country.

17.4.1   *National Intellectual Capital*

Figure 17.1 shows a biplot built from published data about NIC scores according to Lin and Edvinsson (2013). In this biplot, NIC components scores (FC_sc, HC_sc, RC_sc, PC_sc, MKC_sc) are expressed as red vectors and countries are represented by points associated to blue labels. The dimension of the labels tries to convey the quality of representation in the graph.

The distances between countries express dissimilarity in behavior in relation to TP. For example, Sweden and Denmark, which are very near in the biplot, have very similar behavior in relation to TP. Austria and Bulgaria, which are far apart in the graph, have very dissimilar behaviors in relation to TP. The angles between vectors representing variables indicate correlations: large correlations are represented by small angles (as with RC_sc [relational capital] and PC_sc [procedure capital]) and angles near 90° (as between FC_sc [financial capital] and MKC_sc [market capital]) represent zero correlation (orthogonal or independent).

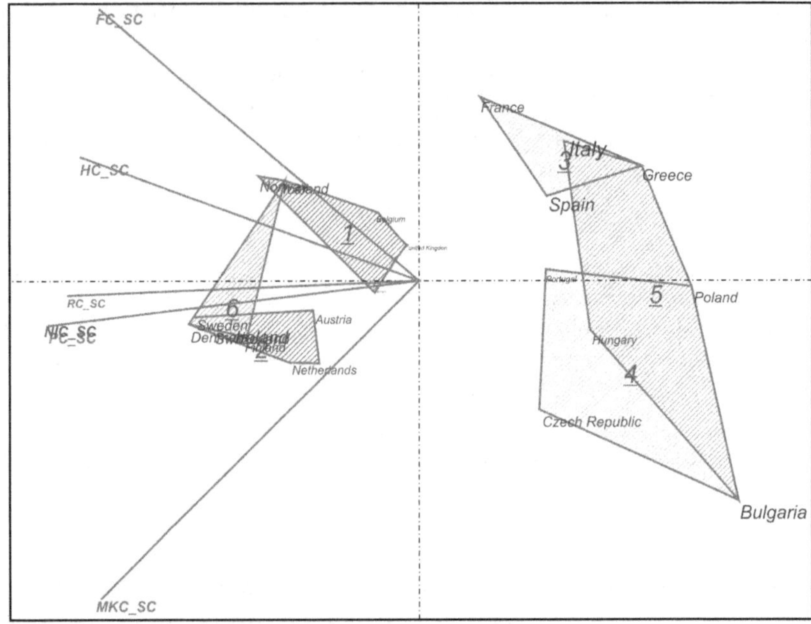

Fig. 17.1   NIC for European countries in 2011

A vector representing NIC has been added to this figure as a supplementary variable (not used for the biplot calculation). Observe that this vector for NIC, which is identified by a square with an X, almost coincides with process capital (PC) and makes a small angle with the horizontal graph axis. This means that the countries with greatest NIC (and its components) appear on the left and the countries with smallest NIC are on the right. Using an automatic cluster analysis procedure (distance: Euclidean; aggregation criterion: Ward) applied to the coordinates of the countries in the graph, these have been organized in four clusters, whose composition and characterization (both in terms of NIC components and NIC) are presented in Table 17.1.

In this biplot, two additional polygons can be seen, labelled as 5 and 6. These additional clusters were obtained with queries selecting, respectively, countries with smallest NIC (cluster 5) and countries with the greatest NIC (cluster 6). Cluster 6 includes countries with NICs above the third quartile (36.1), namely Denmark (39.1), Finland (38.6), Iceland

Table 17.1 Automatic characterization of country clusters in the function of NIC components

Cluster number	Cluster composition	NIC components					
		FC	HC	RC	PC	MKC	NIC[a]
1	Norway			4.70		5.44	32.79
	Iceland			To		To	To
	Germany			5.91		6.10	34.29
	UK						
	Belgium						
2	Austria					6.23	38.59
	Netherlands					To	To
	Ireland					6.82	39.58
	Finland						
	Switzerland						
	Denmark						
3	France	9.44	5.49				24.71
	Greece	To	To				To
	Spain	9.59	6.96				30.91
	Italy						
4	Bulgaria	8.65	5.49				24.71
	Poland	To	To				To
	Czech Republic	9.27	6.88				25.29
	Portugal						
	Hungary						

[a]An automatic characterization with NIC only

(36.2), Sweden (39.6), and Switzerland (39.2). Cluster 5 corresponds to countries with NICs below the second quartile (28.3), namely Bulgaria (24.7), Greece (25.9), Hungary (27.9), Italy (28.0), and Poland (25.4).

Thus, Fig. 17.1 has a topology that is very well defined and meaningful in correspondence with NIC scores and its components scores. The left side of the figure shows the NIC components with large values and the countries with the highest scores for those components. The right side of the figure shows the NIC components with small (smaller than average) values and the countries with smaller scores for those components.

17.4.2 Relationships Between Countries and Trust Perceptions

Figure 17.2 shows a biplot built from 23 variables selected among those presented, with corresponding TP values whose meanings can be seen in

ERCAS15. We excluded all variables that represented variations (change, delta) and only included variables from 2012, 2013 and 2014. The variability (information) corresponding to this biplot (in relation to the information contained in the original data set) is 51.8% for the first axis and 16.3% for the vertical axis, totaling 68.1% for the entire biplot.

As can be seen from this biplot, the 23 variables representing TP were automatically clustered (distance: Euclidean; Aggregation criterion: Ward) in five well-defined clusters, containing variables with large correlations between themselves and small correlations (larger angles) in relation to variables in other groups. To see if each one of those five variables groups are manifestations of a single concept (in this case, something that could be called *type of trust perception* [TTP]) and can be replaced by just one latent variable, Cronbach's α was calculated for each one of those clusters; the results are displayed in Table 17.2. Table 17.2 shows that all identified variable clusters may be replaced by

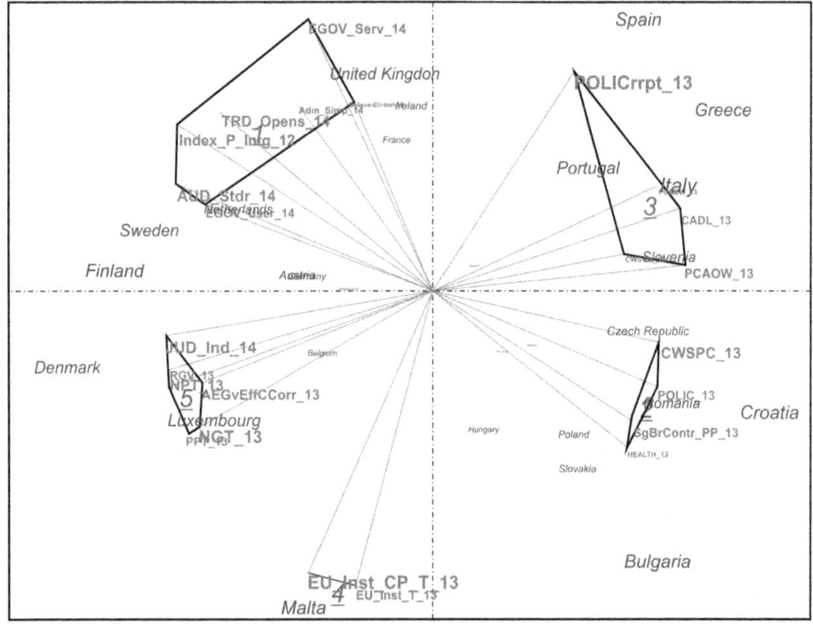

Fig. 17.2   Biplot of 23 variables related to TP for European countries, organized in five clusters

Table 17.2 Content and Cronbach's α for the clusters in Fig. 17.2

Cluster number	Content	Cronbach's α
1	E_GOV_Serv_14 – Electronic Government – Services (2014) AdmSimp_14 – Administrative simplicity (2014) BelieveEInt_Corrpt-13 – Believe in Corruption in European Institutions (2013) TRD_Open-14 – Trade Openness (2014) IPInteg_14 – Index of Public Integrity (2014) E_GOV_Users_14 – Electronic Government – Users (2014) AUD_Stds_14 – Auditing Standards (2014)	0.783 (0.849 std)
2	SingBDRCPP_13 – Single Bides Contracts in Public Procurement (2013) HEALTH_13 – Health Care Systems Trust (2013) CWSPC_13 – Corruptive in widespread in the Country (2013) POLIC_13 – Police Trust (2013)	0.890 (0.912 std)
3	POLI Corrpt_13 – Politicians are Corrupts (2013) FCHBCpt_13 – Favoritism and Corruption Hamper Business Competition (2013) CADL_13 – Corruptive Affects Daily Life (2013) CIV ServCorrpt_13 – Civil Servants Are Corrupt (2013) PCADW_13 – Political Connections Are the Only Way To Succeed in Business (2013)	0.868 (0.878 std)
4	EU_Inst_EU_13 – Trust in the EU and its Institutions (2013) EU_Inst_EP_13 – Trust in the EU and its Institutions. EP (2013)	0.927 (0.928 std)
5	JUDInd_14 – Judicial Independence (2014) RGV_13 – Regional Government (2013) NPT_13 – National Parliament (2013) AEGVEffECC_13 – Assessed Effectiveness in the Government Effort to Combat Corruption (2013) PPT_13 – Political Parties (2013) NGT_13 – National Government (2013)	0.428 (0.966 std)

one latent variable (not directly observable), given the high values of Cronbach's α.

The countries associated with cluster 1 are Austria, Finland, Germany, Netherlands, Sweden, and the United Kingdom. The countries associated with cluster 5 are Belgium, Denmark, Estonia, and Luxembourg. Groups 1 and 5 correspond to countries with highly advanced economies and democratic institutions that are perceived as trustworthy. For groups 2 and 3, greater concerns about corruption manifestations and less trust in political and social institutions and government integrity were identified. The countries associated with cluster 3 are Greece, Italy, Portugal, Slovenia, and Spain. For group 2, the associated countries are Bulgaria, Croatia, Romania, and Slovakia, where trust is lower (especially trust in police).

17.4.3   Relationship Between Trust Perceptions and National Intellectual Capital

In this section, it is presented evidence that supports the idea that it is possible to predict TP given countries NIC scores. The biplot in Fig. 17.3 was built using only data from the 17 European countries (out of 27) for which there was complete information for TP, ERCAS15, and NIC scores (Lin and Edvinsson 2013). This dataset is formed by 17 rows (corresponding to countries) and 29 variables ($p = 5 + 1 + 23$). The first five

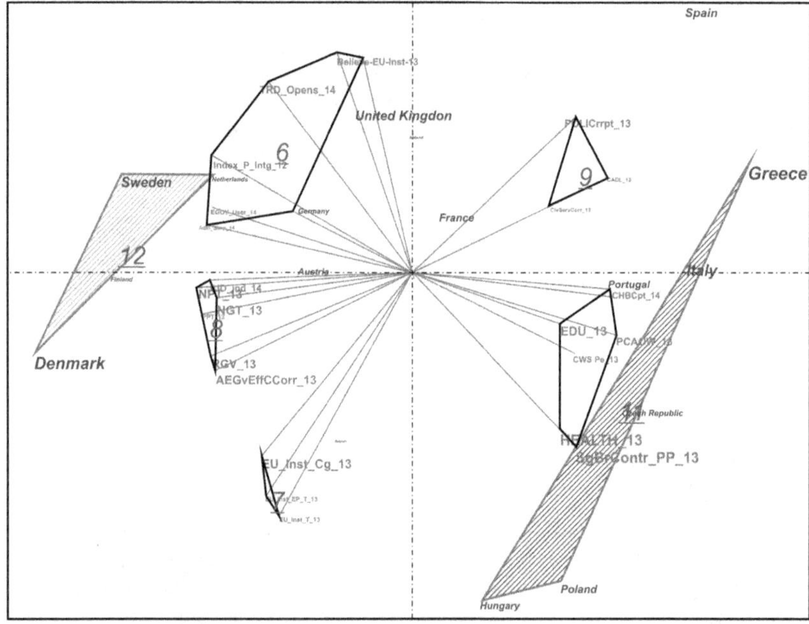

Fig. 17.3   Biplot of 24 variables representing trust perception in the 17 European countries for which there is information about NIC

variables correspond to mean scores of NIC components, (FC_sc [Financial], PC_sc [Process], RC_sc [Renewal], MKC_sc [Marketing], HC_sc [Human Capital]) for the period from 2005 to 2010. Adding these five scores, NIC_sc [National Intellectual Capital] is obtained. The following 24 variables are the same as those already identified in Sects. 3, 4.1, and 4.2. relative to Trust Perception Biplot in Fig. 17.3.

The difference between Figs. 17.3 and 17.2 is that, now, the data covers only 17 countries. Thus, some slight differences in cluster compositions are expected, without significant changes in the biplot's meaning. In Fig. 17.3, variables have been organized in five clusters (labelled as 6, 7, 8, 9, and 10) with contents and meaning similar to those in Fig. 17.2 and Table 17.2. Although the labelling of these clusters is different, their meanings are very similar to those of Table 17.2. In addition, this biplot also presents the country groups 11 and 12, which correspond, respectively, to countries with smaller NICs (less than the first quartile = 28.3) and countries with greater NICs (greater than the third quartile = 35.6).

Table 17.3 specifies the content of the cluster variables in Fig. 17.3 and the countries whose TTP are more influenced by those clusters. That table also includes, in its rightmost column, the corresponding cluster labels of Table 17.2 whose meanings are closest. In the case of cluster 9, there is some ambiguity between clusters 2 and 3 from Table 17.2.

The analysis of the biplot in Fig. 17.3, as well as of the biplot in Fig. 17.2, supplies empirical evidence that NIC predicts TP globally. Specifically, by knowing an NIC score and its components, it is possible to predict the TTP. This is not the same as saying that there is a causal relationship between NIC and TP in European countries; however, this hypothesis should be studied in future work.

17.5 Chapter Summary

This descriptive study using biplots has shown that, in a holistic perspective, there is evidence of a global relationship between the NIC score (and its components) and specific types of TP, as characterized in Tables 17.2 and 17.3. This relationship supports predictability. It has also been verified that, when clustering TP variables, the clusters obtained support the idea of types of TP, called TTP. Here, latent variables subjacent to those clusters of indicators can be used as theoretical constructs (intangibles) in future model specifications. Based on these findings, it has also been shown that NIC scores (alone or with their components) can be used in strategic plan-

Table 17.3 Correspondence between labelling and the meaning of the clusters in Figs. 17.2 and 17.3. Each cluster number (left column) corresponds with variables that compose the cluster and countries whose PPT is influenced by those variables. The rightmost column shows the equivalent cluster labels in Table 17.2

Cluster number	Variables	Countries (NIC_sc)	Correspondence with Table 17.2
6	EGOV-Serv-14 Believe-EU-Inst-13 Index-P-Intg-12 EGOV-User-14 AUD Stdr-14 TRD-Opens-14 Adm-Simp-14	Germany (34.3) Ireland (34.5) Netherland (35.9) UK (32.8)	1
7	EU-Int-EP EU-Int-T	Belgic (33.5)	4
8	AEGV-Eff-CCCon-13 VER-13 JUD-Ind-14 NPT-13 PPT-13 NGT-13	Denmark (39.1) Finland (38.6) Sweden (39.6)	5
9	Civ-Serv-Cov-13 POLIC Compt-13 CADL-13	Spain (28.4) Greece (25.9) Portugal (28.8)	2-3
10	Sg Br Comb-PR-13 HEALTH-13 CWS Pe-13 EDU-13 PCADW-13 FCHB-Cpt-14 POLIC-14	Hungary (27.2) Poland (25.3) Czech Republic (29.3)	3

ning for the formulation of national policies, involving both concepts (NIC and TP). For example, it seems appropriate, based in these findings, to suggest that an investment in education (HC) is a sure way to generate trust in political and other social institutions. Also, the study supports the idea of exploring possible causality relationship between NIC and TTP. If this relationship is confirmed, future studies should explore this kind of relationship for modelling and simulation in support of strategic planning.

When comparing this study with other studies that relate trust to social capital, it is also possible to conclude that the relationship is not only focused on social capital. Rather, it is more comprehensive because it considers the various dimensions of intellectual capital, referred in the studies of Lin and Edvinsson (2011). Some authors (e.g., Bannister and Connolly 2011) considered that technology and e-governments can help in the positive perception of trust by the citizens. However, according to the results of this study, these factors are not enough to improve this perception. For example, countries such as Portugal have low levels of trust perception; however, according to Lörincz et al. (2010), Portugal has digitization of government at the level of countries such as Sweden, Austria, or Ireland. Thus, some other aspects of intellectual capital management can help these countries to improve trust.

In conclusion, improving trust in public administration can be achieved through strategies to increase the management of intellectual capital. Countries where the trust level is lower may use benchmarking processes in relation to the countries with the best trust indicators in order to improve the performance of trust.

REFERENCES

Asiaei, K., & Jusoh, R. (2015). A multidimensional view of intellectual capital: The impact on organizational performance. *Management Decision, 53*(3), 668–697.

Bannister, F., & Connolly, R. (2011). Trust and transformational government: A proposed framework for research. *Government Information Quarterly, 28*(2), 137–147.

Bontis, N. (1999). Managing organizational knowledge by diagnosing intellectual capital: Framing and advancing the state of the field. *International Journal of Technology Management, 18*(5), 433–462.

Bouckaert, G., & Van de Walle, S. (2003). Comparing measures of citizen trust and user satisfaction as indicators of 'good governance': Difficulties in linking trust and satisfaction indicators. *International Review of Administrative Sciences, 69*(3), 329–343.

Cumming, D., Hou, W., & Lee, E. (2016). Business ethics and finance in greater China: Synthesis and future directions in sustainability, CSR, and fraud. *Journal of Business Ethics, 138*(4), 601–626.

European Commission. (2015). *JRC science and policy report – Trust, local governance and quality of public service in EU regions and cities.* Luxembourg.

European Commission. (2016). *European semester thematic factsheet – Quality of public administration.* Brussels. Retrieved from: https://ec.europa.eu/info/sites/info/files/file_import/european-semester_thematic-factsheet_quality-public-administration_en.pdf

European Research Centre for Anti-Corruption and State-Building (ERCAS), Hertie School of Governance. (2015). *Public integrity and trust in Europe.*

288   F. MATOS ET AL.

Berlin. Retrieved from: https://www.government.nl/documents/reports/ 2016/01/18/public-integrity-and-trust-in-europe

European Union. (2014). *Sixth report on economic, social and territorial cohesion. Investment for jobs and growth. Promoting development and good governance in EU regions and cities.* Luxembourg.

Gabriel, K. R. (1971). The biplot graphic display of matrices with application to principal component analysis. *Biometrika, 58*(3), 453–467.

Galindo, Mª Purificación V. (1986). Una Alternativa de Representación Simultánea: HJ-Biplot. *Questiió: Quaderns d'Estadística, Sistemes, Informatica I Investigació Operativa.* Retreived from: http://dialnet.unirioja.es/servlet/articulo?codigo =2360880&info=resumen&idioma=SPA

Grimmelikhuijsen, S., Porumbescu, G., Hong, B., & Im, T. (2013). The effect of transparency on trust in government: A cross-national comparative experiment. *Public Administration Review, 73*(4), 575–586.

Guiso, L., Sapienza, P., & Zingales, L. (2006). Does culture affect economic outcomes? *Journal of Economic Perspectives, 20*(2), 23–48.

Hain, D., Johan, S., & Wang, D. (2016). Determinants of cross-border venture capital investments in emerging and developed economies: The effects of relational and institutional trust. *Journal of Business Ethics, 138*(4), 743–764.

Hamm, J. A. (2016). On the cross-domain scholarship of trust in the institutional context. In *Interdisciplinary perspectives on trust: Towards theoretical and methodological integration.* https://doi.org/10.1007/978-3-319-22261-5_8.

Inkinen, H., Kianto, A., Vanhala, M., & Ritala, P. (2017). Structure of intellectual capital – An international comparison. *Accounting, Auditing and Accountability Journal, 30*(5), 1160–1183.

Jordahl, H. (2007). Inequality and Trust. *IFN Working Paper,* (715), 1–21. https://doi.org/10.2139/ssrn.1012786

Kim, S.-E. (2005). The role of trust in the modern administrative state an integrative model. *Administration and Society, 37*(5), 611–635.

Kim, S., & Lee, J. (2012). E-participation, transparency, and trust in local government. *Public Administration Review, 72*(6), 819–828.

Leana, C. R., & van Buren, H. J. (1999). Organizational social capital and employment practices. *The Academy of Management Review, 24*(3), 538–555. Retrieved from: http://www.jstor.org/stable/259141.

Lin, C. Y.-Y., & Edvinsson, L. (2011). *National intellectual capital: A comparison of 40 countries.* New York: Springer.

Lin, C. Y.-Y., & Edvinsson, L. (2013). National intellectual capital in Israel and financial crisis impact. *International Journal of Knowledge-Based Development, 4*(3), 245.

Lörincz, B., Tinholt, D., van der Linden, N., Colclough, G., Cave, J., Schindler, R., Cattaneo, G., Lifonti, R., Jacquet, L., & Millard, J. (2010). Digitizing Public Services in Europe: Putting ambition into action. *RAND Europe,* 7–8.

Mayer, R. C., Davis, J. H., & Schoorman, F. D. (1995). An integrative model of organizational trust. *The Academy of Management Review, 20*(3), 709–734. Retreived from: http://www.jstor.org/stable/258792.

Morgeson, F. V., III, Vanamburg, D., & Mithas, S. (2011). Misplaced trust? Exploring the structure of the e-government-citizen trust relationship. *Journal of Public Administration Research and Theory, 21*(2), 257–283.

Nahapiet, J., & Ghoshal, S. (1998). Social capital, intellectual capital, and the organizational advantage. *The Academy of Management Review, 23*(2), 242–266. Retrieved from: http://www.jstor.org/stable/259373.

OECD. (2015). Trust in government. In OECD Publishing (Ed.), *Government at a glance 2015* (pp. 156–157). Paris: OECD Publishing.

Ortiz-Ospina, E., & Roser, M. (2016). Trust. *OurWorldInData.org*

Rose, R. (1994). Postcommunism and the problem of trust. *Journal of Democracy, 5*(3), 18–30. The Johns Hopkins University Press.

Rousseau, D. M., Sitkin, S. B., Burt, R. S., & Camerer, C. (1998). Not so different after all: A cross-discipline view of trust. *Academy of Management Review, 23*(3), 393–404.

Tolbert, C. J., & Mossberger, K. (2006). The effects of e-government on trust and confidence in government. *Public Administration Review, 66*(3), 354–369.

Vairinhos, V. M., & Mª Purificación Galindo. (2004). Biplots PMD – Data Mining Centrada Em Biplots. Apresentação de Um Protótipo. In *XI Jornadas de Classificação E Análise de Dados*, 1–18.

Van de Walle, S., Van Roosbroek, S., & Bouckaert, G. (2008). Trust in the public sector: Is there any evidence for a long-term decline? *International Review of Administrative Sciences, 74*(1), 47–64.

Wang, X., & Wan Wart, M. (2007). When public participation in administration leads to trust: An empirical assessment of managers' perceptions. *Public Administration Review, 67*(2), 265–278.

Welch, E. W., Hinnant, C. C., & Moon, M. J. (2005). Linking citizen satisfaction with e-government and trust in government. *Journal of Public Administration Research and Theory, 15*(3), 371–391.

World Bank. (2017). *World development report 2017: Governance and the law.* Washington, DC: World Bank. https://doi.org/10.1596/978-1-4648-0950-7.

Index

© The Author(s) 2018
B. Kożuch et al. (eds.), *Managing Public Trust*,
https://doi.org/10.1007/978-3-319-70485-2

291

CPSIA information can be obtained
at www.ICGtesting.com
Printed in the USA
LVHW081158280620
659213LV00023B/2054